Motherhood is about raising and celebrating the child you have, not the child you thought you'd have. It's about understanding he is exactly the person he's supposed to be. And if you're lucky, he might be the teacher who turns you into the person you're supposed to be."

—Joan Ryan, *The Water Giver*

PRAISE FOR 1,000 LAST GOODBYES

"In this powerful and heartfelt book, Samantha shines a light on the devastating impact of addiction and offers invaluable guidance for loved ones struggling to navigate this challenging journey. Through personal experiences and profound insights, she reminds us that addiction knows no bounds and that even seemingly harmless substances can lead to destructive behaviors. With compassion and wisdom, she urges readers to abandon catastrophic thinking and embrace a mindset of hope and resilience.

By celebrating small victories and acknowledging forward progress, we can make a real difference in the lives of those we care about. This book serves as a roadmap for establishing compassionate boundaries and providing loving support, ultimately helping individuals find their own path towards a better life.

What sets this book apart is its genuine understanding of the complex nature of addiction and the ever-changing landscape it presents. Rather than offering simplistic solutions or quick fixes, the author encourages readers to embrace the uncertainty and embrace communication skills that can help combat further decline. I was deeply moved by the author's determination to share her son's words from archived audio recordings. Each page is infused with authenticity, offering solace and personal perspective to those who may feel lost or alone in their journey.

In conclusion, if you are looking for a heartfelt and compassionate guide to navigate the challenges of addiction, this book is a must-read. It provides valuable insights, practical advice, and most importantly, a sense of hope. I wholeheartedly recommend it to anyone who wants to make a positive impact in the lives of their addicted loved ones."

— Jason Coombs, MPC, author of *Unhooked: How to Help an Addicted Loved One Recover,* and CEO/Founder of Brick House Recovery

"I recommend every parent looking for a roadmap to dealing with loving an adult child struggling with addiction read *1000 Last Goodbyes*. You will identify with Samantha's story and realize that you are not alone and have the ability to help empower your child." — Leesa Starrett, LPC, owner of Leesa Starrett Wellness Center

"Whether you are interested in learning more about the true nature of addiction or have lost someone to addiction and are looking for a good perspective, you will find what you are looking for here! Relatable and easy to read, this book takes you intimately into the world of living with a child's addiction. All the stereotypes fall away as you get to know the author and her son. Honest and gripping!" — Susan Sek, author of *Welcome to the Tribe, Sorry You're With Us* (2021), and *Still Welcome, Still Sorry* (2021)

"Intimate, emotional, and scientifically accurate. I'm an addiction medicine specialist in South Florida. I will be recommending Samantha Waters' book to all my patients and families. It's definitely a timely book given that we are in the midst of a severe opioid crisis." — Dr. Chuck Smith, author of *Understanding Addiction: Know Science, No Stigma*

"Chaotic drug use has become more common in our society as the opioid crisis expands with fentanyl's relentlessness and pervasiveness. As those with substance use disorder descend further and further into their addiction, their family members are left with a cornucopia of alarm, despair, confusion, hopelessness and helplessness. Sometimes the harder someone tries to help the worse the situation can become. Samantha Water's "1,000 Goodbyes" chronicles the tale of a mother-son relationship completely engulfed by the dangers of chaotic and chronic substance use. Waters' experience causes a complete crisis of faith, her faith shaken in God and her religious Mormon background by the lack of answers concerning her son's medical condition. The refrain of the book becomes how could this happen here, with my family, with my child, from my religious background, a common attitude for those parents affected by their child's substance use disorder. Waters even seems to lose her faith at times. Realizing substance use disorder has no discriminatory barriers, Waters becomes engulfed by the chaos of her son's use. Families in the midst of this crisis often do not know what to do, rightfully, as there is very little support or guidance for those with substance use disorder and their families. The realities of the wellness and rehabilitation services that often lack foresight about how those with SUD behave when discharged from care can be daunting, making those with SUD reluctant to seek treatment and their families often lost in the shuffle. Crawling out of the hole of SUD requires so many layers of support and love that is often lost to the dauntingly dark nature of SUD and the impacts it has on loved ones. Encountering rehab brokers shakes her faith in the medical system that is allegedly set up to help those with SUD but all too often is in stark contrast to that goal, some places being dysfunctional and outright seedy. Dealing with rehab centers, hospitals, infections, and other medical problems becomes too commonplace. The disturbing nature of the experience never leaves Waters. Realizing the cruel nature of the world and attitude the general populace has toward those with SUD, Waters comes to a certain type of cynicism that feels all too common for families. Observations about those with SUD offer a heartbreaking insight into a mother's love and painful realization of the struggles of her addicted son. In a whirlwind of life, Waters fights to keep a semblance of the positive memories she holds of her son in the face of absolute terror. Water's criticisms of society's handling of SUD is an important issue in finding the way to move forward with regards to SUD and all of the people it affects. Social media influencers take their script from the medical system, and the medical system, in all its prejudices and dysfunctions, does not offer a wide-scope plan to treat SUD. In the age of fentanyl poisonings, the stakes are as high as ever. Water's book is part of a greater narrative of affected persons of the opioid crisis who are not using opioids, the societal casualties of a phenomenon so great no standing empire has yet to solve." — Emma Guzikowski, Truth Pharm

"This book is relatable and well written. By the second or third page, I was in tears! The author writes so well, and I'm feeling it deep in my soul (having been through the same feelings of despair)." — Renee, mother of recovered person with substance use disorder

"As a person living recovered from substance use disorder but still struggling to overcome my addict mind, I have a unique insight into many of the experiences expressed in this book. I just see them from the other side. This book offers the raw truth from a mother's perspective about addiction, SUD, our broken system, and the recovery industry as a whole, and it is sure to open the eyes of many yet be deeply relatable to so many more. Change is needed in this system, but as we battle on the front lines of this epidemic, our most powerful efforts lie in the real-life stories we share. THIS is what I think of when I imagine a mother's love and what I pray I'll never have to experience as a mother." —Shianne Anderson, a person in ever evolving recovery, Certified Peer Support Specialist, Certified Recovery Coach, Harm Reduction Advocate

"I think this book would be helpful to anyone dealing with addiction and the rollercoaster of emotions that go with it." —Ed Bisch, founder of Relatives Against Purdue Pharma (RAPP)

"A very informative, heart wrenching story by a mother doing battle to save her son. This book will help you see that you are not alone." — Christopher Bunton, author of *Made Free: Overcoming Addiction*

"This book shows you the power of loving someone no matter what. It teaches all of us how to have more empathy and patience with the humans around us. Samantha's love for her son is something we all need to learn from. Any parent or family member that has been affected by addiction should read this book." —Honesty Liller, Certified Peer Recovery Specialist, CEO of The McShin Foundation, woman in recovery from an opiate addiction, and author of *Scattered Pink*

"Oh, Samantha. How I know the pain of trying everything to get them help. Just one more time. Just one more person. And to wonder if they are alive. Are they freezing? Are they hungry? Where are they sleeping? I am sorry you had to do this journey. Unbelievable how God knew we had similar pasts and connected us. You are a Warrior and never ever let anyone tell you should of, you shouldn't of, because you did everything you knew to do at those moments. Your book is extraordinary. I pray that God leads you in meetings, guides your footsteps and blesses lives with your story and book. May it flourish and exceed beyond your thinking. I love it. Many abundant blessings. Thank you for honoring me with the ability to read and review this awesome book. I have been humbled. My heart is with yours in this and so many others. Thank you so much for writing this book. You're a strong woman. I am going to pray over every page because I know Yahweh is going to immensely bless this." —TonniLea, Amazon bestseller, motivational speaker, healing conference producer, host of TonniLea TV

"I LOVED YOUR BOOK … so deep and so raw and such a passion for the desire to save your child. You held all of it, you held every emotion, and decision until it almost broke you. You were relentless. That's what we do for our children! You are an inspiration. Your words/experience/knowledge will serve as a glimmer of hope in many mothers' eyes. Thank you from the bottom of my heart." —Mom of a twenty-one-year-old son in recovery

"[Samantha Waters is] an incredible storyteller. [She has] captured the heartbreak and state of terror that we live in over fear for our kids (no matter how old they are). …I would have a hard time skimming [her and her] son's story. It's that gripping." —Rebecca Ponton, journalist and author

"Brilliant. Painful. Useful. Addiction shrinks the world. Incomprehensibly small, until I can no longer see the only person I have ever been able to save; me. The author eloquently lays out the details of the struggle to guide her son to freedom. The form fitting body cast continues to tighten as support dwindles; words become narrative that no mother wants to hear or endure. The "answer" is woven through the entire book. This heart-wrenching story puts the solution within reach. Is she still looking? Will she find it? Will you?" —J.F., person in long-term recovery

"Samantha Waters' heartfelt story is a valuable contribution to family members navigating addiction. *1000 Last Goodbyes* is a healing journey that exemplifies taking one's pain and turning it into purpose." —Ryan Hampton, addiction recovery advocate and author

1000 Last Goodbyes

One Mom's Quest to Find Peace While
Navigating Her Son's Addiction

Samantha Waters

In a contemporary memoir, stories are told as the author can best recall. Dialogue, events, and dates in this life story are as accurate as possible according to the author's perspective. Names and some locations have been changed to protect privacy.

Scriptures marked NIV are taken from the NEW INTERNATIONAL VERSION (NIV): Scripture taken from THE HOLY BIBLE, NEW INTERNATIONAL VERSION ®. Copyright© 1973, 1978, 1984, 2011 by Biblica, Inc.™. Used by permission of Zondervan.

Visit https://samantha-waters.com/
Follow Samantha Waters on Facebook
https://www.facebook.com/profile.php?id=100048657729945
Instagram samanthawaters1000
Twitter Shablee27
Medium samantha-waters.medium.com
https://www.linkedin.com/in/samantha-waters-50b606200
Parler https://parler.com/
Linktree https://linktr.ee/samanthawaters

ISBN softcover 978-1-958533-26-0, 978-1-958533-28-4
ISBN hardcover 978-1-958533-27-7, 978-1-958533-29-1
Library of Congress Control Number 2023903870

crippledbeaglepublishing.com
Printed in the United States of America

Table of Contents

Why?

When I was growing up in the seventies, I loved to watch all the shenanigans of *Gilligan's Island.* The scariest scene of that comedy occurred when one of Gilligan's adventures landed him in quicksand. I sat in my parents' 80-year-old mud and brick house on Main Street in small-town America and watched, horrified, as Gilligan sank deeper and deeper into the dark unknown pits of CBS Studios while the Skipper and the Professor worked to save him. They finally succeeded at the last minute with cheers and smiles all around. Thirty-five years later, in the summer of 2020, I found myself on my own deserted island in my own sinking quicksand.

My little family had finally shattered after years of walking the thinly veiled line between supporting and showing tough love for my son Mason, who was addicted to opiates. I couldn't bear to say his name to anyone without bursting into tears or creating conflict with my new husband. Due to my family's unwillingness to seek any sort of family recovery, and with the whole world distracted by the pandemic of COVID-19, my hope for my child's recovery seemed like a dim, distant dream.

I trudged through each day in a fog, doing the bare minimum at work, feeling like a wounded puppy who had been given the task of pulling a sled full of supplies to starving children through the Alaskan wilderness. I just couldn't see the forest from the frozen tundra. The exhausting confusion of what my role was had taken its toll.

Some experts and/or professionals in the field of addiction recovery often say that addicts must hit "rock bottom" in order to realize they need to change the direction of their lives. There seemed to be no rock bottom for Mason and only quicksand for everyone else involved. Once it started to slide, the sand avalanched into a full-blown sinkhole.

I kept wondering, *Where is this elusive rock bottom and what will it look like for my son?*

The bank repossessed Mason's $40,000 truck. He lost a custom-built home that he constructed day and night to perfection. He lost his business and his twelve-year marriage with his high school sweetheart. He hadn't seen his kids for nine months. He had a gun held to his head by a drug kingpin. He fled the state, running for his life. He was arrested again and again. He faced four lawsuits and the Internal Revenue Service (IRS), who demanded over $200,000. Rock bottom? Not yet.

I remember that after each one of these events, Mason called me in his signature "controlled panic." sometimes in tears (certainly when he realized his marriage was over), and said, "Mom, I'm gonna turn this around. I'm gonna make everyone proud. I'm gonna make up for it all." But with every bad decision, he furthered the chaos and took all of us with him into the quicksand. I wrote letter after letter to addiction specialists, famous people, presidents, and even entertainers like Taylor Swift and Eric Clapton. I wrote to influencers and former addicts like Tiffany Jenkins and Russell Brand. I begged and pleaded for someone to help us. When I heard that the creator of My Pillow was into drugs before he made his millions, I looked him up and wrote to him for help. I learned later that he does have a recovery site: Lindell Recovery Network. I watched the Garth Brooks special on Netflix and thought since he came close to alcoholism, maybe he will care. When I wrote to him, I promptly received a request not to write personal messages to Garth.

The friends I confided in quickly went silent because I was pathetically immersed in and obsessed with controlling the outcome of my son's addiction. My underlying propulsion for every single letter, every single phone call, was that he was going to get better, or I was going to die trying.

I just wanted and needed help.

I was going to find my Nicodemus to save my family and my son, like Mrs. Frisby from one of my favorite movies from childhood: The Secret of NIMH. I hired a bankruptcy lawyer, a tax accountant, an interventionist, and even a private investigator from San Francisco when I hadn't heard from Mason for seventeen days. I even secured a documentary to film it and had the trailer scheduled. I threw it all on a credit card, not caring how much the life of my son cost. I tossed rope after rope into that quicksand to save my child. Little did I realize that my son and I had *become* the quicksand. Both of us. His brain was completely hijacked by the horrible obsession to use, the physiological cravings for more and more, and the daunting worry that he could never succeed at recovery. I was drowning in enmeshment; on the verge of losing myself. Mason and I were both fighting our worst enemies— ourselves. I could not understand why he couldn't see the devastation of using and just stop. I figured if I read one more article, bought one more book about addiction, posted in one more discussion in an addiction support group, then I could pull us out of the ground for good. I made a fake Facebook profile so no one on my friends list would learn that my son was addicted.

In that summer of hopelessness, every breath I took was labored by a heavy sense of dread. My heart ached so badly that I rarely went a day without a deep, gut-wrenching cry. In my mind, my son was already dead. I had him halfway buried. At work, I wrote instructions for the person who would replace me when my son died. I lived in utter dread and misery. As a mother, I had reached into every nook and cranny that I could think of to "cure" my child.

One day, amid the heat of the summer sun, I sat in my car in my driveway, listless and defeated. I was in such a deep, dark emotional space that I couldn't imagine living through another day. I stared at the sun beating down on my colorful flowers, their delicate petals trying to withstand the heat—ironically just as I felt. Would I fade and die too? As the familiar wave of despair hit me, I felt the tears welling up and my throat squeezing tighter. I heard my voice begging God to take my life in exchange for lifting the obsession for drugs out of every cell of my son's body. I meant every word as I came up for air, breathed, and begged again.

The pages that follow chronicle my story of coming back from the moment I knew I was dying with my struggling son.

To this day, I can never shake the connection between this boy ... and the bread that gave me hope, and the dandelion that reminded me that I was not doomed. — Suzanne Collins, *The Hunger Games*

PART ONE: THE RISE AND FALL

Messenger Goodbye

August 20, 2019, this book was born. As I sat alone in my little condo wondering about and fearing for my son's safety, I wrote from the depths of my heart and from my pain as I felt it. And so, my story begins in what I thought would be a short lesson on inconvenience. I was about to find out, in real-time, how daunting a path lay ahead of us all.

I wrote, "I don't know if my son is alive tonight. It's a Friday night. He lives 400 miles away from me. I haven't heard from him all day after not seeing him online for sixteen hours. I know most people don't keep track of their grown children for days or maybe even weeks, so why do I? Because with substance use, worry is raised to a whole new level because of the risk factors involved. Every moment, every action could be life-altering. Any minute, like hundreds of other moms, I could receive "THE CALL." This self-torture is grueling day after day and even year after year, for some families.

"Why don't I just call him? Well, I could. After all, I ordered him a new phone from Walmart's pickup service a few weeks ago because his previous one broke. That's three phones in three months, but that's a different story that only moms of addiction can relate to.

"I don't call him because, frankly, he probably won't answer. Worse, the call may go straight to voicemail, meaning the phone is not charged. Then do you know what I'll do? My resolve that I've held onto all day will break, and I will lose my mind. Again. I will immediately burst into tears. Then I will check the booking reports for his county to see if he was picked up on one or two current warrants. If I do see him on there, it will ignite the cycle of tears and the fear for his life that I have endured for months."

Thus began this book. My son has been in the legal system since early 2019. He was pulled over by the drug and task force for reasons he told me developed after he was trying to help a girl whose boyfriend was not treating her well. He said he saved her life. (The "boyfriend" is now serving prison time for federal drug trafficking, and she is a new mother and still clean.) That's all I know. I've learned that it's better for me if I don't get the details. The lifestyle, with all its risk taking, is foreign to me. I still can't fully admit that my ambitious and successful son, the leader of the family, the guy everyone could count on, is labeled by society as an addict and now a criminal.

But back to that night. I continued to write.

"If Mason actually is in the booking report (which I sadly have bookmarked on my home screen), at least he is safe, right? As a professional nurse, I know the risks to his health if he's living on the street, so jail may be the safer option. However, I also know how overcrowded jails are. Many are understaffed. It must be annoying as heck for guards to hear countless inmates say they are sick and dying from withdrawals. Until one does. Then they must cover their behinds to make sure they weren't negligent. That is just one of my worst fears these days, and I have a lot of them.

"The absolute worst fear, and the main reason I cannot call, is what happens when I can't reach him. I wait and pray and cry and call again—sometimes twenty times—just begging God to make him answer. I send text after text to please be okay because I just **cannot** bear to have him gone. The thought of it is too painful. Losing a child is tragic enough, but losing a child over and over in your mind is torture also. This ambiguous grief is emotionally exhausting. It's like a roller coaster whose operator went home and you can't get off. Should you jump? Just when you see a green grassy spot to land on, then up, up, up you go. The anticipation builds to a pleasant crescendo of peace and a feeling that maybe just maybe, this is all a dream and you can go back to your regular life stressors. Alas, the steel rattles as sparks fly off the track and you are tossed and turned as your stomach drops again. This ride is a sure recipe for emotional upheaval. If only you were given the details to all of it when you walked into the park of parenthood.

"Sooner or later, the green *light-of-life* on Messenger will magically appear again. It might be a few days before he reads my many messages and even longer before he replies, but at least I know he's alive. The relief floods through me, and suddenly I can actually get on with my day and maybe smile or laugh at a joke someone tells. Seeing him alive online means that maybe I was overreacting. Seeing him alive online means there's more time to save him."

This scenario has played out over and over since December 2018. Maybe I should have learned to not cry wolf, but any parent, child, sibling, or spouse of a person struggling with addiction understands. We are conditioned to think the worst, especially after reading or hearing about one more (famous or not) overdose death.

I soon found the previously unknown world of Facebook support groups for moms of those addicted! It was like a secret world unearthed–full of heartache and pain. There are thousands of members. The similarities across the stories are shocking and heartbreaking. Some may wonder what these mothers did wrong. What kind of childhood did they provide? Many will say, "My child had a solid childhood with both parents, safety, nutrition, education, sports, music, play dates, a trampoline, a wooden play set, a dog, etc." On the other end of the spectrum, parents will admit to broken homes with generations of addicts and some parents went through addiction themselves. It doesn't matter the background. What matters is the current, daily pain and damage, the churning chaos and disappointment that addiction creates for everyone involved with the person who fights a substance use disorder.

The stigma of addiction is still rampant, as those who have zero experience think it's just a matter of poor upbringing, weak character, or lack of discipline to "just quit." The irony amazes me. If people could "just quit" *anything,* then no one would be obese. Or anorexic. Or dishonest. Or promiscuous. Or obsessed with his/her smartphone. If people could "just quit" there may be no casinos because people would realize their odds. If people could just quit, no one would be murdered because people would understand the consequences. There is no "one reason fits all" explanation.

Despite the classification of alcoholism in 1956 and addiction in 1987, or at the bare minimum, "hijacking of the brain's circuitry, a reprogramming of the reward system, and lasting, sometimes permanent, brain changes."[1] The stigma still exists that addiction is a moral failure and that addicts are just pathetic, lazy, criminal imbeciles of society.

---

[1] https://dana.org/article/how-addiction-hijacks-our-reward-system/

I would later see the great divide between the "need" to call it a disease in order to justify the insidious nature of the behaviors, versus choice which would indicate that it's just a matter of willpower and possibly suggest a defect of character.

I believe that those addicted are a unique brand. If you can think of the weakest, most pathetic person you know who is *not* addicted to drugs, imagine him having a horrible flu, a rumbling stomach-churning garbage out both ends, a spinning head ready to explode, blurred vision, hallucinations, hot flashes followed by freezing, sweating then shivering, rinse and repeat. Now imagine him driving, or even walking, miles to find a "doctor." Your loved one is then told there's a one-hundred-dollar cash fee and a five-hour wait in order to have *instant* relief. Would he have the strength or fortitude to do it? You may say that it would be stupid to do that.

What if the problem is not stupidity? What if it's actual strength? What if it's fortitude, persistence, loyalty (even if it is to an evil substance)? What if it's actual, raw, will-to-survive strength? How many weak people do you know who couldn't survive one day of that misery? There are worse things than being a drug addict, but a lot of those things aren't as blatant. In other words, people with substance use disorder aren't inherently bad people just because they couldn't stop at a few beers or they chose a different stress reliever than current laws allow. In fact, Jeff Cloud stated the following about the people society shuns in any scenario:

> *They don't realize that the people they are restricting access to society are those who are:*
> - *Creatives - willing to find ways to live outside of the box, those who get inspired by challenges to find their own solutions.*
> - *Rebels - who have been misfits many times in the past so they are immune to being excluded.*
> - *The Wild Ones - with deep connection and reverence to the land, who know nature has everything they need.*
> - *Old Souls - who have seen this all before and have been persecuted over lifetimes for doing things differently.*

- *Optimists - with an inner knowing of what really matters who can adapt their perspective to see the blessings that difficulties can bring.*
- *The Stubborn Ones - who will not bend to coercion no matter how tight you squeeze, who will find ways to adapt to obstacles before going against their truth.* [3]

I would never justify chaotic substance abuse, just as I would never wish the pain of addiction on anyone. I'm only saying that it takes a combination of strength, personality, bad luck, timing, and a certain set of circumstances to create a full-blown problem. It also is a problem that can be "fixed" (in theory). At least someone on drugs has an excuse for being a jerk. I know people whose personalities will never be fixed and they are as sober as the morning rooster. As Sam Snodgrass writes in his article "Opioid Addiction and the Myth of Powerlessness," "We're not narcissistic hedonists. When we hurt the ones we love, we hurt too. And what is sad is that we don't understand why we do the things we do … We don't understand because no one has explained to us that the changes within the brain at a cellular, molecular level, what we call opioid addiction, is an acquired disease of brain structure and, thus, function, which is manifest not as compulsive drug seeking and use but, rather as behavior directed towards the survival of the individual."[2]

Even if they do understand the mechanisms of brain changes, yet still can't seem to stop, it does not mean they are deeply flawed or "broken." This survival is what I witnessed with Mason for the first few years. When I first came to the stark realization that drugs could quickly end Mason's life, I planned his funeral. I listed songs. I practiced what I would say to ANYONE who contributed to his addiction in strong words. I even found the words for his headstone. These words may not apply to every person with a substance use disorder, but after hearing my son had had a mafia gun to his head after hiding for twelve hours in a shed with no food or water after driving a bullet bike one hundred miles in the dust and wind to deliver a "package" to avoid being killed;

---

[2] https://medium.com/@samphd87/opioid-addiction-and-the-myth-of-powerlessness-a128dc54d114

[3] https://samantha-waters.com/2022/10/10/excerpt-from-1000-last-goodbyes-2/

these words felt right. They speak volumes about the strength of his fortitude.

> *It is not the critic who counts; not the man who points out how the strong man stumbles, or where the doer of deeds could have done them better. The credit belongs to the man who is actually in the arena, whose face is marred by dust and sweat and blood; who strives valiantly; who errs, who comes short again and again, because there is no effort without error and shortcoming; but who does actually strive to do the deeds; who knows great enthusiasms the great devotions; who spends himself in a worthy cause; who at the best knows in the end the triumph of high achievement, and who at the worst, if he fails, at least fails while daring greatly.* [3]

The passage is from a Theodore Roosevelt speech in 1910. I read it in Brene Brown's book *Daring Greatly* shortly before starting this book. You might question the "worthy cause" part, but if you are trying to save your own life, no matter the situation, it's always a worthy cause. And addicts must feel like they are in survival mode because their brain tells them, "Get dope or die."

When I first heard this quote, I dropped to my knees. At that time, I was so sure that my son could beat addiction soon—he just needed a little more time. I told myself, "He's stronger than most people. He doesn't take any guff from anyone. Who could possibly get inside that fabulous brain to change this incredibly talented entrepreneur, hunter, craftsman, and fisherman? How could anything reduce my funny, enthusiastic, brawny guy to a thin, scavenger on the street?"

Back to the topic of raising perfect children who would never do anything to ruin their lives. Frankly, I thought my family was in the clear. All my five kids came from the same dad. We raised them in the open country, surrounded by mountains, rivers, and trees, with lots of room to explore and play and develop self-confidence, pride, and curiosity.

---

[3] https://blog.ted.com/5-insights-from-brene-browns-new-book-daring-greatly-out-today/#:~:text=The%20credit%20belongs%20to%20the,knows%20great%20enthus iasms%2C%20the%20great,

There, they could imagine for themselves lives beyond their wildest dreams. We provided sports out the wazoo in hopes of keeping them busy as far into their teenage years as possible. I repeatedly told them of my brother's death by suicide after he was involved with drugs in 1981 and said so many times, "Addiction runs in the family, so make sure you watch that." Other than the devastating effect my brother's death had on me for decades to come, the only other "substance issue" experience I had was my paternal grandpa being an alcoholic. I warned my kids. That was enough, right? They could just "choose" moderation in all things, or better yet, abstain. Case closed. Mason's voice on audio, August 30, 2019:

I distinctly remember my mom telling me many times that I was at risk for drugs, but I was never one to follow the rules. I might have used to help with my confidence sometimes, but I know that my addiction to drugs did not come from trauma, and no one will accept that. I just don't like being called a sheep and grouping all addicts into twelve steps. I know that's not fair to say because it has helped some. I just know it's not for me. I just like to get high and no one will accept that, and that will never change.

Should you shield the canyons from the windstorms you would never see the true beauty of their carvings. —Elisabeth Kubler Ross

First Hello

July 25, 1986. "I HAVE TO GO TO THE BATHROOM. NOW!"

"No. Wait just a few more minutes until the doctor gets here."

"I CAN'T WAIT. JUST LET ME GO TO THE BATHROOM!"

"It's the middle of the night, and he has to come from another town, so just breathe."

The next thing I knew, I felt a huge hand pushing me back onto the top of the bed via my gorging vaginal area as it pushed a bulging huge baby head back up inside me. I felt my body give as I tore from the front of my privates back to China. I didn't know what hurt worse, my bottom, my throat from screaming, the pain from that HEAD-THING coming out of me, or the sensation of a hand inserted into my cervix. That hand belonged to a stranger I had met only two hours before.

Finally, the doctor appeared. Without even putting on gloves, he delivered a force of nature into the world who immediately commanded attention from anyone who walked into the room, including the doctor.

The baby's face was a definite steel shade of blue. The thick umbilical cord was wrapped around his neck so tightly it took the doctor several tries to remove it. When he finally cried, a sign of relief was felt around the room. Oxygen was thrust through his nostrils, and everyone around him began poking and prodding.

I remember his swollen eyes that night as he tried hard to open them through the gunk. Finally giving in to rest, he slept while the world awaited. I was in too much pain to realize the danger he was in at the time, or what effect the lack of oxygen of all those minutes might be having on him. Plus, I was young (barely eighteen) and had another young child at home.

A week or so after that traumatic night, I went back to the hospital and asked if I could take a picture of the birthing room. This was 1986, so there weren't cameras everywhere you went. I don't know whether we actually forgot ours, or we were just too Mormon-y to even consider taking a picture in a room where I had "too much" skin showing. I laid my little pudgy boy on the clean bed without nurses seeing me and snapped a picture. I still felt raw, like I was in a dreamworld of motherhood, trying to figure out my body and how to maneuver life as an eighteen-year-old mother of two. I was sore and scared, but I thought maybe I would be okay.

The next week, I was sitting inside First Security Bank with him lying in his carrier, the kind that tipped upside down sometimes to make the baby slide right out onto his head. (So, I've heard, anyway. That NEVER happened to my baby boy or any of my other kids.) Soon, a lady stopped by and said, "What beautiful coloring your baby has!" I looked down at Mason. I remember the moment. He was so pretty with his tan skin and chubby little cheeks. So innocent and perfect. That was the first of many moments when I should have relished in the proud moment of being a mother and having everything be okay. I did, but *gratefulness* was a word I didn't really understand yet. Life was a series of problems to be battled with a David and Goliath view. I was the little guy fighting, except I had no tools or sling. I viewed my life with a victim's mentality, focusing on what was lacking versus what was abundant. I didn't know how to be just happy and content. I was taught that we were always "less than" because of our social status. I don't think I even said, "Thank you."

Mason grew up to be a healthy, strong, tall, broad-shouldered, all-American boy, as all good documentaries say. He had so much energy he could have been a poster child for attention deficit disorder (ADD)— that story comes later. He was always testing the limits, trying new things, digging ditches for "flood" control, tracking the biggest deer, finding the best camping spot, or seeing what rule he could skirt just for fun. He either wore a huge smile or a mischievous grin, sometimes looking at you from the side to gauge your reaction to his antics. He constantly laughed and made people laugh with his sarcastic outlook. His sense of humor was unabashed. Mason was pleasant and fun to be around from an early age. He always came with an idea or thought or some new conspiracy, like organ harvesting.

Despite being a second-born child, he had strong leadership characteristics. I believe he is a combo of red/yellow in the color code, but he told me once that he did that test and it was like a rainbow of colors. He struggled in the educational system. Holding still while

29

writing, reading, and focusing in general was a struggle. He just wanted to get outside and play and scheme up a new plan. I've since learned about oppositional defiant disorder. He has admitted that if someone told him he couldn't do something, all he could think about was doing it.

Although lacking scholastically, he still had the persona of someone who was going to make a difference. His brother, Callan, said in November 2019, "Everyone knew that Mason was going to do BIG things. We could just feel it." And he did! He worked hard for years and years on a plan. He dropped out of high school in the middle of his senior year because of a credit miscalculation. He went right to work. Slowly and steadily, Mason mapped out details and enlisted his brothers and wife to join him in his venture. Together they built a concrete business, flat work, basements, and devised Mason's grand project: power substations. He did all of this, mind you, on the side. His regular job was line division foreman for an electrical company specializing in new construction of power substations.

I will never forget the day he changed that situation. I have repeated this favorite rags to riches story many times since. In 2015, Mason called me from the interstate. He was stoked. I had never heard such excitement in his voice. "Mom, you'll never believe what just happened. I was driving home after a rough day. All my visions of having my own business and being able to keep all the money that I'm making for this company, for myself, just actually seemed plausible! I KNEW I could do it! So, I pulled off the freeway, drove to the company office, walked into a meeting full of businessmen, and proposed my dream to them!"

He told me he almost gave up right after that because only in the awkward silence that followed did he realize how he looked. He looked down at his hands and clothes. They were covered in hardened gray and white mud. He started shuffling around, wondering, *What the hell am I doing?* At the last possible second, as he was turning around to walk out, the men broke out in nodded agreement with his ideas and welcomed the deal with hardened cement dust handshakes. His enthusiasm and motivation propelled him into action.

He did it. Success at 28. There's no question. Since his wife had finished nursing school, he was able to start a year sooner than planned. He took that day and flew. Rain, snow, or sleet, the boys worked their tails off. From building pig farms with a $2 million-dollar contract out in the rural desert to maneuvering a 500-foot crane between dorms on a busy college campus in the city, my boys hustled. They also worked without any financial backing, office, or official secretary, other than his wife. Mason's gross revenue the first full year was $70,000. He set a goal to double it. He reached $1 million the next year, set a goal to double it, and reached $3 million the next year. From the first little junky flatbed trailer he bought, as we all stood around looking at it with wonder at the possibilities, to having almost fifty vehicles and equipment all over the state.

He soon learned that hard work and owning your own business come at a price. Working out of town, toiling for long hours, and battling business emergencies are hard on a marriage and rough on a body. Concrete is an especially hard, dirty, and unpredictable job. It requires extensive study of the elements, the soil conditions, and precise measurements. It involves the strenuous use of every muscle in the body during hard, fast, steady movements before it dries. If these steps are missed, thousands of dollars are lost.

The physical toll at the end of the day and over the years makes young vibrant men feel and look a lot older, quickly. Mason's workers poured 14,000 cubic yards of cement at the pig farm alone. The work called for long days, late nights, and tiring trips back and forth hauling equipment and workers to the middle of the desert in summer. What happened at that pig farm in 2016 would change the course of Mason's life forever.

The road that is built in hope is more pleasant to the traveler than the road built in despair, even though they both lead to the same destination.
— Marion Zimmer Bradley, *The Fall of Atlantis*

A PIG Mistake

It was another hot day on the job of the $7.1 billion-dollar buyout from Chinese company Shuanghui International. They were building massive pig farms in a rural town. Barely a dot on the map, the town would be home to the largest pig farm takeover in America. Mason won the cement contract for over $2 million, and he was stoked. This was his big break, but, in more ways than one, that pig farm was evil.

My other boys reported always feeling sick out there. My daughter would have to throw away her husband's clothes because the dried mud was always a sick shade of green. Maybe it was the earth's way of warning them that life as they knew it would drastically change. If we all had crystal balls, would we even get up in the morning if we knew what was going to happen? When the alarm clock rings in the first few mornings of the movie *Groundhog Day*, the realization that the main character knows everything that is about to happen kills his motivation.

My son told me that his years of casual "use" were manageable and even helped him achieve more than he might have without use. Similar to the glass of wine at the end of the day that's sophisticatedly promoted to middle-aged women as a stress reliever. I would find out later that the Sacklers specifically marketed their pills as a way for people to "think" they are getting their life back in the form of something they never knew they needed [until they were hooked].

Pork Problems

I hate this chapter. I didn't want to write it because it represented such an advancement of addiction. For years, I blamed this one person who "introduced" the practice of crushing and smoking pills to my son. I know the person. He was the old addiction stereotype and stigma that I carried: a wiry-thin, slightly scroungy guy who likely had a rough childhood. The guy you see in the corner store without his shirt on, the guy you avoid, the guy who is a lifelong dabbler in the old drugs that are a little "safer." When you get to know him, he's likable, in a way. Such a guy worked for my son. I was later told that he considered it a success to get the boss "hooked."

I learned from some sources that every pill popper will eventually have to increase his dose or change his drug of choice. I think in my naivety, I "hoped" that Mason could just stay there (yes, I know, mothers of addicts resort to wishing for a lesser evil). That's not what happened. He knew from the first inhalation that he "was f-cked." The drugs went straight to his midbrain to activate the pleasure center to fire up the dopamine receptors in anticipation of the reward. It's that same feeling of well-being that runners get as a result of endorphins releasing from the hypothalamus and pituitary gland.

Once a person realizes he can increase those pleasure centers and **feel good,** leading to possibly feeling more *normal*, he is likely to continue self-medicating to fix his problems. If he has poor impulse control to begin with, like Mason with his ADHD, he is more likely to engage in poor coping skills in order to find that relief. People with ADD have a history of being shamed so often for getting things wrong they are more likely to cover up (lie), cheat, and even steal in order to get that balance of feeling good and even **doing good.**

It's a survival mechanism, one that comes with years of being told that if they would just listen, quickly put away their school stuff, be on time, or just control themselves, they would be "okay." The trouble begins when this cycle no longer works for those intentions. Mason clearly stated this in his voice recording to his first nurse practitioner before being administered ketamine in a medical setting. The problems start to build after this daily/weekly/monthly/yearly cover up of habits, desires, and effects. I would learn much later–almost too late—that finding someone to be honest with was another one of Mason's quests, because it's not easy to find someone that these negative consequences have not affected.

During my years-long, intense search for answers, I went to the infamous pig farms. I don't know why I had demonized them so much. I was shocked at how massive they were and how many there were. All my boys busted their butts for that place, sacrificing their time and applying their talents to complete that project. I stood there overlooking the desolate valley filled with pig farms. I told them they had stolen my son's soul. I demanded they give it back. I was desperate for a do-over. I wanted Mason to have some sort of "back to the future" reset that would rid him of this damaging plight. Unfortunately, there wasn't a DeLorean in sight.

If you achieve something good with hard work, the labour passes away, but the good remains. If you do something shameful for the sake of pleasure, the pleasure passes, but the shame remains. —Musonius Rufus

A Fertile Field

I'm the mom of a heroin addict. Really? Is that how I must define myself from now on? Everybody knew heroin was that destructive habit that happened in some other place, like Florida, which is close to Cuba, or Chicago back alleys, or New York. But Utah? *Mormon* Utah?

And why heroin?

And how does one jump from a few pills to smoking or using a needle? I would soon set out on a journey of questions like these and earn an education that I never wanted. I didn't know it then, but my smart, entrepreneurial, driven, funny son was a textbook poster boy in the right (wrong) place for this evolution.

My first question was, "Where did heroin originate?" Heroin was first found effective for coughs in 1899, despite concerns that heroin might be a dangerous poison. The "early studies" touting that heroin posed no risk of addiction are nowhere to be found, of course. Even at that time, scientists discovered that in order to remain effective the dosage had to be increased. Shocker.

Even though they knew of its addictive qualities in 1902, it was still thought to be safer than morphine. Heroin was finally banned in 1924, creating a huge underworld business for smugglers and cartels. Since its habit-forming qualities are far-reaching, it is one of the most difficult to cure. Sudden withdrawal can cause cramps, convulsions, and even respiratory failure, yet detox methods are still not covered by most, if any, insurance companies. In contrast, most companies do cover alcohol treatment. Compared to morphine, the post-convalescent treatment, both psychological and physical, is longer and more difficult.

Dr. R. Joel Bush, MD, FASAM, spoke at the UVU Addictions Conference in February of 2021. With permission, I have included three important slides from his presentation.

OPIATE ADDICTION
WHERE DID IT ALL BEGIN?

- 1898: BAYER MARKETS HEROIN* AS A COUGH SUPPRESSANT
- 1906: PURE FOOD AND DRUG ACT ENACTED BY CONGRESS (FOCUS ON LABELING)
- 1914: HARRISON NARCOTIC ACT PROPOSED
- 1916: OXYCODONE INVENTED (UNIVERSITY OF FRANKFURT, GERMANY)
- 1920s-1950s: OPIOID RX AT AN ALL-TIME LOW
- 1938: CREATION OF FDA
- 1950: PERCODAN* (OXYCODONE/ASA) APPROVED BY FDA
- 1955-1975: VIETNAM WAR (44% UA TESTS + FOR HEROIN)
- 1960: FIRST METHADONE TREATMENT PROGRAM ESTABLISHED
- 1970: CSA PASSED AND SIGNED INTO LAW (SCHEDULES I-V)

OPIATE ADDICTION
WHERE DID IT ALL BEGIN?

- 1973: DEA ESTABLISHED
- 1970s -1980s: ERA OF "OPIOPHOBIA"
- 1981: BUPRENORPHINE FIRST APPROVED FOR USE IN US
- 1986: WHO RECOMMENDS AGAINST OPIOIDS UNLESS NO OTHER OPTION
- 1987: MSCONTIN* APPROVED BY FDA
- 1990: FENTANYL PATCH APPROVED BY FDA
- 1992: SAMHSA AND CSAT CREATED BY CONGRESS
- 1990s: CHRONIC PAIN MANAGEMENT HIGHLIGHTED AND ADVOCATED
- 1995: OXYCONTIN* APPROVED BY FDA IN ORDER TO REDUCE ABUSE POTENTIAL

OPIATE ADDICTION
WHERE ARE WE NOW?

- LATE 1990s: CURRENT OPIOID EPIDEMIC BEGINS
- 1998: PURDUE PHARMA SPENDS 207M$ ON MARKETING FOR OXYCONTIN®
- 2001: TJC INTRODUCES AND REQUIRES PAIN AS 5TH VS
- 2000: DATA 2000 SECTION PASSED
- 2002: SUBOXONE® APPROVED BY FDA (SCHEDULE III)
- 2000-2010: PHARMING BECOMES POPULAR
- 2010: HEROIN BECOMES LEADING OPIOID OF ABUSE
- 2013-2015: IN US, 27K INFANTS BORN WITH NAS, OPIOID OVERDOSE DEATH RATE GROWS TO OVER 52K
- 2016: CDC OPIOID GUIDELINES RELEASED
- 2020: HEROIN USE, COVID-19, REDUCED RX LEAD TO CURRENT STATE
- 2020: OPIOID OVERDOSE INCREASED BY OVER 38% FROM PREVIOUS YEAR

The Oxy-morons

Heroin, oxy, roxy. Good heavens! *Bittersweet* may describe the oxymoron of oxys. Every generation seems to have its drug, from the hippy marijuana movement of the 1970s to the endless marketing campaigns of the alcohol and tobacco industry. Although tobacco has seemed to decrease in popularity, alcohol continues to be widely glamorized, especially in country music. Check out the words to Justin Moore's country song, "Why We Drink," which tells us that we can drink for any and every reason.

Miss Mentelle, a graduate student with a website on Tumblr, said it best in her 2017 article titled "What the Hell is the 'Opioid Crisis'?" Her main points are paraphrased below as additional information to the slides above:

- *In the 1970s, opioids were used for terminal cancer patients (addiction wasn't a concern).*
- *In the 1990s, with the explosion of chronic pain diagnoses, the federal government was desperate to provide more effective ways to treat pain.*
- *Drug companies saw tremendous opportunity, as using opioids only to treat end-stage cancer limited profitability.*
- *Early studies "declared" that opioids posed no addiction risk, so doctors began writing millions of opioid prescriptions.*
- *By 2010, the federal government panicked and started cracking down on opioid prescriptions.*
- *Addicts were cut off from their prescriptions, and the supply of OxyContin and Percocet on the streets dried up.*
- *When doctors stopped prescribing, addicts sought drugs illegally.*
- *Mass addiction can't be cured by cutting off legal drug supplies and offering addicts no assistance, so many addicts resorted to heroin.*
- *It's impossible to tell how potent a specific dose of heroin may be, so overdoses became common.*
- *Victims of the opioid crisis get treated like sub-humans. We consider them … selfish, stupid, and weak. But they didn't come out of nowhere. They deserve our empathy, and our understanding.*[4]

We can talk forever on WHY. *Why* can't people just stop using drugs? *Why* do they have this mental obsession to use, even when the physical cravings are controlled? "Why?" is the million-dollar question. The reasoning differs for every addict, but the bottom line is the changes made in the brain chemistry make it extremely difficult to "just stop." Their REASONING isn't functioning at top speed (excuse the pun), so

---

[4] https://missmentelle.tumblr.com/post/161464040242/what-the-hell-is-the-opioid-crisis

they follow the path of least resistance: search for the high, find a way to get the high, experience the high—which is NEVER as good as the last time—then panic in anticipation of the sickness that is about to come if they don't find the next high. It's a full-time job. My son told me once that he could run three businesses with the same time and effort he puts into this exact cycle. He said running all over town, earning and spending the money, bumming rides, finding places to sleep, forgetting to eat, wheeling, and dealing, are all exhausting. Despite that, habits are hard to break, and the fear of not being capable of recovery is always in the back of their minds.

The stigma of addiction may never go away, but there's progress. Many families who used to be ashamed to put the cause of death in obituaries for fear of shaming the family or tarnishing the deceased's legacy are now doing it. The opioid crisis that has people arguing over disease versus choice and enabling versus tough love, meanwhile is destroying dreams and entire families. Whatever the cause, never in a million years do people think their last days on earth will be spent desperately searching for some "death juice." Most are conditioned to think that they deserve this endless lifestyle and believe they lack the skills to pull themselves out without resources.

This is another reason I wanted to write this book. I tire of the memes and comments like, "Where were the parents?" or, "You either choose drugs or your family. It's as simple as that." It's not simple, I found out. I used to hold those opinions too. I thought those addicted were weak losers who just chose crappy lives for no reason. Addiction and the opioid crisis are complicated, messy, and painful for everyone involved. I believe there is never a singular cause for starting or a "one-size-fits-all' solution to help someone recover. Notice I said to HELP SOMEONE recover. Many may spout off memes, complain about break-ins, or claim homeless people are an abomination to society, without really offering a practical solution or making any effort to help. Someone told me, "All he has to do is get through the few days of withdrawals, and he'll be in the clear. I did it with soda, and I'm fine." Research shows that's not true with opiates. Withdrawal from a substance shouldn't be a crime or a punishment. Withdrawals are a medical condition and a very harsh one that people don't deserve *to suffer* just because they "chose" to partake. I don't pretend to have all the answers. Does anyone? What I absolutely do know, is that taking the drugs away and expecting everything to be okay is not accurate for the majority of people deep in addiction. There has to be the strong desire to want a different life, followed by a commitment to changing circumstances and habits. There usually is a time gap between wanting a different life and the sudden revelation to do it.

This book explores that gap.

What was a revelation through all this is that the responsibility does not lie only with the addicted one. Recovery involves a steadfast commitment[5] from the person, but also everyone around them. Seeking out their own personal recovery of coping and communication skills in order to change the dynamic of each relationship. There are reasons people start to use, whether it is experimentation which may or may not lead to addiction; or full-blown escapism from a life that is too painful to bear. Whether we like it or not, the life before addiction contributed to this dynamic. It's easy to forget this, due to the far-reaching consequences of addiction. Also, none of this sounds like powerlessness to me, by the addicted one or the family, but I wouldn't see that until later.

You hypocrite, first take the plank out of your own eye, and then you will see clearly to remove the speck from your brother's eye. —Matthew 7:5

---

[5] In *Recovery!* by Stanton Peele, he states: True recovery means taking the focus off the substance or behavior and putting it back where it belongs—on your values and life's purpose......the opposite of addiction is not *abstinence*....It's *intention and what you seek in your life*....."https://www.amazon.com/Recover-Empowering-Program-Thinking-Reclaim/dp/073821812X Italics added.

The Perfect Storm

What was happening in this strange field of drugs between my son's birth year of 1986 and 2016, what I call "The Pig Farm Decline"? Many will say those decades were a fertile breeding ground in the making.

In the chapter "Two-Thousand-Year-Old Questions" of *Dreamland, The True Tale of America's Opiate Epidemic*, author Sam Quinones, a former *Los Angeles Times* reporter, wrote extensively on the subject.

> *A neurologist-turned-pain specialist was speaking at a conference, and a lady told him she had been waiting ten years to say, "You killed my brother!" He was shocked, but truth be known, there were thousands of stories of chronic pain-ers being given narcotics because of a newly mistaken belief of their non-addictive qualities.*
>
> *The "newly mistaken belief" originated in 1979 with Dr. Herschel Jick's "assumption" that less than one percent of pain patients prescribed opiates ever developed addiction. This conclusion came about because (he stated) only four out of 12,000 patients became addicted after a brief stay in the hospital.[6] He later admitted it was taken out of context, and the statement was transposed 600 different ways by drug companies trying to push the safety of their drugs. Even more outrageous was that this "study" was actually a letter to the editor at the New England Journal of Medicine by Dr. Jick, using his personal database of hospital patients.*
>
> *Dr. Katz later stated, "New conventional wisdom on opiates has emerged. It was not only ok, but it was our whole mission, to cure the world of its pain by waking people up to the fact that opiates were safe, all those rumors of addiction were misguided, the solution was a poppy plant, it was there all along, the only reason we didn't use it was stigma, and prejudice, once it became 'clear' that pain patients weren't going to become addicted…we were now liberated to use that solution that had been in hand the whole time."[7]*

---

[6] https://en.wikipedia.org/wiki/Addiction_Rare_in_Patients_Treated_with_Narcotics
[7] https://samquinones.com/dreamland

So, with this theory in mind, the statistics on Netflix's documentary, *The Business of Drugs,* are not surprising. "By the 2000s, most of the country's 100 million chronic pain users were being prescribed even by general practitioners who had little time and training, the kind that Purdue pharmaceutical targeted in marketing campaigns." It's not surprising that prescription drug overdoses rose exponentially from there. In a 1998 Purdue promotional video for Oxycontin, which was the "new drug made in 1996 to replace MS Contin whose patent has expired," a nice businessman in a powder blue, satin shirt calmly claimed the safety and efficacy of the drug. He would tell the physicians to just stop saying that they can't use strong pain medication to treat chronic pain because addiction is less than 1% [likely]." Thank you, Purdue, for changing that percentage. At the time I write this, an opioid overdose happens every eleven seconds. Purdue's profits hit $1 billion in the first four years, and the market of prescribed opioids is valued at $25.4 billion, according to my sources.

The National Institute of Drug Abuse reports overdose deaths of 92,000 in 2020.[8] This is actually up from 2018, when there were 67,367 drug overdose deaths in the United States.[9]

In 2015, drug overdoses killed more Americans than gun violence and ended more lives around the world than the Vietnam War.[10]

In 2016, the *New York Times* reported drugs as the leading cause of death for people under age fifty. [11]

I could quote statistics all day long, but they don't mean squat when you are living through the evil reality they represent. I mean, one, especially when he or she is your loved one, is one too many.

---

[8] https://nida.nih.gov/research-topics/trends-statistics/overdose-death-rates

[9] https://www.cdc.gov/nchs/products/databriefs/db356.htm#:~:text=System%20Mortality%20File-,In%202018%2C%20the%20age%2Dadjusted%20rate%20of%20drug%20overdose%20deaths,rate%20in%202017%20(21.7).

[10] https://www.vox.com/policy-and-politics/2017/6/6/15743986/opioid-epidemic-overdose-deaths-2016

[11] https://www.nytimes.com/interactive/2017/06/05/upshot/opioid-epidemic-drug-overdose-deaths-are-rising-faster-than-ever.html

Who is to blame? We live in a society right now filled with people who are quick to blame others in lieu of personal responsibility, but we can't deny the facts. There are ripe breeding grounds for why people choose what they choose. When I watched the Netflix documentary about the drug reps, I couldn't believe it. I actually remember this era because I worked in health care. I saw this in real time. I was taught that pain is the fifth vital sign after body temperature, heart rate, oxygen saturation, and blood pressure. We were told to ask the patient's pain level (between one and ten). We were to assume that the patient always told the truth. There were no ifs, ands, or buts. Study after study was shown to us on how patients can't heal from surgery if they are in pain. The information seemed legit and reasonable. What wasn't shown to or even questioned by the average nurse or physician is who sponsored those studies. Netflix's *The Business of Drugs*[12] includes interviews from the pharmacy reps regarding the studies. This would be followed by more revelations in documentaries such as *Dopesick* and *Painkiller*.

I remember the good-looking pharmaceutical reps who came in with their low-cut, silky shirts and tight skirts. They were always made up with gobs of makeup and they brought goodies—edible and functional. We always looked forward to the treats or useful knickknacks boasting drug company logos. Reps who offered cool pens (nurses love cool pens) or mugs won favor. The doctors weren't getting pens; they were getting bigger things, like gift baskets and weekend trips. Eventually, there was a price limit put on these gifts. We nurses, as minions in that system, had no idea the price would be much higher when all these pain pills became a systemic and national nightmare. Little did I know how much it would personally affect me.

We spend millions of dollars to remove pain from our lives. It's why so many people get hooked on painkillers. The body becomes addicted to painlessness. That tells you a lot. —Henry Rollins

---

[12] https://www.netflix.com/title/80199963

Hello Jail

The little boy's hair gave way to the hot breeze as it blew the soft blonde locks over a head that seemed too big for his little two-year-old body. He giggled in delight at the water splashing on him as he waved his arms, which were held tightly by puffy, vinyl, made-in-China water wings. I snapped a picture of his big, wide smile, not knowing that just two miles behind that picture, across the highway that weaved between the red-rock sandstone, there was a brand-new jail which would hold this little boy's hands in steel—not vinyl—some 30 years later.

Washington County was settled in 1852 and named after the first President of the United States, George Washington. The city to the east of the jail is named Hurricane, after a whirlwind blew off the roof of a buggy owned by an early settler, Erastus Snow. He said, "Well that was a hurricane! Let's call this Hurricane Hill." Early Mormon pioneers, who found the hot desert difficult to maneuver, named the area Purgatory. Roadside America would describe the jail naming as: The Local Government, probably one with a sense of humor, decided to name the correctional facility Purgatory.[13]

My fiancé Liam and I waited in the deserted, echoey hall of that gray, cinderblock jail. There was a strange sense of apprehension in the air. This longtime happy destination town now held a strange sense of foreboding. In numbing shock, I stared through the tiny, darkened glass window. Behind that door was stuff seen only on TV: criminals, some hardened and angry, others pale and restless, looked like lost dogs. Others appeared neutral, listless, and indifferent toward their predicaments. All had lost their freedom due to their own poor choices or unfortunate sets of circumstances. The correctional officers stood vigilant, paid to control other human beings who had lost the ability to control themselves. The horror of the legal system had now penetrated the sanctity of my little family.

---

[13] https://www.roadsideamerica.com/tip/30763

As a mother, I had tried so hard to mold my family into functional, loving, successful humans, yet here I was, listening to the bail bondsman's voice drone on about how drugs had taken over the town, how officers couldn't keep up with the revolving door, and what a tragedy it was, yet the situation made them a "dang good living."

I thought, *Well, good. I'm glad we can endure the pain and humiliation of our son being arrested for drugs to help you buy some specialty cheese. Now get me out of this nightmare!*

This was Mason's second arrest. Liam and I made the agonizing decision to bail him out and get him into rehab, which he had previously refused. We seized the opportune moment to bargain. I would soon learn how very valuable these windows of opportunity were. We took off on the four-hour drive through the desert and arrived in the dark of the night. This was the first of many "On Call for Chaos" (OCFC) moments.

Like the experts had proclaimed for years, most drug users progress through different drug types and ingestion methods due to the need for more and more of a high. My son had said several times through the first year or two of his heavy pill addiction that he would "never use a needle." When he walked through that heavy steel door wearing a big smile because he was so happy to see us, I expected to feel relief. Instead, I was shocked. I hadn't seen Mason for nine months. He looked like he had fought through a war zone. Instead of the happy golden blonde curls from 30 years ago, his moppy brown hair lay slumbering over his long eyelashes. At the pig farm, he started smoking pills. Now, apparently, he was using needles.

As he sat in the bail bondsman's office across the street, in his tan cargo shorts, I tried to snap pictures of him to send to my daughter, Haven, who anxiously awaited news of the minute-to-minute progress. I was hesitant to document the moment permanently because I was in shock at his rail-thin legs and arms plus I didn't want to shame him by exposing him to our morose curiosity. My once strong, broad-shouldered, tanned son had lost 85 pounds and was now ghost white. Dark burn marks and scabs covered his skin. His hair was dirty. *Can you shower in jail?* I wondered.

I guessed that five days eating jail rations couldn't make up for nine months of running all day long to find money, buy dope, use the dope, then hustle to find more money and more dope before the agonizing sickness attacked. Over and over, day after day, this is the life of an on-the-street heroin addict. The stark reality of the situation was almost more than I could bear. The ride home was better, sort of. On the way home, we listened to him talk. He told us about people he met in jail as he played country songs on his phone. He was so happy to be out, to have music, to stop at the convenience store and get food. He told us stories of drones, nicknames for all the drug dealers, and how to spot an SUV that belongs to an undercover drug enforcement task force. He was giddy, funny, and grateful. He reached up several times from the back, squeezed my shoulder, and said, "Thank you, Mom. Thank you." It reassured me we were doing the right thing; however, the next nine days would test that assurance.

Your beliefs become your thoughts. Your thoughts become your words. Your words become your actions. Your actions become your habits. Your habits become your values. Your values become your destiny. — Mahatma Gandhi

Home Detox

Trying to detox your heroin-addicted, thirty-three-year-old son on your couch on your own, was one of those things that I thought, "How hard could it be?" Just like the time I said the same thing about a six-week cherry picking job followed by the six longest, stickiest, stinkiest, six weeks ever known to man. These nine days were exhausting, similar to having a newborn. I had grabbed my mail the day before we picked up Mason and ten days later, I saw it unopened on the table. I had only had time for Mason and nothing else.

I thought he had detoxed in jail, but he actually used in jail, so we started over at home. The shaking, the chills, the sweats, the lethargy. He could hardly get off the couch, and when he did, he was suddenly ravenous.

He would beg, "Don't leave me alone, Mom. I want to use so bad." We didn't leave him alone. We had bought $330 in groceries which were gone in three days. We took him to a real barber. While Mason sat stoically in the chair as the barber took nine months of hair off and gave him a clean shave, I went outside to make phone calls. I desperately tried to find anyone who would write a prescription for medication assisted treatment (MAT). Mason had tried Suboxone before and said it "didn't work" for him, one of his many "Nothing works for me" statements that keep him stuck. I quickly realized that we were not prepared for a detox. I realized Mason needed medication assistance or rehab, or he was going to run to find what he needed to keep from being sick. Since it was a Friday, no one was taking new appointments. Plus, he didn't have insurance, so our options were limited. We bought CBD oil and vapes. In a plain, white, rundown building in an old strip mall, I saw my first glimpse of kindness. After picking out $140 of specialty oils/vapes to help with withdrawals, Mason went outside to smoke. With a tinge of secrecy, the boy behind the counter handed me two small lotion bottles and said, "Put these on his scars, it might help fade them." I felt my eyes sting with tears of appreciation. The last few days had been so stressful, such new and unwanted territory, yet I was so glad to have my son back after a year of shock, disappointment, and powerlessness. We never used them, but to have that non-judgmental gesture of kindness from a stranger warmed my heart.

Next was a visit to the clinic to have the cysts on his arms taken care of. Yup, the first time you read that I'm sure you think, "*Wow, I'm glad my child…*" but, never say never. Life with an addicted loved one is one of constant questioning, as in, "Is this really happening?" I asked that question as I stood in a medical exam room and watched my son scream as a doctor drained a two-inch-wide, flaming red, infected cyst caused by **MY SON STICKING A NEEDLE IN HIS ARM.** The irony. A meaner person would say, "Feel the pain. You deserve it for injecting poison into a perfectly healthy body." But a naïve, simplistic, and tired mom trying to hold back the tears, I answered my own question. "Yes, this IS happening, but, finally, he has hit rock bottom…." If wishes were fishes.

We took a drive up the canyon. I watched Mason's eyes wander, as if in a daze, around the familiar and beloved scenery. This kid used to hunt and hike every mountain range in the state. He knew the backcountry, the back roads, the front roads, and every river in between. He talked to some guys with camouflage backpacks on. Always an easygoing, friendly, talkative guy, he could make friends anywhere. I thought, *GOOD, this will MAKE HIM want to get back into hunting, and camping, and fishing, and going on vacations with his kids.* I wanted to ask, "Remember your kids? When did you last see them?" *Yes, talk away my lost, now found, son. Talk as much and as long as you want, so you can get back to LIFE.*

As I watched my tired, worn-out son, with his shirt inside out and his arms wrapped in blue adhesive bandages, I snapped another picture. I was so hopeful that some *thing*, anything, would spark his interest in something other than scavenging and scrounging. I truly thought he was on the way back. I didn't think the process would be easy, but I thought, *YES, YES, YES! He's doing SOMETHING, he's making progress.*

The next few days were filled with anything and everything to keep his mind occupied and get his body healed. We ordered thick, yummy shakes from the drive-in his grandpa used to take Mason to when he was little. We visited a saltwater spa to detox his skin and reduce inflammation. Afterward, as we sat in the dimly lit snack room, with peaceful spa music playing, Mason was lying on the big round LoveSac. He jokingly threatened to "hide the LoveSac and walk out with it." Surprisingly, he candidly opened up about the allure of drug use. Of course, I recorded the conversation.

"Not having drugs is like being on a diet. All you can think about is what you're not supposed to have."

That was the first lesson I learned regarding the mental obsession that addicts face.

I heard a famous actor who was addicted say that the best way to recover is to stay home and watch movies with your mom. That week we did. We watched episode after episode of *I Shouldn't Be Alive*, handpicked by me, of course, because I had already watched them and knew the ones I wanted him to see because each show ended with great life lesson speeches by the survivors. (No enmeshment and controlling the outcome issues here.) Mason especially liked *The Secret Life of Walter Mitty* and said that we all need to be like Walter Mitty in the sense of having courage to take the first step to be happy AND not just daydream about it. Ironically, the ongoing theme of *Walter Middy* is to let go of the things that are holding you back. When he overcomes his reluctance to get in a helicopter (with the drunk pilot, no less), he exhibits the courage to live out his dreams by leaving his old (shy) life behind.

Mason's sister Haven came up to help us one day. We all went to the department of motor vehicles to get his driver's license reinstated. He sat in the chair and held my daughter's little baby girl. He said, "I feel guilty because I don't even hold my own kids." As she leaned her little blonde head against his chest, I said, "Well, now you can start." I snapped a picture of that moment and when I look at it today, I can feel what I was thinking at the time: *Yes! Look at those pathways in his brain reformulating new and better ways of thinking and doing. Remembering family and babies and following the law and leading a normal life doing normal things. YES, YES, YES, we were on our way.*

Those moments were too good to be true and too wonderful to last. Mason's court date loomed, and it would occur back in the evil town from which we had rescued him. I had called to see if it could be zoomed into but they said no. Little did we know of the two years of Zoom-only to come. Mason agreed to let me drive him, since he didn't have a car and didn't have a place to stay. While he was in jail, his nice top of the line fifth wheel camping trailer was taken over and had turned into a landing spot by the "crowd." The camper became a hot spot and he, rightly so, didn't dare go back to it.

One day at work, I was about to lose it emotionally. The stress of actually being a nurse and trying to help people who were in a sort of recovery themselves was challenging. I was drawing blood once on a patient, and she said, "My veins are so good I could be a heroin addict, couldn't I?" I literally gasped, held my breath, and tried to gain control of my voice, and try not to pass out with the needle still in her arm. I didn't know how to respond. I felt like the space after a sneeze when no one says, "Bless You." Could I bless myself? In the past I would have laughed and said, "Yes, you could." Laughing about addiction was the furthest possible reality from my life. Now, I would hide in the bathroom to regain my composure after these situations. One particularly teary-eyed, challenging day, the medical director happened to have some free time. I asked him if I could talk to him. I told him about my son's situation. He suggested some promising solutions, such as ketamine injections and ibogaine therapy. We had already looked into ibogaine but could never get the $6,000 needed to go out of the country. He told me, *"If you don't get him to stop, the drugs will slowly disintegrate his entire body without him realizing it, because they are just trying to survive the cravings and obsession minute by minute."*

So, now, while sitting in the office for the ketamine injection that he agreed to do, I recorded my son's first actual interaction with a medical professional regarding his addiction. I will always be grateful for the kindness and respect shown by this lady to my son as she asked questions that were bringing this serious healthcare problem into the open to be talked about and treated.

September 3, 2019.

Audio recording:

Mason: *It's overwhelming for me to think of staying sober a month or a year or even a day. The reason I haven't been successful is I can't get my mind back to where it used to be. Sleep is one huge advantage of drugs. When I am clean, I cannot sleep. So, the temptation to use just to sleep gets the best of me.*

Medical professional: *Are you depressed?*

Mason: *I don't know because every time there was a problem, I would use. I don't feel like I've had to deal with reality for the last few years. When you are using every day, you don't feel pain because it's masked by heroin. Except the panic attacks that would come. A majority of issues led to my drug use. I overwhelmed myself with too much responsibility, promised way too many people, too much stuff. So, when I couldn't deliver like I should, and wasn't sleeping, I went to more drug use to try to help me increase my productivity. I had had a little bit of drug use with pills here and there, and when you first start that, you feel like you can do more. But I started getting physically dependent. When you wake up, you just think you have to have it… All of a sudden, I couldn't do anything without it. I went to heroin overnight because my pills got cut off and heroin was cheaper.*

I remember, when I would quit, I would realize that if I used the day before, I got half as much done and realized that I can't do that. I'm not myself, you know? [At] a certain point I [knew heroin] wasn't helping me, but I was physically dependent on it somehow…I got stuck, kept thinking, "Maybe next week, I'll start." I had to literally get locked in a room to stop.

*I've tapered myself off before, but never planned on staying sober…I've gone back to using because it's so overwhelming to see all the crap I've caused. **It's easier to just use again.***

That last line is important. I believe that is why, despite all the talk of recovery in that appointment and despite having an amazing experience with ketamine, the day Mason had to return to the trigger town for court, it *seemed* all for nothing. We drove four hours to make it to court. We listened to my favorite guru Matt Kahn chant, "I am the light, the light I am," over and over again. My son, ever the funny guy, rolled his eyes and mouthed the words. I called the LDS temples and added his name to the prayer lists. I even added some of his using friends, asking him to spell their names for me while I was on the phone. Finally, we arrived at the courthouse. Mason wore shorts, which violated the dress code. They wouldn't let him in the courthouse. He had ten minutes before his appearance in front of the judge, so I drove like a maniac down the street to Kmart and literally ran down the aisle, grabbed a pair of Levi's, and ran them back to the courthouse. They turned out to be skinny jeans. My son is NOT a skinny jeans type. He was sitting in the front seat, wrestling, and squirming, trying to pull the tight things over his huge cankles, when he said, *"I would rather be in contempt of court than wear skinny jeans!"* But he was on time.

His brothers and I arranged to get stuff moved out of one of the lots that Mason was using for his business. We hustled like crazy to wrap up things that had unraveled during his nine-month slide into addiction. But Mason had other plans. After ten days clean, even with a Kratom taper and CBD oil *and* a ketamine treatment, my son wanted heroin more than anything else.

The first night we stayed at his brother's house turned into a big argument that tore at my soul. These two boys, who had often been at odds with each other yet had somehow worked together for over ten years, had now switched positions. The tables not only turned, but they also flipped upside down and lay on their sides. Mason was no longer threatening to fire his younger brother for not getting work done. Instead, Mason, the captain of the sunken ship, was being held in contempt for his atrocious actions that sank the business and the many people involved in it.

That night, out on the patio in the dark desert, away from the bright lights of the city, my prodigal son sat smoking a cigarette and reflecting on the last two weeks: the first in jail, the second detoxing. He had spent the second week battling his hovering helicopter mother, who was desperately trying to keep him away from the lifestyle that had stolen him for the last nine months. How must he have felt to be a thirty-three-year-old man, entrepreneur, dad to two precious, innocent children, and now ex-husband of a twelve-year marriage who had lost everything and needed his mother to babysit him? He needed me there, physically, because he couldn't control the demon that ravaged his every thought. He also needed my resources (money) because he had nowhere to go and no job to help him start over.

As we looked up at the night sky, the stars began to appear more and more, twinkling in the dark, clear night. We found the North Star, the Big Dipper, and then he said, "Look, there's a drone. You can tell because it has sparks around it and seems to be hovering." Then a distance away, there was another one, and another one. We counted four or five curved in a line around us.

I was horrified. *"Oh my God, are they watching you? Us? Right now?"* My voice shook with fear. My paranoia, fear, and utter disbelief were on high alert after a week at my first real look inside the ugly drug culture. The jails, withdrawal symptoms from hell (including the gut-wrenching sound of vomiting in the middle of the night, after which he lay there shivering almost into a seizure); infected cysts and torn up trap trailers. *Could they possibly be after him again?* I asked myself. *Can we not even sit out and enjoy the summer night? What has my little family's life become?*

The weekend was exhausting. After the disagreement at my younger son's house, Mason insisted we stay somewhere else the next night. We were finished with court but still had thousands of dollars in equipment to move out of a storage yard. After court, he remembered a truck that had been at the mechanic's for over a year. We (I) paid the mechanic $1,200 (on credit cards) to get it out and get licensed. Enter my first real view into the world of so-called enabling. As mothers and loved ones of addicts, we are often caught up in the dilemma of overthinking what the right thing to do is in every single situation. It's like when your kids forgot their homework or gym shoes when they were in school. You either imagined your child suffering while the other kids "progressed" and you ran the items to the school, or you refused to rescue him and went on with your day, trying not to think of him in the corner, being made fun of, yet hoping the experience would teach him to be more responsible.

At this junction with my son, I had zero idea of the power this drug had over my son. I had zero idea that my son would be anything but grateful for all my efforts. I had no doubts that as soon as he was "better" and started working again, he would pay me back all I had spent. Such was his usual character, as one of the biggest hearted people I knew.

My attempt to babysit him that weekend was disastrous. On the way home, the usually pleasant trip was the first of a few times my son would become belligerent toward me with argumentative and angry verbal assaults. I had prided him on never doing this, especially as I read about others' negative experiences with their addicted loved ones. Who knew it was coming to a theater near me?

He spent the whole trip arguing while picking "glass" out of his arms, from "bongs" that had exploded over the last year. Liam, who was out of state, played counselor on speaker phone for a while and I thought it was very helpful. I didn't realize it then, but a week off drugs is not near enough to absorb anything reasonable and practical in the damaged brain. My son continued to argue about all the reasons that he just needed to get back working and not be wasting all this time talking about "recovery." It was all too much. I soon had to call for help from my daughter. My ex-husband met with him, and they made temporary work arrangements, but right after we left, he washed his hands of the whole thing because he saw my son's tracked arms. I mean, he's an IV heroin user. Did he miss that memo? I'm not sure if he thought the arms would magically get better or what. I admit, it is easier to walk away from something you don't understand or feel powerless over. Plus, with the ongoing popular theme of "just let them figure it out," it seems morally virtuous to cut someone off "until they get clean."

The emotional turmoil of wondering if I should just leave him there, go home, and give up on getting him help exhausted me. I didn't know what to do. I didn't know what "help" would look like. At that time, I didn't have the moms' support groups, a counselor, insurance, or any sort of plan. We literally lived minute by minute. My knowledge at that point consisted of thinking, "Isn't there some sort of blue book that has all the answers?"

Liam, who was out of state, jumped in a truck and started driving the twelve hours in the middle of the night to get home to help me with him. By the time he arrived, however, Haven had come to our house and picked up Mason because I couldn't stop crying and was becoming fearful of him. This caused another huge fight between Liam and me, only adding to my sorrow and pain. I recorded one of Mason's "conversations" during this time. Mason gives a profound explanation for why he thinks people in addiction keep using.

Mason's words on audio: 09/08/2020:

> *When you are using every day, you are living in luxury. You're trying to get the best feeling of life every day, so you're making your dopamine every day. Like with any luxury, every day can get bad. Say you love lobster and steak. If you eat them every day, they're gonna suck and you're never gonna have your favorite meal again. You can't top it anymore. So, heroin. The high feeling is like the highest you can get in your pleasure center—your dopamine high. And you're there every day, so every day sucks.* **There's nothing to look forward to,** *and that's what has changed with me. And that's a big fuckin' deal.*

Looking back, listening to his voice from that weekend, I realize now that he was trying everything possible to get back to the lifestyle. Back to that town. His brain was all over the place, so intertwined in this issue that I'm sure he felt completely overwhelmed at achieving ANY success at recovery. He had so many irons in the fire in the form of loose ends of a failing business and strained family relationships, which were all burning up in smoke. He was a lost and tormented soul, in my opinion.

When he left, as usual, I thought it might be the last time I ever saw him, so I snapped a picture of us. I look at it now, me with my now familiar swollen, sad disappointed eyes of a mother, who begged the camera, "Please help us, anyone."

I learned that addiction can become progressively more chaotic, and fatal, unless something intervenes or the person has a "come to Jesus moment." Every step of the way seems to have the human psyche try to justify its experience by saying, "At least my son isn't doing [this/that]. At least he still has a job. At least he still takes care of his kids."

In the world of addiction, we know that catastrophic thinking contributes to our projection and paranoia. We ARE grateful, even in the midst of our worry, that our child is still here or not as "bad off" as some. Unfortunately, with addiction, that line is crossed quickly. Even teenagers with marijuana habits can have negative behaviors. So, to say, "It's just marijuana," is not an option anymore. With the poisonous drug supply, we can't downplay anything. There is so much at stake. Rock bottom can be death nowadays, so it makes sense to learn every possible communication skill to help combat further decline and "raise the bottom up." We have to decide what we can live with, without remorse. There are so many regrets from people who have lost loved ones, people who adhere to my dad's favorite line, "If only I knew what I know now, I would do it all again." But we can't live in that place. The mental gymnastics that our mind does contribute to our projection of worst-case scenarios and paranoia. This journey changes daily and there are no clear-cut answers.

My goal for this book is to help loved ones find a place from which they can operate with compassionate boundaries, loving suggestions, and to celebrate *any forward movement* towards a better life for those struggling. It would take me years to learn to congratulate him if there was a decrease in use; mostly because I couldn't come to terms with the overall situation. As Mike Brown of Never Use Alone[14] states, "If we started celebrating small victories, we'd attend a lot less funerals."

Of course, every death is a different scenario and a tragedy regardless of what led up to it, but I learned that if I can stop the all-or-nothing thinking that recovery or a situation has to be a certain way, on *my* timeline, the overall outcome may be better. If I can help even one person have some kind of hope and assurance that they are doing the right thing in that moment, for their situation, then this whole book is worth it.

---

[14] https://neverusealone.com/

There are two things a person should never be angry at, what they can help, and what they cannot. —Plato

Aloha Goodbye

After Mason made a beeline back to his world, my entire two weeks of taking time off work, buying Kratom, CBG vapes, seventy-dollar spa treatments, rubbing his back while he shook uncontrollably, and filling the tub with warm water, Epsom salt, and lavender for my vomiting son; appeared to be all for nothing. I sank into another hopeless pit. I couldn't drown in my disappointment for long, however, because I had a wedding in only two months, and in Hawaii!

Yes, I was getting married for a second time, and this time on the beautiful island of Kauai. Liam had whisked me off to Niagara Falls earlier that year to propose to me in the Skylon Tower revolving restaurant in Canada. Now he was getting antsy and made it clear that it was time to focus on us. *Imagine that?* I pulled together the location, the wedding package, flowers, and dress, and ordered like crazy off Etsy. Then I had everything shipped directly to the hotel. Liam made all the travel arrangements and paid for everything in advance. We were set.

I thought having a destination wedding would be less work, but it turns out that picking places and decor from a shiny internet page plastered with wonderful beach photos is a bit deceiving. The beach we picked out turned out to be a dump. We were scared to even walk up to it, and my future father-in-law didn't dare leave the car alone because we had seen so many abandoned cars shot up with bullet holes! We quickly left that area and went in search of a better beach.

The next day, my son, Luke, was walking out behind our hotel and came back excitedly to tell me he found the perfect beach! Sure enough, right there in the hot island sun, in the silky white sand, was a picturesque large, white bark beech tree resting on its side. The iconic Sleeping Giant Mountain range in the background completed the perfect spot.

I called the wedding planner and asked to move the ceremony. She said, "Sure! Beach permits are good on any beach!" The wedding went off without a hitch. When I walked through the foliage-lined path toward the beach to be married, I felt a twinge of sadness for the missing pieces of my family. My oldest daughter, my son, and their kids were absent. Then, my other two sons met me and walked me into a spectacular view of rushing blue-green waves.. They had Liam facing the ocean and when I came within about ten feet, they turned him around. He could hardly contain himself as he looked at me. On that Hawaiian beach, with the preacher, the guitar player, the photographer, and my smiling family standing in the sinking hot sand, I forgot all my problems and was focused on the future.

We had an amazing Hawaiian ceremony with perfect weather. We included my daughter via the Marco Polo app video. The days that followed were filled with family, adventure, and amazing serenity on the tropical island. We enjoyed a much-needed break from our life that had revolved around addiction since my husband and I met.

Home Depot

Liam had met Mason for the first time under the bright lights of a Home Depot parking lot on a humid summer night eighteen months before that day. We had traveled four hours to our favorite vacation place. As we walked to Mason's truck, my excitement in having them meet was quickly dashed when I realized that my son was under the influence. They had a quick talk about divorce, lost loves, and broken relationships because my son was feeling defeated in that area. The strong, funny, driven son that I knew was buried under the burdens his addiction had caused. At one time an old-school story of success, failure, and rising from ashes, my son now appeared lost. He had drawn the map to success, but his ink was disappearing. My son could usually reprint the map, re-dip the ink pen, and forge through the barriers that life throws at us. But not that night. That night, he was forlorn. That far-away look in his eyes, even as he tried to act brave for the new guy in the family, told me he wanted to vanish.

That beginning was the only version of my son that my husband knew. That version was what caused this momma so many tears and sleepless nights. That version sent the family into havoc and dysfunction. Liam didn't see the hero that an entire family admired, the brother who would do anything for anyone, the friend who cracked jokes and made every day more pleasant, the businessman who hired family and friends, the provider who enabled employees to get to work, the giver who took his family on trips to Jamaica, Cabo, San Diego, and Disneyland. I wanted Liam to know the son who called me one day and said, "Now I understand why it takes you so long to get your patients out of bed after hip or knee surgeries because I just spent an hour getting [my employee] back to his truck after hurting his back. He wouldn't let me call an ambulance."

After that Home Depot parking lot meeting, my son sent me this text:

"Don't tell him I'm using, sorry, I'm embarrassed. I'm sorry you had to see me f-ng up. I don't want to do it anymore, sorry."

Liam would say later that he always felt like Mason was some sort of caricature of another person, yet not a fake one. A real one. It was strange, in a way. Liam would be madder than heck at him, but the minute we met up with him, all was forgotten. That's the magic of Mason's persona.

So now, after returning from Hawaii, we had only five days before we were OCFC again. My daughter had taken over being "on call" so I could enjoy my wedding and vacation. One night, she sent Mason a pizza, some shoes, and a new phone from Walmart pick up because he was literally walking around town barefoot and hungry. It had still been under a year of this downhill slide and none of us really knew how to best help him. He had been arrested twice and still appeared terribly embarrassed and sorry about it all. He was so good at not asking for much. Then again, every few months he got desperate and asked for one little favor which, of course, would be the "thing that will turn everything around." Just one more tank of gas, one more meal, one more phone, and he could get a job and make money again.

But one night he was hanging around a gas station (the same gas station where he had once spent thousands a month on gas for all his company vehicles), when the clerk called the cops on him for being in the bathroom. I don't know the whole story, even after calling the store and talking to the manager to see if she had seen his bag of belongings anywhere. That was all he had to his name, and I wanted it back. Out of parental pride, I had to throw in that Mason used to spend thousands of dollars there. She stated it was policy to call the police on someone hanging around suspiciously. All I know is that was his third arrest, and it hit hard. The situation was now serious. I mean, the other arrests were like, "What the hell? What are you doing?" But this one was somber and sad.

So here he was, back in that purgatory of a county jail for the third time in one year. I can still hear his droning monotone voice on the phone, echoing from that jail as he begged for me to get him out. He was beaten down, sick, and wanting out of there, desperately. I could feel the cold, sweaty starkness of his cell. Occasionally, other inmates swore at him to hurry up. He told them to "chill out."

He got angry when I wouldn't run right down and get him (400 miles away). I tried to ignore his calls because I was at work, but when he said he promised his union money to any of his friends who would get him out, I lost it. I went into the closet at work and yelled bloody murder at him to never, ever threaten me with money again, especially after all we had done and spent just in six months, not to mention the five days the previous December that Liam had worked on Mason's screener plant with zero monetary compensation to try to help restart his business that had floundered for months. I was upset and crying when I walked back into my job and tried to act like my son wasn't in jail on drug charges and that the horrible unspoken demon of addiction hadn't completely shaken his business and our family apart. I had to pretend I didn't know that my son could die in jail from addiction withdrawals. I had to be a healing nurse to patients who were struggling with a different disorder: eating. To this day, I keep Mason's haunting voicemails saved on my phone.

When life puts you through a tumbler, it's your choice whether you come out polished or crushed. —Elizabeth Kubler Ross

PART TWO: THE ROLLER COASTER

Intervention Goodbye

Before Mason was arrested that third time, we had been toying with the idea of making the four-hour trip to help him move all his business equipment out of the other storage yards. Some of his high dollar items were disappearing and tensions were getting high with the owners due to his non-action for the last eight months. He also didn't have any vehicles to use or anyone to help him move the odd array of $20,000 in materials, tools, and equipment. The problem of moving a variety of random items from Point A to Point B was hard enough for us, even with healthy brains and valid driver's licenses, but his disarrayed state of mind, manifesting as ambivalence, made the project significantly harder. When we got the news of his latest arrest, we decided it would be easier to move the equipment without his involvement. His propensities to downplay everything and procrastinate were maddening. He truly believed he would fix it all right up soon, when in reality he was facing more potential lawsuits by his inaction. So, we set out for the weekend to do whatever we could in the short time we were off work.

While driving, I saw a post on Facebook about someone who was committed to helping addicts recover because she had lost her son to a heroin overdose. I messaged her about our situation, and she immediately said, "I'll get back to you." What followed next was a flurry of phone conversations and travel plans, arranged in three days, for a private interventionist to come to the jail and whisk Mason away to detox and rehab. Yes, an actual forced intervention. I know it's controversial, especially with the manner in which the TV show exploits SUD peeps, but with the financial situation bearing down on him and his legal troubles mounting, we knew he had to get healthy in order to deal with those situations. We were still naïve about the process of recovery and truly believed that the intervention, detox, and rehab combo would be the key this time. We contacted the public defender, a former cop, handling his case, and he was more than helpful. He sent in an order for the judge to sign so we wouldn't have to make bail.

Anyone else could have bailed him out before then, and then we wouldn't have control over his whereabouts, namely, to get him on the plane for which we'd already bought tickets. Overriding that concern was the statistical fact that overdose is more common when addicted loved ones get out of jail because their tolerance is so low. I could not let that happen! I checked the booking report at least every hour for five days straight, crossing my fingers every time to see those words written in red: IN CUSTODY.

Desert Night

One of the "items" we needed to rescue and fix was his Ford Super Duty 7.3 work truck that he lived in until it broke down in the desert a few weeks before. Since he couldn't fix it, he had literally become homeless. I messaged the only friend of his I knew, and he gave me the truck's exact location. Now we had to get the keys from the jail, but without my son knowing we were in town. If he knew we were there, he would beg us harder to get him out. Liam called the jail and said he was coming to pick up the keys to tow it because he was passing through town in his company truck. The jailer had to give Mason a paper to sign. He signed it without questioning anything, like he always signed things; and we picked up the keys. Mason thought the paper indicated we were getting the truck and then coming to get him. When he found out that wasn't happening, he freaked out, punched the cinder brick wall, swore, and told me over the phone he was going to go back to his cell and kill himself. He said, *"Bye Mom. This is the last time you will talk to me."* I had never heard him like that.

In tears, I called the jail and told the officers that Mason threatened suicide and that he needed to be put on watch. They were less than sympathetic, so I told them to listen to the call and if something happened, his blood would be on their hands. Liam and I then raced across town, entered the jail, and talked to a supervisor. He was able to feign enough interest to calm me down, so we headed to the desert to fix Mason's truck.

After a series of events late into the night, including not having the right wrench, going across the state line to buy $400 in tools, we found out the lug nuts on our own truck were one spin away from falling off while we were speeding through a deep curvy canyon! We somehow managed to drive that truck back into town and hide it behind the hotel so Mason wouldn't see it and take off in it during the intervention. Needless to say, the weekend was exhausting.

Shame

In dealing with these people and situations, I struggled to balance the shame of Mason's failures with my belief that he was still a person who had value. One who had the potential to overcome this. I tried to not make excuses for him, but I was battling my own shame, disappointment, fear, and uncertainty. People like to talk. I knew the word on the street was that my son had gotten into drugs, lost his business, and "hurt a lot of people in the process," as one arrogant old man told me. Some of the people talking may not have been into drugs, but they had their faults. One had basically set him up to fail in his business with a set of conditions that were overlooked by my driven, passionate entrepreneur son, but noticed by his brothers and possibly his wife. Another person I'd known for many years, who, shall I say, was not a sexually "well" person, had a lot to say about how rotten my son was and even took Mason's property as payback for an owed bill. It seemed to be an ongoing theme of mine, at that time, to point out others' sins to balance out my son's. I wanted to scream, *"There are worse things than being an addict!"*

All my efforts were wasted energy, I soon learned. The sad fact is, you typically cannot change people's perceptions of addiction, especially when our loved addicts keep committing crimes to feed their use or harm others through stealing and even violence. Although Mason wasn't doing any of the things that families complained about on support sites; I still had to delete my doorbell alarm app. Seeing the people trying to get into cars and houses hit too close to home when my son became homeless and hungry. The comments would kill me when people would talk about the lowlifes and losers who ought to just "get a job." I feel like most of those people are likely consumed in finding money to not get sick for just one more day. I desperately wanted to separate my son from the "criminals who commit crimes" as Joe Herzanek of "Why Don't They Just Quit" audio CD stated about those who are addicted and break the law, "Not a criminal with a drug problem, but an addict with a criminal problem."

I unfortunately would learn that there are many people who wish death on addicts, thinking they are a hopeless cause. Such people think addiction is the worst sin possible and that any other character defect that people may have is minor by comparison. Addiction does hurt a lot of people other than the one doing the "sin," but the question I kept coming back to was: did that make him a worthless POS? Was I wrong in not wanting to engage in throwing shade and shame at him? How is it helpful to just throw my hands in the air and say, "Yup, you're exactly right. He's an abomination to society, a bad seed, hopelessly flawed, and should be cast out and forgotten." With so many constant negative affirmations, how do people retain any hope of recovery? I know Mason despised being thought of as "only an addict" and treated sub-parly. It wretched his soul to be talked down to–even with the thick skin he had. He still craved to be shown dignity and respect no matter what his disorder looked like on the outside. One of my counselors (on what would be my last visit, of course) said, "If I hold a hand out to a homeless person and he refuses it, then I will walk over him forever after that." He is what I would later call a *one chancer*—three (or one) strikes and you're out. How many *chances* do you give a person to heal? Everyone has that number in their own head, I would find out.

Intervene

The next step was figuring out how to present the intervention plan to Mason. We also had to negotiate logistics and timing so everything could happen smoothly in the two days we were there. We needed to time the intervention precisely as a surprise, but also have time to catch flights out of state. We casually proposed to my son that we might be able to get him out because we found a "bed" he could use for 30 days. This must have sounded okay to him because he had nowhere to go. As long as he thought the truck was still broken, he was out of options. We said the "lodging" would be ready Monday morning just to help him think he only had to get through all of Sunday in jail. The interventionist wasn't flying in until late Monday, and we had to wait to make sure the judge signed the order Monday. I spent those tedious days praying Mason wouldn't get bailed out and constantly checking the booking report to make sure he remained in custody. I feverishly tried to find a replacement for my Monday afternoon shift at my job four hours away. I had zero luck and decided to ride the four-hour shuttle to and from work in order to keep my job. Finally, Monday morning, just thirty minutes before I was to board the shuttle, my boss said she was training someone, so I didn't need to come in. What a relief.

We drove three hours to Vegas on Monday morning to pick up the interventionist, Lance. He went to his hotel room and slept past our designated time to roll out. Between checking the booking reports, keeping my son patient and occupied, waiting for the judge to sign the order, and waiting for Lance to wake up, I was a nervous wreck.

Finally, without any other choice, Liam and I headed to the jail without the interventionist and without the judge's order, which meant we needed to see the bondsman and pay the fine. I wanted to avoid that because I didn't want to be responsible for him getting to his court cases, but hey, he was going to rehab so that meant he would be all cured, right? I truly believed that. Well, that mistake almost cost me $8,000.

Everything went unbelievably well. The interventionist finally woke up. His only words (which Liam and I continue to use often) were: "*I guess I needed that!*" When Liam and I pulled up to our hotel with Mason, he said, "*Cool. My drug dealer used to deal out of here.*" I tried to hide my shock. This was a brand new, nice hotel. There were a handful of trashy hotels in town where they could do their dirty dealing. With addiction, the surprises never end.

Two of my other kids, Haven and Luke, had driven through a horrendous snowstorm to get there and were hiding in the room. Mason was starving, scruffy, and dirty. We had a whole counter full of food. I had packed a bag full of new clothes and items he would need for rehab. He showered, ate, and then stepped outside the hotel to smoke. I texted the interventionist that Mason went outside and that I feared he would run. The guy walked out the hallway door, cool as a cucumber, lit up a cigarette, and made casual conversation with my son. Almost immediately, my son caught on. He smiled and said, "Wait, are you here with my mom?"

To my relief, Mason didn't take off. He came back into the room, and we opened the adjoining door to a room full of his family. The look on his face was one of embarrassment, trepidation, and vulnerability. He had no idea what was in store.

Confrontation

We proceeded to have a great intervention, just like you see on TV. He was uncomfortable and fidgety, but he was open about his struggles, how everything transpired, and how he knew he needed help. He talked of the future and how he was going to make it all up and more. I watched and listened to my younger son, Luke, who always looked up to his big brother, open up honestly about his anger. He stated how Mason's addiction had affected his life, including that it allowed him to take charge and open his own business– something he may not have done that soon.

My oldest daughter, Haven, there with her rambunctious, wobbly-walking baby girl, tried unsuccessfully to keep the tears back. Here was her brother, her best friend growing up, sitting there at everyone's mercy. Now lost in this tormented chaos of the dark world of drugs. Oh, how those two played together as children, roaming the fields in small town America. Making up adventures, dressing up, putting together plays and songs. She had watched with admiration as this little brother, now almost a foot taller than she was, made his mark on the world. He drove his nervous energy and full-on personality into work mode, working all over the western states, grinding day after day, always with the dream of starting his own company. She watched him achieve just that. He even employed her husband for a time. To watch Mason, break down over the last eighteen months, little by little, was torture. Like the rest of us, she believed he could handle it, that he would always prevail. He was persistent in every other goal he ever set, so he could get over drug addiction, right? Yet here he was. Endurance, perseverance, and courage, hidden behind all this turmoil. How could this be happening? Where did this deep abyss develop between two young, innocent children and this moment of adult darkness and pain? Could we ever bridge that gap?

We've talked a lot lately, she and I, about when someone has a hidden secret for so long. It's hard to know where their baseline even is. Who is the old Mason that we knew? Which part of him is the non-drug part? I've heard other moms say this as well. That they don't know their children anymore, but they wonder if they ever knew them, especially if the child started using in his/her teens.

About a year earlier, Haven and I traveled to Mason's town, which was our favorite weekend destination. We met him in a parking lot overlooking the highway. He and his dog, a white fluffy labradoodle, played, as Mason threw deer antlers for the dog to fetch. I took videos and pictures as I always did. I noticed that Mason looked a little rough, but I knew he was incredibly stressed at that time. He had over thirty employees, three different companies, and six job sites. He took on new projects even if he didn't have all that was needed to complete them. Being the boss, he had the responsibility to pull all the things together for these projects.

Looking back now, the patterns seemed to be emerging. He was gone longer and longer. Money was sometimes unavailable. He isolated more and more, leaving his employees to run the jobs without consistent leadership. It seemed like a sinking ship scraping an iceberg. The tip of the iceberg, in that scorching desert sun, melted quickly when an auger got stuck in a forty-foot-deep hole on the edge of a golf course. This was a major problem. He ruminated on it for days, worriedly calling me and telling me his options. He could send a professional diver down the hole at a cost of $25,000 and risk the diver's life, which he did not want to do. He could rip the auger of the hole, to which golf course management said, "No way." I can't even remember the third option or how they solved the problem. I do know it cost a lot of money and took any last wind out of my son's sails.

Nothing was the same after that. He was not set up for that kind of hiccup.

Anyway, that day, my daughter and I noticed he was acting a bit fidgety yet super fixated on random things. He always had ADD, so to pinpoint a time when the ADD stopped and the drug use effects took over is hard. I think he told us once that meth actually made him feel normal because the adrenaline meth stimulates countered his ADD just like Adderall or Strattera did, calming his jumbled thoughts. I learned that it's common for an addicted loved one to use in the beginning just to feel normal, or to gain energy, remove inhibitions, and smooth out social situations just like any other stress reliever might accomplish.

Mason had told the first nurse practitioner who was giving him his ketamine shot, "*I overwhelmed myself with too much responsibility, promised way too many people too much stuff, so when I couldn't deliver like I should, and wasn't sleeping, I went to more drug use to try to help me increase my productivity.*" When substance use becomes a crutch to just get by, addiction takes hold. Any person can go from being a casual drinker/occasional user to someone being in full-blown addiction whose life eventually becomes unmanageable. Jordan Peterson stated in his book *12 Rules for Life: An Antidote to Chaos*, "Order is not enough. You can't just be stable, secure, and unchanging, because there are still vital and important new things to be learned. Nonetheless, chaos can be too much. You can't long tolerate being swamped and overwhelmed beyond your capacity to cope while you are learning what you still need to know." [15] Balance seems to be the key. There are many checks and balances to help that happen and keep those around us accountable in all areas of our life. Did we fail in that early on? Should we have stepped in and helped in some way?

Now, a year later, with the intervention a success, we jumped in the car just in time and made the three-hour trip back to the airport. Mason sat in the back next to Lance, the stranger from the south, in whose hands I had placed my son's recovery. I snapped a picture, of course.

---

[15] https://www.jordanbpeterson.com/12-rules-for-life/

Dropping them off at the airport, Liam and I watched them walk through the glass doors. I collapsed into my husband's arms in relief at our accomplishment. This was big. A small set of unbelievable miracles came together. All was well. We thought.

Then they landed in Chicago on their connecting flight.

Exit the land of delusion where falsehood lives like a king. Let the bridge of faith take you places where your caged soul can take wing.
—Hingori, Guru Sutra: *The Guru Who Won't Keep Spiritual Secrets*

Chicago Goodbye

Three hours later, we got a frantic call from the interventionist. They had landed in Chicago for a connecting flight. "We have five minutes to board, and he's nowhere in sight! His phone goes to voicemail. We stopped to get fast food inside the airport. Mason said he was going to walk around the corner to see what food they had. Now he's gone. You didn't give him any money, did you?"

"Um, yes," Liam said. "He needed a charger, so we gave him $100." You'd think we had committed the ultimate sin. Lance freaked out.

He said, "YOU NEVER, NEVER, EVER GIVE AN ADDICT MONEY! He's probably gone to buy heroin!"

I was sick. I repeatedly called Mason's number from my phone. Finally, he answered, acting his normal *cool as a cucumber* self. He said, "What? I'm almost to the gate. That guy is just crazy." The tension and suspense were incredible and unbearable as we listened on one phone to this mad-as-hell addict turned Jesus-loving interventionist yell at us for being so foolish and on the other phone to my son, who we hoped was running to the airplane's gate.

They finally made it. They were the last two to board. I collapsed into relief. *God, this roller coaster never ends. One minute of despair followed by fear, confusion, and disappointment. Then relief. This kid. This kid.*

To this day, we don't know if Mason tried to score some heroin at the airport. All I know is that two days later, I received the absolute best phone call ever. Mason excitedly told me how wonderful the rehab place was, how grateful he was, how the people there "got it" and "knew what they are doing," how they needed one of these back home, and how he wanted to come home and open one. On and on he went. I couldn't stop smiling. This one phone call that I sadly didn't record, will stay precious to my heart. It was a phone call of hope, of justification that our stress and strain were all worth it. Mason had made it to detox after an entire night in a hotel where he admitted later that he wanted to run.

With so many moving parts surrounding a person in active addiction, happiness is sometimes short-lived. In the days that followed, a strange internet phenomenon occurred. Apparently, after viewing our picture at the airport, the parents of another struggling person called Lance for help. Apparently, when Lance got him to the detox facility, he took a selfie. In the picture, the guy was either passed out, or ducking his head. Only two people know for sure. The image created a huge controversy around health information privacy laws (HIPAA) and the qualifications of interventionists. When I say controversy, I mean intense internet bullying, arguments with hundreds of comments, character bashing of Lance, and many phone calls to the very DETOX, which MY SON WAS IN.

I remember sitting at work, watching in horror, one minute believing our first successful detox and intervention were an answer to our prayers, and the next minute thinking the entire thing would fall apart in a matter of days. The hecklers tore apart the website of the detox facility, saying it shouldn't allow patients to be photographed and that Lance was nothing more than a body broker for addicts and their families. They threatened to discredit the facility and even shut it down. They went into its history and tried to pull up disparities and biases.

I feared for my son's recovery, that his funding wouldn't continue, and even for his life. I knew it was only a matter of time before they found out that he was Lance's last "victim," and our privacy would be breached. I feared he would have to come home before he even made it out of detox and into rehab. Lance's stance was, "They can't hurt me. I'm only helping addicted loved ones, and you don't have to be licensed to do interventions. Just stick by me and we will win over these wolves." I was torn. I did the quickest deep dive into patient brokering ever. I learned that addicted loved ones are a hot property in the recovery world because they represent money from insurance for facilities. Obvious, right? Hospitals need sick patients to function and there was no shortage of addicts with worried, insured families.

I learned that some rehab center recruiters and marketers seek out addicts with the best insurance. The recruiters are then offered a cut from the insurance after it's billed and paid. Sometimes these cuts equal $2,000 to $3,000 per patient. Other parts of patient brokering deal with halfway houses and sober living scams. The rehabs will push patients into these sober living organizations who bill a huge amount (like $1,000-1,500) for urine and drug tests. The worst part is that some will even give drugs to addicts in order to get them to relapse so they can be re-admitted into the system, earning the recruiters financial kickbacks.

Lance didn't back down. He criticized the recovery community right back for wasting their energy on him, instead of helping other addicts.

These people worked in their offices inside rehabs or Suboxone clinics, or they were freelance "licensed interventionalists." They were all supposed to be on the same page—professionals in the field, leaders who were fighting the fight for addicted loved ones. And yet, here they were, acting like middle school kids and trying to bring down a person in recovery who was out on the streets, pulling addicts from the depths of hell. I always cheer for the underdog. Mason didn't have good insurance. He didn't have any insurance. And besides, Lance didn't charge us a fee. He asked only that we pay his expenses. So, how could he be this horrible monster they were saying he was? Oh well. I couldn't worry about his intentions. I had to keep my son in treatment.

The next day Mason called, unaware of all the attention, and said in a voice that reminded me of his excited toddler voice after building a huge bridge and tunnel in the mud. "Mom, I'm with Lance, and I'm ready to move to the next step." I panicked, wondering if they would get mobbed by protestors outside the detox, wondering what Lance would actually do with my child. Would he run him to a halfway house? Would he give him drugs so he would have to go back in? I had no clue how this patient brokering worked in real time. And here my son was in a car with him 1,800 miles away.

Since I was at work, and by this time a nervous wreck, I called Liam and told him to hurry and call Lance. I told Liam to ask Lance about the publicity and allegations and to find out where exactly he was taking Mason. Liam recorded the call for me. Lance was reassuring. Without letting my son know anything was wrong, since he was sitting in the car beside him, he spun his story and encouraged us to not give in, stay the course, ignore people, and that it would all work out. Lance was so good with words. I couldn't understand how he could be in this for a scam. He seemed unfazed by it all. He said he was "doing God's work."

I couldn't deal with all of it anymore. It was too far out of my control. I remember finally breaking through my silent barrier at work and saying to my coworker, "The craziest bullying thing is happening on the internet right now, and my son is right in the middle of it, but he doesn't even know it." She, of course, was confused, but in order to tell the whole story, I would have to tell the WHOLE STORY. I didn't.

Lance did deliver Mason to the rehab place. The first weeks went well. Although, I was incredibly frustrated by the lack of communication. Because of privacy laws, I could not get information. I was also unable to speak to Mason. I called one day to get a letter of confirmation that he was actually there, so I could get his social security card replaced for legal reasons. They sent it to me, and I made an appointment for a social security card. The social security office representative said the letter needed a date on it for proof. I called the rehab center and asked for another letter with a date. They sent another, but this time I noticed that Mason's name was misspelled. I gave up and turned it over to my daughter, who "magically and with a little Photoshop help," fixed up that darn mistake on the letter so we could take it to the social security office for a card.

We called another day to see if they could take a picture of Mason so I could get his passport replaced. All his documents were confiscated in his truck in Las Vegas when he had the gun held to his head. Angry, he called me saying a passport might mess up his insurance with them. *Okay, weird, but whatever*, I thought.

One day the center suddenly told him his insurance had run out and he had to leave. We panicked, not having made travel arrangements or anything. With privacy laws blocking my efforts, and communication with Mason scarce, it was hard to know what was going on. We knew Mason would get antsy and try to leave sometime, so we wondered if he was manipulating us or if he was actually being kicked out. My daughter was finally able to get through to a different employee than usual. In a strong southern accent, the employee promised that the center was trying to get Mason reauthorized, and he was "okay for now." Mason called back, confirming that the staffers were working their butts off to get him approved for more days.

The next week, his "re-authorization" sounded sketchy. He said he was transferred to a fishing cabin deeper in the mountains and that he was bused five hours a day with one kindergarten class of therapy. He said they had billed his insurance $100,000 by that time but were only feeding the patients dinky ham sandwiches. He said the organization was overwhelmed with patients, that counselors were quitting, and that the center didn't have room for him. I couldn't believe it. Were the counselors quitting because of the publicity backlash over Lance's photo? Who knew?

I was livid, but how could I call and complain when I had no idea if the center was scamming Mason or Mason was scamming me? My son was 2,000 miles away from me, with people I didn't know, deep in the Appalachian Mountains with (as we later found out) a different culture of people. I feared what they might do. Yes, he's an adult, but he was completely at their mercy. His brain was hijacked by substance abuse, he had no money, and he knew no one.

It was a stressful time. I'm sure I've watched too many of those murder shows when the killers get rid of the witnesses, but if we were dealing with scammers who had full control of my son, such a situation was plausible.

One day, I called and casually asked the office manager if I could send Mason an MP3 player so he could listen to music on his long commute each day. She said no and sounded weird. He told me later not to say anything to them because they got mad at him for telling me about his "long commute." So sketchy. Later, Lance told us, "You should have called me. I would have had him transferred." I thought, *Oh, okay. " You're the one who told us, "Don't give in to his demands while in rehab because he will do anything to get back to the drugs."*

He finished almost another month. Soon after moving to the fishing cabin, under the supervision of one recovering addict, Mason was somehow able to find his phone. It was on a room search, where he hid the phone in the searcher's own backpack and retrieved it later. All recovery bets were off at that point. We saw an immediate change in him. It was nice to be able to talk to him, but I knew the possibility of contacting his old pals was plausible. When he was released, they didn't have a way to get him to the airport. He finally went outside and called Lance on his own phone, and said he needed a ride to make his plane. He walked back in where the supervisor said, "Hey, we found you a ride. He just called."

Mason said, "No, you didn't, you liar. I found that ride."

His follow up care was a yellow sticky note in his wallet with the name of a Smart Recovery office in our town. Overall, I'm glad he went. I enjoyed hearing his stories about the geographical area, his peers, and all the shenanigans of the facility. That said, some tales were scary, with counselors doing inappropriate things. We found out later there might have been some improper insurance billing and kickbacks. Two years later I learned that a Medicaid claim was still open in that state in his name. I have never been successful in obtaining his medical records despite eight-plus attempts.

I know that my son made it seventy-three days without use, which was the longest period he'd been substance-free in a long time. All that we did to make this happen was a miracle, and I don't regret any of it, including Lance's involvement, and neither does Liam. He connected with my son and did an amazing intervention. When I picked Mason up from the airport, he was a bit dazed still, unsure what was next, but he appeared excited about life, glad to be home, thrilled to see his children for the first time in close to a year, and to get back to work. I recorded our conversation. Below are some of his comments fresh from rehab. Notice how they match what is told to him, but he still is trying to reconcile what his beliefs are.

Jan 22, 2020:

Addiction is a lifelong disease. There's no cure, but it's a decision. I hate when people say they'll be an addict forever. I AM, but I'm not gonna advertise it. It doesn't have to define you. When people say they can't stop smoking, that's a myth. Since I lost my truck, I didn't have the money, so I just started shooting. But the last twenty days in rehab, something happened. I've stopped obsessing about it. I used to think about getting it and selling it.

Here's the thing, though. It's not like you start talking to people, then decide to use it. You don't go visit your drug dealer to see how his kids are.

Your subconscious does everything for you.

Looking back, I did certain things that led up to my relapse. I got two empty rigs (syringes) BEFORE I got heroin. Obviously, I planned to use it. But the last twenty days, it hasn't even been on my mind.

This goes along with recent brain images of addicts while they were anticipating a fix, showing that the prefrontal cortex becomes highly activated in the areas of executive functioning.[16] I would learn later that brain scan changes don't necessarily mean disease. Falling in love creates brain changes too. One of Rylee's favorite podcasters, Dr Andrew Huberman states that dopamine is "tacked to pursuit more than it is to outcomes."[17]

I was always grateful for Mason's sober time. Even with the increased risk of overdose being significantly higher (some reports say 40% higher) if they resume use after, these times always brought my son back. Back to family and life and reconnecting even if it was for just one more time. I needed to be more like dopamine, to just enjoy the journey and not be attached to the actual outcome.

Healing is painful. It means disinfecting deep wounds. It means experiencing the pain for a season in order to put it in the past for a lifetime.
— Emilyann Allen

---

[16] https://dana.org/article/how-addiction-hijacks-our-reward-system/

[17] https://www.youtube.com/watch?v=z-mJEZbHFLs

Guilty Goodbyes

Zero. What an awful number. Especially if you're staring at it, in blaring red neon on the heart monitor. I was sitting next to my 86-pound dad in the hospital, listening to the slowed beeping of the monitor. His gaunt, pale, sunken face haunted me, but it didn't stop me from climbing into the bed beside him, knowing I would never get the chance again. The COPD he had battled for years had finally overtaken his lungs, causing him to go into unconsciousness when they wheeled him into the emergency room from the ambulance a few days prior. Now, in his room, before the nurse left, she had said it was only a matter of time until he would slip away. She came back into the room and told us this was it–his heart rate was fading fast. My mom and I sat in silence. My mama, stricken with her second bout of lung cancer, sitting on the chair with her colored scarf covering her chemo-ridden scalp, was nervous and scared. She didn't know quite what to do. I laid my head on his chest and watched his lifeless body slip away as I stared at the machines for verification. I told my mom to come over and say goodbye. Suddenly, I heard his heart beating strong again. I said, "He's alive! Go get the nurse!" My dad raised his right arm, as if it were a flailing last attempt to beat this disease, then dropped it to the bed. He was gone. Years of smoking took his life and then my mom's just four months later.

So why then, twelve years later, were my oldest daughter and I standing in a convenience store on an Indian reservation in the middle of December– waiting in a long line of people who were all there for the same reason? To get a carton of Lucky Strike cigarettes for half the price. It was for my son, of course. Wasn't everything? While he was in the rehab out of state, he was allowed to smoke. Remember life with a person in active addiction has you doing things you never thought you would. We were thrilled to have found these cigarettes for him because we had searched online on how to send some directly to him. Apparently, that's not an option and illegal so that kids can't buy them.

It took me back to that little girl carrying a handwritten note to the grocery store forty years earlier: "Please let Samantha buy one pack of Pall Mall" And they let me! What a circle of life!

Turns out, though, that even if both your parents died of lung related diseases, directly as a result of smoking all their lives, the shock of finding out that your kids smoke has completely worn off when you realized your son is a heavy IV drug user. To *only smoke* is HUGE compared to THAT world. We were thrilled to be able to do that for him, as long as he was in rehab, and they were allowing cigarettes to help with the absence of the drugs.

Let's talk about guilt. Ugh. Brené Brown made a fortune by speaking about healing shame, but guilt is an entirely different monster. Al-Anon teaches:

I didn't cause it,

I can't cure it,

and I can't control it.

This is the motto for all in family recovery to help them feel better about being "powerless" in the journey of addiction of a loved one. Truth be told, as moms, we all seem to keep this little tinge of guilt inside us to bring out on particularly bad days. Not the days when you are completely, insanely angry. Not the days when you yell, cry, or try to beat (figuratively) any possible common sense into your (mostly adult) child about the causes and effects of their actions. No, it's the days when you see a dad with his kids sitting in a restaurant. It's when you pass a construction site with a huge crane, and you wish beyond anything that your son was running that job or even getting paid to show up every day.

It's the days when you meet a new coworker, and you are petrified he or she will ask about your family. How are you going to say, "I have another son. I don't know where he is or what he's doing because, well, he struggles with which master to follow, I suppose."

Those are days when you casually look at an old picture, evoking such bittersweet memories, that you completely break down, pleading to God for a do-over. To just take you back to a certain time and you'll do it all again. You'll do it right this time. You'll take that little boy in your arms and say, "Do you know how wonderful you are? Do you know the challenges you will face and how strong you will have to be to say no?

Do you know you will have a beautiful little girl with towheaded hair like you had and a cute little boy with your now thick wavy hair and your smile who will idolize the ground you walk on, if only you will stay the course?"

Remembering your innocent child and all the things you wish you had said or done is a hell only a mother knows. "They," the experts, say, that in order to process this trauma of loving those with addiction, you have to let go of the guilt. But I know I will always have a tinge of guilt about things that *may* have left him feeling empty as a little boy. He always stated that he had a great childhood, that he's one of the twenty percent of those affected who wasn't abused, but that doesn't mean he didn't have trauma or have an environment that left him unable to manage his emotions or process pain.

I remember sitting in the grass, under the shady sour green crab apple tree, by the red brick house on the corner of Main Street. My best friend and I were watching the cars go by. We were 12 years old. This was our spot to view the world and make all our plans. We were preteens and unaware of anything outside our little town except what we saw on the three channels on our TV. We would walk down to the Dairy Queen, then back up to that faithful old apple tree, and sit and talk about the future as we saw it. We asked things like, "Do people who have ugly kids know they are ugly? If we ever have ugly kids, let's promise to tell each other the truth," and, "I'm sure the only way anyone will ever have kids with me is if I accidentally get pregnant."

Wait, what? Was that how low my self-esteem was? How could that be? I had two parents my whole life. I mean, they didn't sleep in the same bed or ever show affection. In fact, I used to fear coming home because my mom always threatened that my dad's things would be out on the road. But, hey, we were "intact." There was NO fractured, single parenting in our house. We did have weeks we called "starvation weeks," when there was literally no food in the house. We lived on pasta in V8 juice and TV dinners the other weeks. My parents worked hard. Really hard. They were poor folks. They each came from large Mormon families. My mom had fifteen brothers and sisters. All were born at home, except the last baby girl who was born in the hospital and died. My dad had thirteen brothers and sisters, and his parents actually divorced then remarried each other, I think twice, which was rare in those days. Dad told me that his mom got pregnant with him in 1932 and his dad "had to marry her." Allegedly, my grandfather beat my dad from the beginning, often calling him a mistake.

My parents grew up in pure survival mode so they raised us in pure survival mode. NOT THRIVE-AL, SURVIVE-AL. My role in the house was the peacemaker and to prevent my mom from going into one of her "moods." Those moods were torture. The saying, "If mama ain't happy, ain't nobody happy," could have been on our family crest. I remember coming home from school and being able to FEEL the heavy darkness from a mile away. She would lock herself in the bathroom for hours and just not talk or sit at the kitchen table staring into the abyss and chain smoking. When she wouldn't answer a simple question, I would resort to sliding papers under the door, with riddles or tic-tac-toe or the old dot and box game, where you drew dots in squares then each took turns drawing one line between the dots in order to see who could make the most boxes.

I didn't know it then, but this begging for validation and being the peacemaker in the house makes a child develop an acute sense of inadequacy, hence the apple tree conversation.

So where does a small-town girl with a developing sense of inferior ego and poor communication skills find a husband? Well, her friend sets her up on a blind date to the local basketball game at the ripe age of fifteen, and she ends up having a beautiful baby girl a year later while her friends were at the junior prom. In all fairness, I had a great husband who was a great father for twenty-four years. The problem was that I was a child raising a child. Even so, I loved being pregnant. I loved having amazing little humans inside me. Mason came when I was barely nineteen.

We moved to the big city where I drove my little yellow 1977 Ford Pinto in and out of the busy city streets— a small-town girl completely out of her league. Luckily, I had great in-laws who were helpful and nonjudgmental. My parents, even in their dysfunction, were great grandparents to my kids. But I still had this apple tree self-esteem issue.

The trouble with "getting pregnant" in a small Mormon community is the amount of shame that you may internalize. Stack that onto everything else, and you have a mom who tries to live out her worthiness through her kids. From the get-go, I set out to prove that I was worthy of having these beautiful little children. I mean, they were perfect. They were innocent and playful and curious and bright and just so beautiful. Did I mention beautiful?

I loved my babies. Their jerky, kung fu fighting motions, their feet–climbing invisible mountains. Their curious fingers. The smell of babies! I reveled in the glory of this amazing thing of creating a living, breathing life. An emotionally healthy person would bask in this sublimity and exquisiteness, but not this small-town, still shame filled girl. Nope, she had to prove herself worthy of their essence. She had to see them shine, so SHE would shine. To see them as perfection, to cover her imperfections.

Subsequently, I spent many years attempting to make my daughter a star. I did this through various activities such as: modeling, extras in movies, and little girl pageants. Even though we weren't rich, we spent time and money on gas, dresses, photo sessions, contest fees, and photo contests all over the state. It was an addiction. And where was Mason? On the sidelines. I have videos. I see this little boy, playing on the floor by the chairs. I see his sweet, innocent, chubby cheek face and big, gorgeous lips looking up at me for approval, for love.

Did I give him enough?

I can almost see the frazzled young mom, trying to do it all and have it all, being impatient with her husband, with her kids. I thought my value was somehow dependent on having my children achieve everything that I didn't. I had to prove that it was okay that I "got pregnant." I imagine my grandmother back in 1932 feeling the same shame. Back then, it would have been a worse tragedy. In 1983, not so much, but shame is shame. No matter where or when.

When I think back to those years, the first two verses of Bette Midler's, "Wind Beneath My Wings," always come to mind. Although the context of the song doesn't fit, and I am not placing ANY of these words on my now grown-up beauty pageant girl, or even Mason, but the words hit deep for the pain my son might have felt all those years, possibly setting him up to prove himself worthy. Worthy of love, of success, of awards, of just *being*.

We all have stories like this. Not many people can say they had a completely trauma-free, functional childhood. Many people with the worst childhoods grow up just fine. Was I enmeshed in my daughter's pageantry for all those years? Did I ever run my kids' homework to school when they forgot it? Did I make my kids stand up for themselves or did I come to their rescue? Of course, I did, but what am I going to do about it? I was young, but even if I had waited to have kids, it still would have been my first experience with every situation. **You don't know what you don't know! People do better when they know better.** To be fair, I wasn't a whole lot different than those around me. The culture in Mormon Hood was to achieve. It was all about sports, the awards, school functions, medals, and eventually sending your kids on missions for the church and being married in the temple.

Addiction Gene

In 2009, the National Institute of Health published an article on genes and addictions. They admitted that, "The moderate to high heritability of addictive disorders are paradoxical, because addictions initially depend on the availability of the addictive agent and the individual's choice to use it."[18]

This could explain why kids growing up in the same house can still have different experiences and personalities that leave them susceptible to addiction.

So, if this gene exists, I think it skipped me, like the twin gene supposedly does. Did I pass it on to my offspring? Both my parents

---

[18] https://www.ncbi.nlm.nih.gov/pmc/articles/PMC2715956/

smoked almost their entire lives, my grandpa was supposedly the town drunk, and my brother became involved in some sort of 1970s drug which contributed to his death. I still have no desire for alcohol or cigarettes and have never even tried marijuana.

What I do have is the propensity to be obsessed with whatever "project" I'm currently interested in. I wasn't one of those perfect children who had to excel on the surface *for their parents,* but I may have felt the need to cover up deep-seated insecurities and validation. Quite frankly, my parents had zero expectations or discipline. The pageants with my daughter, endless scrapbooking, even opening up a craft and scrapbook store, along with my obsession with self-help books and conferences, plus my lifelong Diet Coke habit, are all telling of my need to find/have something outside of myself to make me okay. Or maybe I was just active and involved—who knows?

My son is a lot like me in many ways—obsessive, easily frazzled in the sense of focus, and overwhelmed at times. He told his sister during his addiction, when he finally caved into having social media and got barraged with messages and texts; that he would read only the first four words or so. His brain just can't focus on the rest. As explained in the next chapter, I feel like he learned to hide his ADD and impatience with hard work, funny jokes, and always throwing another new idea into the mix in order to keep the subject moving along when he got uncomfortable.

There are many books about ADHD which reference the hunter theory including *Driven to Distraction*[19] and also Gabor Maté's *Scattered.* The theory is from Thom Hartmann from his book *Attention Deficit Disorder: A Different Perception.* Gabor quoted that the high percentage of North Americans who have ADHD may be descendants of yesterday's hunters who were quick-witted, fast on their feet, restless, and individualistic (like my son). They contrast with non-ADD populations, whose ancestors were farming people and stalling, patient, hardworking

---

[19] https://www.simonandschuster.com/books/Driven-to-Distraction/Edward-M-Hallowell/9781442370319

traditionalists (my second son).[20] So one conclusion is that today's ADHD people are leftover hunters in a farmer's world. I haven't read Hartmann's recent books on the subject but I don't think we live in a farmer's world anymore. I think social media is making everyone more distracted. The topic is explored in Johann Hari's new book *Stolen Focus*.

At one point, not too long before writing this book, I was still fraught with immense guilt. If only I had made him join the military. He idolized the Navy Seals. Then he would have had enough discipline and willpower to overcome this. If only we had more money, we could have nipped it in the bud at the beginning and whisked him off to Mexico for Ibogaine treatment and he wouldn't have lost everything.

For months after he lost his house, I wished we had apartments for him to live in. I even looked for a house to buy for our retirement and "let him stay in it until he got on his feet." I wrote to many rich people begging them to buy my grandchildren a house! Then I read Brenda Seal's book, *Son Down, Son Up*. Guess what? Her son had most of those things, yet it didn't stop him from continuing to use drugs. We all know the saying, "If a mother's love (or money or power or fame) were enough, there would be no addicts." It's true. What works for some may not for others. Hence, rock bottom is subjective, as is tough love.

My second counselor literally sat there and stared at me as I described, between tears, this emotional hellhole I was living in, how I couldn't talk to anyone about it, and how if Mason would only get better, then, of course, I would feel better. That was that.

He asked, "Do you think you caused this?"

I said, "No, of course not. I mean, I could have paid more attention to him when he was little. I could not have started him on Adderall. (Or made him take it more consistently, and for longer.) I could have noticed the signs. I could have believed he was not immune to losing control of his life just because he was the strong one. But what good does that do now? I just need him better."

He said, "Listen, you are never going to get past needing him to get better until you resolve the idea that you may have caused this. Because

---

[20] https://drgabormate.com/book/scattered-minds/

guilt/pain and healing/peace are separate, you can't work on them simultaneously."

"Well then. Just skip to the healing part of it," was my answer. "I'll get over my guilt."

He said, "No, we can't skip steps. Since you can't control the outcome, you have to work on being okay with whatever happens. And to be okay with whatever happens, you have to work on your core belief in yourself and your role." He said the KEY WORDS, "The chances of Mason getting better are just as likely as him not. As a mother, what are you gonna do with that revelation?"

I never went back to that counselor because he gave me no direct answer to my goal, which was to make my son better. But he was right. I HAD to resolve my inner conflict about why this was happening, how I was contributing to the problem, and why addiction had hit my family. I missed my family. Why didn't I better appreciate all those times BEFORE more? On and on …. I mean, isn't addiction messy, ugly, and evil enough? Do we have to relive our pain and suffering over and over again by using the power of guilt to punish ourselves more? It's ludicrous! At some point, you have to ask, *What am I getting out of this sorrow, this constant sadness in the pit of my stomach, this going through the motions of life while dying inside for my "problem." Just kill me now, God, because I cannot watch this play out."*

Part of my warped reasoning was, *"If I can find a REASON he's like this, then we can help SOLVE the problem, right?"* NO. In my quest to learn as much as possible about addiction, I learned that my son's choices were my son's choices, just as my choices in early parenting were my choices. During all this introspection, I HAD to work hard at figuring out where the enmeshment ends—where I end and Mason begins. Where does the role of a parent stop and a son's responsibility for his life begin?

After wrestling with the guilt, I still had a big hurdle to get over: *I was not responsible for what the rest of my family felt or chose to do regarding this trauma.* I cried so many tears over my perception of my family's role in Mason's addiction. My fantasy expectations were that we all do a group huddle (weekly, of course), arms around shoulders, on what to do that week to pull the wayward son back into the fold.

It seemed no matter what I tried, I only made the experience worse for everyone. So, not only was I losing my son to this nightmare, but also my family members were all at odds with the situation and with my role in it. All this daily self-torment came on top of not knowing how it would end, or when, or if ever, is the definition of ambiguous guilt.

It's hard to describe the daily in-the-pit-of-your-stomach fear and sickness and utter despair of not knowing whether your child is going to be one who survives to tell his story, or if only you will be left to tell his story. It's like riding in an airplane and wondering where the pilot went to school, how many flight hours he's had, or what happens if the radar breaks. You will drive yourself insane by not trusting the process. You must trust that you will land where you are supposed to. That will happen only if you can master your mind and let go of the absolutely desperate need to control the outcome of the situation, all while simultaneously trying to figure out where you went wrong. Hmm, maybe that therapist was on to something.

A bridge can still be built, while the bitter waters are flowing beneath.
—Anthony Liccione

Loss of a Wizard

I could feel the coolness of the home sewn patchwork quilt on my face as my warm tears fell onto its colored squares. I plucked at the little strips of yarn that arose from the middle of each square. I seldom remember having bed sheets, but these beautiful quilts that my Grandma made kept me warm for years. My slanted–ceilinged room was on the second floor of my 1912 childhood home and always had its drafts, but the cold Utah winter winds blowing through the old wooden windows was nothing like the chill I felt in my bones that day. This day, I had thrown myself onto my bed in a slurry of tears wrought with confusion, anger, and stunned disbelief after learning of my brother's suicide death at the young age of twenty-four.

He was my wizard hero. He was my stability in a dysfunctional, sometimes bitter home. He had a brain beyond anything I've ever seen. I compare him now to Elon Musk or Steve Jobs. I always felt like he could have invented Nintendo. With the wide-eyed naivety of a little girl in a small town poor family; I suffered the confusing deep pain of suddenly losing this hero to some evil thing called drugs, which no one dared talk about. After coming home from a mission for our church, my brother somehow started using LSD. It turned him into a depressed listless soul plus a few episodes of destructive rage directed onto his car. I'm not quite sure since it was never talked about. He ended up hooking up his car's exhaust through his trunk and running the engine while he sat in the fumes. Guess who saw him out on the lawn working on his car a few days before? Yes, the little twelve-year-old girl who didn't know any better. I thought he was just washing his car. Little did I know, he was setting up his own death.

My grief stretched beyond what my twelve-year-old could comprehend. This had to be some kind of cruel joke. My brother, my "wizard," the smartest person I knew. My protector from the madness of my dysfunctional childhood where there was never enough money and where there were never enough explanations.

My only sister was the oldest, a hippie-era freckle-faced redhead who was our second mom at night while my first mom worked nights at the turkey processing plant. My mom wore knee-high black rubber boots to work. She arrived on time every night without fail and cleaned it so perfectly that the inspectors eventually stopped checking her work.

Three boys followed after my sister, and then I arrived. My mom wanted a girl so badly that she was thrilled when I came out (no ultrasounds). I was the object of everyone's attention for the first few years—or at least that's what the old super eight movies portrayed. Me on a sheetless mattress, in a barren room, playing with a brightly colored Jack in the Box toy. Maybe my anxiety started there—with the popping up of the clown-like jack face.

I suffered from my brother's death for over a decade before I could even process it or talk about it. Was I now subconsciously trying to redeem that situation in my own mind? How could I possibly lose another of my allies? I had had so few in my life. God help me.

Now some forty years later, my obsession with the addict masquerading as my son was consuming my mind, body, and spirit almost as fast as Mason's illness was consuming him. One thing I realized I was fighting for was the immense loss of the relationship between my son and me. He used to call me and talk for hours, as he would drive long distances for his job. He would come and stay with me when working in my city. He and his older sister, Haven, were my best friends in that sense. They loved to talk about the parables of life and relationships. He called me one day and said, *"Since you're such a deep thinker, I thought you would appreciate this…"* I don't even remember what "THIS" was. It was just a fact that he could share with me. When I felt these conversations slipping away, I started recording them. I treasured every interaction, of course, to the point that I "may" have started my enmeshment and the immense feeling of the need to fix him. Could it actually be for purely selfish reasons? For me? For how I felt? For what I perceived as a loss? Me, me, ME! But, to my credit, a lot of my heartache was for the kids involved. My stomach would turn in knots every time I thought of him without his kids and having them not being able to know him as we all did.

I would soon start to wonder if he was looped and suckered so deeply into this horrible deal by his ADD brain and by the stressors he faced with his fiercely driven work mentality. By the time the house of cards started falling, it was almost too late. Never too late to turn around, people do that all the time. It may take many attempts to flip that switch in the brain, which only they can do. At this time, it seemed impossible for him to see the ripple effect he had on others that I was so desperately trying to get him to see. He had learned so many ingrained coping skills for many years that he seemed unable to change them without a severe interruption in the cycle. The definition of addictive behavior is repeated compulsive drug use despite negative physical and social consequences. He was certainly racking those up.

My empathy and search for understanding of this unraveling affliction helped me cope. Although I didn't realize it or accept it at this point, my other family members coped in their own way too. They all have completely different personalities. They had to detach in order to function and survive. My boys were starting new relationships, families, jobs and moved away from the area. My girls were trying to live their own lives, finding their own happiness. My grandkids felt farther away. To me, the silent suffering and distance between us, physically and emotionally, meant the collapse of my entire family. It meant the loss of our vacations together. Our family messenger groups. Our particular brand of humor and fun we always had while camping or having Christmas parties. To me, losing the battle of my son's addiction meant I was losing my family too. And that was pure torture to me. I cried many tears over this situation that was definitely a casualty from the addiction itself, but also a testament to our weak communication and problem-solving skills. No one person's fault—except maybe me.

The Loss of Me

One day a memory came up on my Facebook. It was a picture of me and my older daughter at a storytelling festival just three years earlier. I looked fabulous! My hair, my skin, my smile. I was with my grandkids on a cool summer night listening to fantastic entertainment, unaware of what the next few years of my life would entail. I compared it to my pictures now. My videos of myself that I had sent to my son, begging, crying, pleading. My hair was sparse and dry. My skin is thick and blotched. My spirit was worn out, completely drained. I was in destination mode, basing my entire emotional and physical life on another person's actions or some elusive event in the future that was out of my control. "Just get better already!" I wanted to scream! "Geez, is it so damn hard? Is it?"

After his last detox without rehab, Mason was standing at my counter eating and I said, "I need to go get a haircut, but I have to wait for my head to heal."

He said, "Heal from what?"

I said, "My nerves. I have sores that I pick at, so I have to wait for the scabs to heal."

"What do you do that for?"

"Um nerves, I guess."

"Well, just stop it," he said.

"Touché," I retorted back.

I realized the disconnect from his actions affecting others. Or if there was realization, it was too painful to bear. This was another moment when I realized no one was going to save ME. I had to start taking care of myself. There I was, out of shape, emotionally unstable, stuck in my own mouse wheel of sorrow, twenty pounds overweight, gray hair that I couldn't color until my sores healed, and my sores won't heal until I got control of my emotions and nervous picking habits. Not to mention my polycystic ovarian syndrome (PCOS)[21] was kicking up, which always happens with weight gain. That entails losing more hair, gaining more weight, increased mood swings, and increased acanthosis nigricans on elbows and underarms[22]. I mean, I was truly a train wreck. And I wasn't even the one addicted. How did I expect him to help

---

[21] https://www.mayoclinic.org/diseases-conditions/pcos/symptoms-causes/syc-20353439#:~:text=Polycystic%20ovary%20syndrome%20(PCOS)%20is,fail%20to%20regularly%20release%20eggs.

[22] https://en.wikipedia.org/wiki/Acanthosis_nigricans

himself with a warped brain if I couldn't even model healthy behavior by helping myself. I had to find a way out of this place so I could help him out—*If and when* he wanted out.

We seem to want to show someone how much they are hurting us as if that will bring us relief from the pain; yet it is shown over and over again that it just doesn't work. If they could feel your pain, then they could feel their own pain and not be covering it up in the first place.

In one of my favorite video documentaries "Restoring the Shack", William Paul Young talks about when his wife asked him if he missed her. He stated: "My misser was broken." I believe this is especially true in addiction. So many things are broken that others desperately want fixed –immediately.

The human psyche will do many things to avoid pain, as I should know, working with eating disorder patients. They will do anything to avoid eating too many calories and will go to unbelievable means to exercise them off. This includes standing, squatting, crunches, stretching, basically any form of movement at any and every chance they get. I've seen them hyperventilate for two hours to avoid drinking two ounces of Boost. When so much energy is spent every hour of every day contemplating how to do these things, it starts to affect other areas. They will lie and deny all day long about their intentions with movement or food. With addiction, we seem to take these behaviors personally. I guess you could say eating disorders don't affect others as much as addiction does, but here is what I kept wondering: If eating disorders and addiction both have DSM codes, and each is classified as a disorder/disease, why is the "cure" drastically different? They are both self-sabotaging conditions with negative consequences. The negative consequences for one of them is made worse by it being criminalized.

Over and over, I read in support groups, the frustrations of families who continue to be shocked at the audacity of what their loved ones say or do not say-or do- or don't do. I understand that everyone needs to vent once in a while, but there are some groups that border on toxicity. It doesn't seem helpful to continually objectify and demonize one person as the one who holds the key to fixing it all. *The unhealthiest one!* It seems to me that those in chaotic use can't even give themselves proper care, physically or emotionally, as is obvious by the poisonous, risky lifestyle they lead. I assume the support with families in eating disorders doesn't sound like, "After all the food I bought her, she still doesn't eat it. She **must** not respect me."

Eating disorder patients do face society's expectations of body image that contributes to their thwarted thinking. Then they're suddenly hit with: "Now you are TOO skinny!" Along that same note, as it relates to addiction: If you went to your twenty-year class reunion, 100 pounds heavier than high school, and someone said, "Wow, you look like you've gained a HUNDRED POUNDS!" Would that surely make you realize your predicament? "Golly, you're right! Maybe I should do something about that." We all know when we're missing the mark on health, or our goals, or whatever, but can we easily fix those problems even with a non-hijacked brain? No. It takes focused discipline and commitment every single day to achieve those goals. It's hard even on a good day to do what we are supposed to, and it doesn't happen by people telling us what a loser we are. We, as humans, have enough self-hate talk. I know constructive criticism is needed in life to help us set goals at work and to help set checkpoints so that we don't go farther down a scary path, but when the brain is full-blown chaotic control (when drugs or alcohol affect their *daily* decisions), it's too late for blame and shame to be constructive, in my opinion. I'm not a doctor, but I am a nurse.

Lorelie Rozzano, author of the Jagged Little Edges books, stated:

Why do we make people who have lost the ability to fight for their lives, responsible for making life and death decisions? We wait for those suffering to hit rock bottom, to reach out for help, and to come to their 'senses.' But SANITY IS NOT MAGICALLY RESTORED TO HOPELESS INDIVIDUALS WHO HAVE LOST THE WILL TO LIVE. When scared and dope-sick, your physiology changes, causing blood to go to the body parts you need for survival-muscles, heart, lungs, adrenal glands, and the brain. This means all conscious brain activity is re-routed to your reptilian brain while the actions in your frontal brain, the thinking and feeling parts, shut down. The message is, "Get dope or die. [23] (Used with permission.)

My son described being in that rat race for so long and searching for a way to "stay well" daily, that nothing else matters. This cycle may start as a way to 'numb out' but quickly turns to an ever-spinning rat wheel. The risk of death is known, but the search for relief, supersedes that knowledge. It's definitely heart-wrenching to think of someone being that desperate, lost, and unable to break free of the cycle. I have come to believe that sometimes it is a form of self-sabotage that we all do on some level, even if ours isn't noticeable or hurting others. Other times, it's just a plain old ugly consequence of trying to find some joy.

I think of when I was a little girl riding my bike all over the dusty country roads–one of my greatest joys as a child. Inevitably, my pant leg would get caught in the bike chain. Soon it would force me to a rolling stop to fix it, but not before turning my 1970s-flared pant leg into a greasy seemingly unfixable mess. I would carefully try to go backwards on my pedals, while pulling hard on my clothing, hoping the chain would disengage. I'm sure someone would be laughing saying that I chose to get on the bike, so get yourself out of it. Yes, I could do it myself, or I could enlist some help but no matter what, I can't fix myself *while on the bike.*

Not while caught in the chaos.

Sometimes you do have to go backwards in order to move forward.

One day while writing this chapter, today actually, I woke up with a migraine from hell. I could not move my head without vomiting. I became so dizzy trying to make it to the bathroom that I stayed in there for an hour, not daring to move. My younger daughter, Rylee came to see what was wrong, and I asked her to go get me a 7-Up because that cured everything when I was a child. At one point, with my head pounding and unable to keep medicine down, I begged out loud, in tears, to please make it stop. Please, anything.

---

[23]

https://www.facebook.com/recoveringaddictandauthor/posts/2416662548381427

This. Is. Exactly. How my son describes withdrawals. He said he has been so sick, unable to move, to even get his phone, and there would be people there, doing drugs in front of him, who wouldn't help him. This help, of course, is to give him some of their drugs. And no, they weren't doing it like some emergency rooms or pharmacists do. "I'm not contributing to '*your problem*.'" He was telling me this in the context of how he couldn't ever be a "mean'" drug addict. When someone is sick or broke, he can't stand to not help them. He said he realized finally, just like with his business, that the people he helped would not necessarily be willing to help him back, and that's one big lesson he learned for the first couple years. At that moment, I was both proud and jealous that these people got the best part of my son and *we didn't*, but that even in dire and disparaging conditions, my son showed some kindness. I wanted my big-hearted son back!

He said in those moments of being sick, he wished death upon himself. His pain-filled, sleep-deprived, hijacked pathway, trauma, and loss-covered brain was only running on two cylinders. Or cells. The GET DOPE OR DIE cells. I can't imagine in those moments, if he were to receive demands from one of the many sober people who missed him and need him to step up and get better, like immediately. It's like running through the airport late for a flight. You cannot stop and care about anything. You simply don't have the capacity.

In the book *Understanding Addiction*, authors Dr. Charlies Smith and Dr. Jason Hunt talk about salience. They write, "In the field of neuroscience salience refers to those things that grab our brains attention. Our brains are limited, after all. We can't possibly process all the information and stimuli that come at us. Saliency is the brain's way of determining what's important. It's a survival mechanism. If you're dying of thirst, water becomes salient and your brain focuses on that." [24]

On the contrary, what if the message was received of "Hey, I was thinking about you and wondering how you are today?" That might open up a conversation of what he could do to feel better without making his situation worse. I learned later to never ask questions if the

---

[24] https://www.youtube.com/watch?v=suipVqm7szY

response would anger or disappoint me. *I learned to give statements of fact and love, not questions of morose and virtuous sounding curiosity, with the underlying intent to spew my unsolicited advice and "recommendations."*

Vegas

One day, I found myself in Vegas. How ironic that would later become. I felt confused. I had just been at work, it seemed. I had been gathering the medications for my patients. The handyman had just brought in a new red Sears rolling toolbox to replace my medication cart, or so I thought. But as I pulled open the drawers, they were full of random things I didn't need. I searched everywhere. I went into the closet to look. Nothing was making any sense. He wouldn't have taken my medications, would he? Good lord, he would be in trouble. I set out on the hunt, finding myself walking into another building. I started recognizing buildings in Vegas. I looked at what time it was. I needed to get these medications passed out to the patients within the hour. How could I get from Vegas to my job in that length of time? I sat down on some steps, and the frustration and confusion were too much. I just didn't get it. I realized I needed to call my boss. How would I explain this? I would have to tell her I must be having a case of temporary delusions. But is it possible to be delusional yet know you are delusional?

Soon, a guy stopped by. He said, "Hey, I know what you need," which was followed by a sexual offer in exchange for a ride. Of course, I wasn't going to take him up on that. Weird, so weird. The frustration and the horror of realizing where I was versus where I needed to be and how powerless I was to fix it (because my brain could not think of a solution) were paralyzing.

Luckily, I woke up. Yes, it was a dream. I was so relieved. I have never had a dream that felt so real. As I lay in bed thinking about this, I thought, *Oh my hell. How he must feel like that! Knowing he was screwed, yet not understanding fully how he got there, or how to get out, must be maddening.* Now imagine if I were sick too. Imagine if I were dying for water, and that "guy" with the offer just happened to have some water. It would seem that his water was my only chance at survival at the moment, and that I could "figure out the rest later." (Mason's most famous words).

This is *my* story and not my son's story because I truly don't know how he feels. I don't know what it's like to battle these demons. I don't know what it's like to not have a bed at night. I can't imagine wondering where my next meal is coming from. Furthermore, I can't imagine not CARING where my next meal came from. I can't imagine being reminded of all my failures every time someone's name popped up on my Messenger- like MOM! The internal eye roll of what have I done wrong now, what a mess have I made of someone's life, even when high, must get old. Pair this with ingrained ADD coping skills learned all his life and you get a perfect storm for the addicted ADD brain. More on that later. Thank you, Gabor Mate!

This story isn't my other kids' version of the story. I suspect they are still angry or suffering greatly at the trauma of losing their brother and their friend and enduring the problems addiction caused. They each have a unique perspective, pain, and wounds to heal in their own due time. They have restructured their lives with steadfast courage and grit. I'm truly proud of all of them. I love them so much and I admire a lot of things about them too. I miss many people and their sweet smiles and joking around. I miss what they contributed to our family, not just Mason. This book is written in the context of my journey through addiction to help other mothers, but that doesn't mean I wouldn't write a book about my other kids, if the need arose.

We all grieve the loss of and miss his talent, his stories, his impact on so many people he touched and taught or made laugh. Everyone seemed to know Mason was a larger-than-life thinker and do-er. He just had that aura about him. Part of that was his restless brain. He was always thinking, thinking, planning. He always said that's why he and his brothers made such a good team, because of their differences. He was a big picture looker. A risk taker. The youngest is a firehouse of energy, always working in the present moment, focusing on perfection at what he was doing on the job, detailed, strong, and funny. Passionate yet easygoing, joking around, making work pleasant for everyone around him. The middle one is quiet, steadfast, strong, yet sweet. He was able to notice things the other two missed because they were so enthralled in their own roles that required a bit more ego. Steady and strong, like a backstage man who the show could not run without. The epitome of Alabama's 80s song "40-Hour Week."[25] He's an old soul, thoughtful and introspective.

Mason was a legend in the industry, at least that's what he used to tell me. I once went into a big office to pick up a check of his as a subcontractor and in pure Mason form–he asked me after if they had a statue of him up yet. It did seem that everyone in his industry knew his name. From inspectors to equipment drivers all over the western states and Ohio, too; everyone has a Mason story. And Mason had a story about everyone.

He has a way about him that made everything seem like an adventure. He is a big kid at heart, with huge dreams and visions. His brand of humor with sarcasm makes every interaction with him pleasant and fun. That kind of drive and personality made him a popular guy in any environment. He has a strong voice, tall, buff, and broad-shouldered. He looks people straight in the eye and holds their attention. A wallflower he is not. This led him into his daredevil, always searching for something else, a risk-taking attitude. He loved to embellish a story or tell it in his own funny version.

After my deep dive into learning every single thing, I could find about addiction and then ADD, I learned that this daredevil (workaholic) approach is classic with severe ADD children who grow up with a (sense of having) a lot of failure, discouragement, and a chronic sense of inadequacy due to being so neurophysiological tuned out and distracted. Society and school just don't allow for this and the child is left feeling somehow flawed. They spend their life proving that theory wrong, although deep down that's the only way they know to be true. And possibly to stay safe from uncomfortable emotions or situations.

With one hand, you change what you cannot bear. With the other hand, you bear what you cannot change. —Nkwachukwu Ogbuagu

---

[25] https://www.youtube.com/watch?v=S-G2J3RzURA

Rhabdo Goodbye

In October 2018, about a year before this, when things were just beginning to unravel, I texted my younger daughter, Rylee, who lived in the same town as Mason. It was midnight. "Can you go to Walgreens and get some salt tabs and take them to your brother at Sleepy Inn Motel?"

"Mom, I'm an hour away and I have to be at work in the morning."

"But I'm three and a half hours away, and he will go into kidney failure if you don't."

"Tell him to call an ambulance. Last time it took me five hours to get him into my car."

The "last time" she's speaking of was over a year before that, when we were vaguely aware that my son 'might' have a pill problem. Now all that seems minor. More than anything, I wish I had realized how much worse it could get. What would I have done if I knew?

On June 17, 2017, she went to his house and found him almost paralyzed on the couch. She spent close to five hours trying to get him into the car so she could drive him to the hospital. He couldn't walk, and every time he tried, his muscles would spasm and send him to the floor. He refused to call an ambulance and kept thinking if he drank salt water, he would be able to walk. When she finally got him to the hospital, he was admitted and diagnosed with rhabdomyolysis, a muscle-wasting condition. I'd only heard rhabdomyolysis happening when elderly people fall and lie there for hours or days. It can lead to kidney failure and organ damage if not treated. My son's creatine kinase, the enzyme that measures muscle damage, was 2046. Normal is under 200. We still don't know for sure why he got it, but we figured it was a combination of stress, working so many hours, and—as we now know—possibly his drug problem. He came out virtually unscathed, but of course, we thought it was the wake-up call for him to start slowing down and taking care of himself. I thought, *I hoped.*

Yet here we were again, a year and two months later, with another attack. Now he was in the middle of nowhere, hunting elk, staying alone in a hotel with his trusty, fluffy dog Ruby2shoes. She was a high-energy labradoodle Mason paid to have flown to him, after his last dog was run over. The dog was his constant companion.

This was my first real "on call for chaos" moment. Liam and I headed south in the middle of the night, stopping at every convenience store to find salt tablets. Having no luck, we sat in the darkened Walmart parking lot about an hour away from home, wondering why a simple salt tab was so hard to find. We soon heard that Rylee had finally bought some Pedialyte and made the drive to him. She said he was fine, and she would be staying with him the rest of the night.

We headed back home, relieved. The next day, my son called and asked a strange question about preventing such an experience in the future. "Can I just inject salt water into my muscles?"

"No, son. No, you can't. Please don't even think of that again."

"Oh, I won't. I'm scared of needles. I was just wondering if it would work."

To this day, I keep jars of pickle juice in my fridge because apparently it has the electrolytes needed to solve that problem. I was in a health store recently buying vitamins for Callan when an elderly lady came in asking for pickle juice! The store said they were out! So it really was a thing! The few days following that incident, Mason was in and out of cell service areas, which sent me into fitful nights of wondering if he'd had an attack, was alone in the desert unable to move or call for help, and slowly dying. His few responses were short and semi-informative.

In previous years, it wasn't unusual for him to go out alone to roam the mountains, hunt, and search for deer sheds (the antlers that deer and elk drop every year in anticipation for winter). He was an avid outdoorsman, taught by his dad and grandpa to respect and enjoy the mountains. He reveled in that environment. Solitude in nature was his peace, his bit of heaven. If I had to pick a month when things truly changed in my son's routine and sent him spiraling toward losing his business and family, it would be that month. He started "hunting" every day. One Monday morning when he said he was hunting, I knew something was wrong. It was normal for him to take a week or so off every season for a camping/hunting trip with his dad, grandpa, and cousins, but this week, to be hunting on a Monday morning was strange. Around that time, his cousin, who was his same age, died unexpectedly from a random electrical accident. Mason didn't appear upset, but after his ketamine experience a year later, I think the deaths in his life truly bothered him. "Unresolved trauma," the experts might call it. One more wound to cover up with a substance. That wound fell on top of a mound of others: stress, burnout, painful loss of precious relationships, impending doom of the business and major expenses from time and money lost on drug use.

Looking back now, it seems that was the year that heroin got its sharp hooks into my son. Just a few months after the premature birth of their son, my daughter-in-law told me she suspected heroin use. Oddly, I rejected the idea at the time. I just didn't want to hear it. When you're living in the what-the-heck moments of trauma, human nature puts up defensive measures that include/sound like benefit of the doubt, hope in all things, "not my child" statements, disbelief, and just plain denial. Compile those tendencies with the fact that Mason is an adult, lived 400 miles away, and has always been the captain of the ship of our family. The combination allowed the demon a lot of time to dig its evil talons into Mason's habits and life.

Mason convinced himself (and us) that he could handle it, that he would take care of the problem "tomorrow." Besides, heroin??? In the old (and some new) Hollywood movies, cocaine and alcohol were made fashionable and acceptable. They were (and are) used by the elite in glass-walled mansions at bustling parties filled with glamorous women in black gowns and hotshot men in button-down white shirts and jackets. But heroin? That was for men under a bridge, likely mentally ill people. This very heroin stigma gets in the way of recovery/help because today's heroin users are likely a direct progression from prescription pill abusers—no matter where it leads them. As stated earlier, they are normal people who may have once had productive lives.

During this time, Mason had been living in motels for almost a year because of the uncertainty of where things were going with his house and marriage. I wanted to get him somewhere stable and cheaper. Every effort I made to calm things down had backfired. I learned that involving myself in any other relationships only caused more division and conflict. This caused me much turmoil in addition to the actual addiction. Addiction pits the struggling person against everyone who tries to get between him and it. The tentacles of addiction's nooks and crannies bring out confusion, anger, lying, cheating and basically the worst in everyone. Families are horrified, reactive, and devastated. Not knowing what else to do, they start to turn on each other. With all the different personality types and expectations, this adds fuel to an already hot fire.

The fact was my son wasn't getting better, and I thought he needed an advocate for moving forward with housing and recovery, instead of me trying to fix, force and/or repair past issues and relationships. Somehow this stance of me backing away from playing counselor, a role that I wasn't very good at anyway due to my lack of boundaries; resulted in my daughter-in-law blocking me, and, I believe, my daughter, for almost two years. We didn't see the grandkids from December 2017 until December 2019. It was a tremendous heartache for me. I did not know how to process my son's unraveling life, his failed business, his living in motels, his reliance on shady people, and my not being involved in my grandkids' lives. On top of all that, my work unit was closing up, and I had to find a new job while also navigating a brand-new relationship with Liam.

I was miserable. The pain of navigating the addiction's tornado-strewn path was too much. The heartache of possibly never seeing my grandkids grow up was incredibly sad. I cried many tears. I suffered in silence. My other children knew some of it, but I told no one else, not one soul, about the situation for two years. I wrote a children's book on addiction in honor of my granddaughter, to help me cope. I wanted her to know how I felt during those years, even though I knew I probably couldn't publish it.

At this time, Mason and I were still having long conversations about life and relationships. We strategized endlessly about how to mend the wounds. I told him countless times, "If you would only get clean, you could fix everything," which I truly believed. But he was committed to solving relationship problems without getting clean. The addiction monster was hell bent on keeping this obedient slave under its spell of believing he could have it all. He said, "Mom, even if I can't save my marriage, I'm going to get her to not hate you." Always the fixer, the take charge leader of our family since my divorce; Mason thought he could repair anything, even when he couldn't repair himself. He has a huge heart. He hated to see everyone suffering. His brain was hijacked and still vacillating between the shame of where his addiction had taken him and denying that "it was a problem, and you guys are overreacting. I will straighten everything out tomorrow."

None of us knew what to do, especially as he spiraled so quickly. Each of us kept having one WTF moment after another. We were so deep in pain and discomfort and lack of control of the situation that we started to cover it up by lashing out at each other. Disappointment and unmet expectations elicited knee-jerk reactions that turned into major emotional upheavals that were not conducive to healing. Everything I did seemed to make things worse.

Looking back, it's easy to see the progression of the breaking apart of communication and the dissolution of family bonds as each person fights to come to terms with his or her experience. I was overwhelmed. We all were, but I could only do me. Things were moving so quickly out of control that I had to back away, find my own truth, and absorb the upheaval this disease was causing me and my daily life.

Reunited

During the "possibly shady" rehab experience, the Christmas holiday came. Although Mason was out of state, we had our annual family Christmas party, a thirty-three-year tradition. We rented a beautiful condo in our beautiful resort-turned-drug town and decorated it all up for Christmas. My amazing, wonderful daughter somehow managed, on her own, to invite and persuade my, by then, ex-daughter-in-law to bring those sweet babies and stay with a family she hadn't seen in two years.

With so much hurt and distance between us all, her joining in the Christmas spirit helped mend damaged hearts. We were thrilled beyond belief to see the kids again and to watch all the cousins play together.

This was another unbelievable miracle, and I believe Mason fulfilled his promise to me to help her "not hate" me, if even for a moment.

If there's life, there is hope. —Stephen Hawking

Shed Goodbye

April 27, 2020, 3:00 a.m. "Son! This is why your motivation is so low and why tomorrow never comes and why you feel like you're on a hamster wheel and can't get off! If you want to talk to someone about your serotonin levels and mood, the doctor's volunteer clinic has an appointment for you at three tomorrow." This was the message I sent to my son because I knew he was trying to cut down his use due to money. I attached a video titled "Addiction Neuroscience 101."[26]

He responded, "I wrecked my truck. I have nothing left now. Wish me luck. I'm hiding in a shed, but I'm okay. I'll start walking in a few hours."

"What? Where? Why are you hiding?" I was freaking out. What was this life?

"I'm tired. I'm going to sleep. Cops are looking for me, so I'll have to report the truck stolen." He had wrecked his truck into a rock in the middle center island of the road. He couldn't afford a tow truck (being homeless and all), so he left the vehicle for someone to find and tow. He stayed nearby until cops showed up. He said there were ten of them swirling around the truck, so he took off because he "didn't feel like going to jail."

The proverbial, never-ending "other shoe to drop" had dropped, except there were always more shoes. I was not only the lady who lived in a shoe, but I was also living in the damn shoe factory. I frantically thought of what to do in this obvious OCFC moment. Seasoned

---

[26] https://www.youtube.com/watch?v=M5Mky3Jr960

veterans of addicts and tough love advocates would say, "Do nothing. This is his responsibility to figure out. You can't rescue him every time he wrecks his truck, hides from the cops, has nothing to eat and continues to experience negative consequences that SURELY *someday* will make him change."

But there's a slight problem with that.

I had too many fingers in the fire left over from his first rehab experience. For starters, I had put my address as his when he first came up for air after losing his marriage and home. Then when the bills started coming in, I had written to the IRS in response to the $83,000 delinquent tax bill they said he owed. Then the lawsuits started arriving. When the first one came, for an $18,000 judgment, I went into a full-blown panic attack. I called a friend who had several businesses that I knew had been sued. The advice was, "He's screwed. He better put on his big girl panties and get to work. All he has to do is get that stuff out of his system and he'll be good to go." Sure, tell that to a person with a substance use disorder. Try to tell him ANYTHING. The mistaken belief that detox is all that is needed to "recover" is rampant in people who think addicts are just weak. I even thought that at one time but was quickly learning that it isn't quite that simple. There are many parts to recovery, one being the mental obsession to use even when the physical withdrawals are out of the body.

Of course, I was in fear he would be caught by the ten cops allegedly chasing him. I admit my imagination ran amuck—afraid of seeing him on the news, walking in the tall dead wheatgrass away from a beat-up old shed, surrounded by overzealous uniforms, shackled in old rusty handcuffs, looking gaunt and disheveled, and turning to the camera saying, "Mom, you didn't make it fast enough."

So here we are. Another negative consequence. What to do. What to do. I thought, *surely if I just let him sit there and figure it out with his tired, cold, dirty, hijacked brain and body, he will make the right decision. Which is what? Go turn himself in? Tell them he was scared and left the scene of an accident because he may have drugs in him or on him?*

When they get themselves in so deep, a one-size-fits-all answer may not be practical for every situation. There are just too many moving parts. In this case, all the moving parts were frozen. My son was paralyzed in fear in an old shed in a dumpy side of town. His last truck—his house really; filled with all his belongings, now broken down with a leaky radiator, then towed to join the hundreds of other stagnant vehicles, all with their own stories of demise. *Surely this is rock bottom. Thank you, God, that he didn't hit anyone or injure himself.* Now, when I think back to how the next few days and weeks went, I suspect he had a concussion from that wreck. As a nurse, I should have taken him to the ER, but all I could think of was this was another chance to get him to realize he needs to go to detox.

Just the Friday before this, he had texted me, "Any chance you would get me an Oreo shake and bacon burger from Denny's?" I had done so maybe three or four times that year. Haven had fed him a few times too that I know of. Some tough love advocates don't believe in any of this. In my opinion, it's dangerous to give advice when we know nothing of the entire situation and family dynamics or when only one side of the story is being presented. Every single post I see about asking what to do with a certain situation with a person with SUD is followed by dozens of responses about not enabling them to death. I read, "Walk away. Save your sanity. Don't give him money." But there are just as many posts that read, "I got the call today. My child is gone."

Many parents wish they had done more. They relive their last "tough love" words to their now gone children. One of the reasons I wrote this book is to help parents and spouses have some relief that no matter what their addicted loved one throws at them, no matter what the situation, you have to apply what you know at the time. Whenever someone told me to walk away, I became infuriated. It just didn't sit right with me. On the other end, I admit, are those who live in fear of their child or spouse due to their erratic behavior and have to cut off contact for safety. There are those in the middle who just don't know what else to do, so they limit contact. And finally, there are those who are just fatigued. They see each attempt at sobriety as one more chance wasted and just like my therapist had said about the homeless person— he only gives one chance.

I would eventually figure out that sometimes taking a stance either way is an attempt to gain a sense of control of an otherwise uncontrollable and unbearable situation. We seek a need to feel like we are doing something, and if doing nothing achieves that, then so be it. I do think it can be a smoke screen or a way of manipulating what we want to see happen too. Such as using some threat or ultimatum in order to get what we so desperately want out of another person. Some who defend their decision of "tough love" with "cause and effect" stories on the support groups such as, "As soon as we stopped enabling, they requested rehab/got their act together/and now has been clean for X-Y-Z amount of time." When I casually asked how long it took for that to happen, they would respond 6 months, two years etc. Yet they still insist that their actions were the motivator. I think it's okay to think we are the cause of someone changing for the better, but I also think there is no way to measure all the variables that constitute "success" from either tough love or enabling. I do think it's cruel to tell someone, even in a group post, that "enabling kills," without any data that suggests someone actually killed someone by loving them too much or advocating for them. What a kick in the already grief-stricken mom's teeth to pile on more guilt that she caused her child's death.

I also think it's a travesty for social influencers with big audiences to try to map out a certain pathway for sobriety as a one size fits all solution. Especially with broad statements of enabling and tough love which mean completely different things to everyone. Because of this disparity and divisiveness, there are moms asking if letting their child shower or keeping them on their medical insurance is enabling. That saddens me. We want to move them toward recovery and a normal life by showing them they're worthy of it. How is denying food, cleanliness and the means for recovery doing that?

It is a fine line between "lessening their consequences" which is the argument for enabling – and sparing them *more* shame of their decisions – which is what love does. As if addiction in itself isn't enough of a negative consequence. Most people don't skate by without losing many things by the time the addiction is in control of their lives. Luckily, we all get to choose our response and my choice most of the time was to not add more pain and consequences in order to "teach him a lesson."

In my opinion, addiction is cruel enough. I enable my son to know he is loved and that he is capable and worthy of a better life.

Just because it's true doesn't make it helpful- —Matt Kahn

Lost in Paradise

Imagine a place that you've loved for as long as you can remember. A place where every single smell, tree, or sunset gave you such pleasure and comfort that when you left, you ached to return there. Like picking apples from Grandma's tree, savoring the taste or the feel of the hot air on your skin, breathing in every ounce of sunshine you could. Then suddenly, something unknown sweeps in—like a virus—and poisons all your thoughts, dreams, experiences, and worries.

This is the place where my kids had planned all their hopes and dreams. A place where we could go for a weekend to de-stress, hike, bike, and swim in the red river water (from the red clay dirt). Even my parents loved the area when they were alive. We would drive around looking at all the retirement subdivisions, go to home shows, and dream of winning enough money to move there. It was quite an oasis in itself, with palm trees in Utah, no less! It was similar to the beautiful red rocks of Sedona, Arizona.

I had driven to this once-wonderful place full of happy memories which I now found utterly depressing. This weekend, while my daughter was busy cleaning her apartment and squaring things up with her roommate, I set out to "casually" look for my child. Afraid of what he would look like, I didn't actually want to see him. While driving around the familiar streets, I was filled with trepidation and sadness.

As I was reliving memories, trying to settle the fight between my thoughts and feelings of what that town had become for me, I spotted a ten-speed bike lying beside the road. It looked as if someone had fallen off it, and sure enough, it was then that I saw the body of a man lying motionless off the side of the road, down the hill a little. I quickly sped up, then turned around to go get another look. Could it be my son? Had he "borrowed" a bike? Was this person dead? I called 911 and told the dispatcher it almost looks like the man had been hit and thrown off the road. I turned back around to shine my headlights and look for any movement. I saw none. I passed two policemen I had seen earlier at the convenience store. I turned around to see the guy sitting up talking to them, with ambulance lights swirling around. He acted irritated. He must have been refusing the ambulance. If he was just sleeping, why didn't he pull his bike farther off the road? On my last swing by (yes, I was a nosey, obsessed mom driving around in the dark, looking for my homeless son that I was afraid to see), I prayed that someday, someone would be nosey enough and care enough to call 911 if Mason were lying there.

I never found Mason, but I started to think of how I could best help him with food or shelter or basic necessities if he insisted on staying in that environment. I went to the laundromat and put a $15 credit on the system so he could wash clothes in the future. I went to the dollar store across the street to do the same thing, but I didn't dare tell the "whole story." I was afraid they would deny him entrance if they knew he was homeless. This was when Covid-19 fear was creeping into communities. I bought gift cards, which is a no-no in the enabling world. I couldn't help but think how nice it would be for him to be able to go in and buy water or candy bars.

Even though active users don't care about that stuff, it is still comforting as a mom to do things to help your child stay warm and fed. I then went to Walmart and bought a little red cooler jug. Mason had told me how hard it was to get water since restaurants had closed down their lobbies (again, Covid-19 pandemic issues). He couldn't go to fast-food places to use the restroom or get water. I tried to figure out a neutral place where I could drop off the cooler for him to pick up. I made some calls, found a spot, and dropped off the cooler, towels, water, and a whole bag of granola bars and goodies. Sadly, Mason never picked it up.

So now, we were back home from that weekend and now my child was hiding in a hot shed back there. In the early hours of Monday morning, I was deciding how to help him without "enabling" and how to resolve my shattered nerves. My most hopeful thought was that this supposed new "rock bottom" would work to see how far he had fallen. Finally, after four hours of tormenting indecision, I took off and drove the four hours back down to our favorite town-turned-hell.

Mason agreed to "do what I wanted if I came, but he was going to go get high one last time." I arbitrarily started driving without having a definitive plan. I made what felt like 100 phone calls on the way down. I practically begged people in the local recovery community to help me (by placing a post on a recovery Facebook site—my usual method of finding help). Thanks partly to the new scary Covid-19 pandemic situation, no one would get involved.

On the way, I stopped at Haven's house for advice. She didn't know but agreed to follow me in support. She loaded up all her kids, and we took off southward. To this day, we don't know why we drove the four hours in separate cars. Mason actually mentioned this to her in his humorous way when she picked him up. I hid down the street because I was scared of seeing what he looked like. He said he almost ran when she pulled up because he thought she was the task force in her white Tahoe.

Before we arrived, we spent hours arguing with him on text about what the best plan was. My daughter and I arrived at the town, still unsure where he was because he wouldn't give his address due to being afraid we would send cops. We stopped under a tree, in ninety-five-degree heat, to let her kids run on the grass, while we devised a plan. He argued endlessly. Of course, he just wanted me to give him some money for groceries (to put where?) and to help him get his tools out of the truck at the tow shop. Nope. I had played that game before and lost big time. He adamantly refused to go to rehab, so finally I said, "If you don't need any help, I will just turn around and go home. He finally admitted he had nothing and had nowhere to go. He agreed to go with me.

We left without a concrete plan, but we had our guy. The only problem was that our guy *didn't know what he wanted*. He wanted to continue trying to build his business back up. He wanted to talk us into giving him some money or a ride somewhere. These were strange times as our little convoy trip headed north, Mason in her car and me following behind like an oversized tow car stating the obvious, *"AT RISK CARGO AHEAD—we just want to get it somewhere safe so it can work on healing, life skills and prosperity. Please give us some room and grace."* We stopped at the gas station. I parked far away, still scared to get a glimpse of him, and praying he wouldn't take off. My daughter texted me twenty minutes later saying they had a good talk, and he was sleeping. God, the ups and downs of this journey with an addicted loved one. On the way home, I made an appointment with the bankruptcy lawyer for early the next morning. This was honestly one of our main motivations for dragging him home. I NEEDED those papers signed to call off the wolves from all his business debts in the last year. I NEEDED my address off everything, and the only way was to finalize what I had started and do the "detach with love" that everyone was talking about. I had been begging him to help me get that done, and it was always, "I'll come up tomorrow" or similar procrastinating promises. *(Addiction loves to mess with time management and planning).*

One of the definitions of enabling is cushioning the fall—the consequences of the behaviors of addiction. Numerous times, I've defended my choices as a mother. Every person's situation is different, and I think that someone reading one paragraph or knowing only a small part of someone's situation is not enough information to use to give specific advice. I was in such pain and torment that, every month or so, I would actually post a crying, snot-nosed video on the "moms of addicts" groups to get some support. Remember, outside my immediate family, I was talking to no one about Mason. Some of the advice I received was encouraging and helpful, but I did have to suffer through advice from those who didn't understand the scope of Mason's debt, including what he owed the IRS, and the severity and speed of his fall plus all the ramifications of the debt to family.

He stayed with my daughter that night while I drove the hour back to my house, knowing I would have to drive all the way back to pick him up for the bankruptcy appointment. Morning brought bad news. He was

114

sick. Withdrawals were bad. He said he just needed a little bit of relief and would do anything to find it.

When I arrived at 7:30 a.m. he wouldn't get off her couch to come with me. I was livid. I could feel a fight coming on. In a huff, I walked out the door and to my car. I tried to settle down. Somehow, my daughter pulled through again. I don't know what she told him, but he staggered into the car in the dollar store clothes. Here I was again on a trek in my car with my resistant son, like dragging him to church when he was little. By the end of that day, though, I got what I wanted but at an emotionally exhausting price.

I drove straight from my daughter's house in the country, into the city, and right to the rented lawyer's office. By this time, he had retired, but agreed to finish this case. Another miracle. I dragged Mason into the fancy office building with no shoes on. Yes, that's right. He couldn't find the dollar store sandals I bought him because he was thrashing around so much in the back seat. I said, "Just come on. Your pants cover your feet."

The few minutes outside before we went in were wrought with sweating, shaking, and nausea by Mason. Somehow, he was able to act semi-normal and feign interest while signing the thirty-plus documents. All I could think of was there must be a huge block of denial in his brain. Maybe it was self-preservation, if you will, because if he actually were to feel and think about how much he had lost, his entire dreams splattered in those papers on the lawyer's desk; he would have gone completely crazy.

The lawyer gave him a pep talk about finances and being able to start a new business. Then off we went. To where? We didn't know. I had "arranged" a detox admission but convincing him of that would take another two hours when I absolutely refused to "go find drugs." I snapped a picture of this moment, with him in the passenger seat, reclined back, halfway in and out of withdrawals, and me, steadfastly looking straight ahead through tear-soaked, tired, swollen eyes. I barreled forward, straight to the detox facility. I posted the picture to my private mom's support group and received almost 800 likes because the heartfelt, sad image resonated so much with moms.

Mason went into the hospital detox and sat through the admission process, still nauseated. When they scored him to be eligible for detox, he was three points under. My panic rose and my eyes started watering above the Covid mask they made us wear. I caught the eye of the nurse whom I had been texting to get him in there. I said, "But weren't you vomiting at your sister's house, son?" trying to get another point added on. The nurse interrupted and asked me to go wait in the waiting room. I was horrified he wouldn't get in. I sat in that empty room and prayed with all my might that he wouldn't come through the door and say, "Let's go."

He didn't. They admitted him. Relief flooded through me. The nurse told him he could go outside and have one more cigarette. I was horrified. Surely, he would run then. But he didn't. He sat out on the lawn of the hospital, staring ahead, looking like a lost puppy. Of course, I snapped pictures. At one point, he lay down on the green grass, and my tears welled again. *How did we get here? How did we get into this mess?*

There is no way that anyone, unless he or she has lived through what I've described, has any idea of the constant fear, confusion, and absolute lack of power felt by the addicted loved one. THIS IS A CHOICE? I wanted to scream to the office and hospital building around us, "THIS is what every person who takes a drink to relax after work wants? Pus oozing out his arms and losing money, people, respect from years of addiction? Yes, I'm sure, *all of this* flashes before everyone's eyes before taking those two little pills of hydrocodone for back pain!"

That choice for stress relief does not mean they could ever imagine what that would balloon into.

The next three days were both equal parts relief and pain. Mason asked for candy. I gladly went to Smiths and bought forty dollars' worth because I knew how he craves sweets when withdrawing. I brought him a charger because, oddly, the hospital staff allowed him to keep his phone. He needed to call insurance to authorize another day, and he actually did it. He needed to call the tax guy, which he did. He needed to call his old job to fax something, which he did! What he *wouldn't* do was agree to go to rehab. I had secured him a bed in a private rehab that was fully paid for by his state-issued insurance that we now had. It was a great opportunity this time around (after many, many texts and phone calls of this 'so- called' enmeshed, codependent, enabling mama, thank you very much). All in vain.

Mason was discharged three days later, and I put off going to get him for three hours while trying to convince him to call the rehab place and go. The director told me not to pick him up, just let him find a ride "wherever" if he wouldn't agree to go to rehab. I just couldn't. His dad could. I couldn't. I knew my son, and if he made up his mind, he would just wander the streets of the city to find heroin as fast as he could find a hamburger.

If he wouldn't go to rehab and didn't have a truck to go back to live in, I reasoned it was better if he stayed with me and figured out a job in my town, which was far away from those dangerous, nasty triggers. I picked him up and took him to the same store where we'd bought his work boots after his first rehab.

He went over to the apples and said he had been craving fresh, green apples. One of my stupid little regrets to this day is that I told him I had just bought a whole bag and they were at home. He put down the apple and walked away. It was like watching my dejected little boy from 30 years ago who was denied another toy dump truck. Why didn't I let him buy a stupid little apple to give him a small sense of normalcy? *I mean surely that would have changed everything, right?*

I brought him home for an exhausting week of continued detox. 3 days of professional detox is all his "18 years paid into the system" could muster? He had cysts on his arms that needed draining. He had back taxes to get finished. He had to find a job, housing, *anything* to keep him from going back to that town. I found a program at the local university that was intensive outpatient "Medically Assisted Treatment" (MAT). But it required an ER visit to qualify. I swear to God, I managed to get my stubborn son, still in withdrawals, to that ER and wait five (yes, FIVE) hours to be seen. During this time period, as I waited in the parking garage due to Covid restrictions, I endured many frustrated texts, like, "This is BS, I'm leaving."

I was able to make several phone calls to the MAT program, the ER, and the social worker who was supposed to present the program to him *after* being seen by ER doctors. This resulted in him not leaving, thank God. Every hour, it seemed, I would say, "You're next. They're coming to take you back to a room right now. I just talked to the secretary." He was able to get the cysts drained, get antibiotics, and hopefully qualify for the MAT outpatient program. But we would never find out. This seemed all in vain too. But is it? Possibly saving him from a deadly blood poisoning? And why didn't the hospital detox doctor wheel him down the hall to take care of the cysts?

He did go back for the second visit a few days later to have his cysts packed, but that doctor didn't believe in packing, so he didn't do it. When Liam and I drove to pick him up from the ER, he was standing on the corner waving the red flags used for pedestrians to cross the street. This kid. Always the funny guy. Even in the midst of chaos, he could find a way to be silly. I grabbed my camera but only caught him putting them away. Still, he had that wide, familiar smile on his face.

During this time, we tried to figure out the next steps to get him working if he wasn't going to rehab. It was finally decided he could go work for his brother in a few days after he was detoxed. I took a few days off to stay close. Mason wasn't having any withdrawals except for lethargy. All he wanted to do was sleep.

One day I came downstairs, and he was gone. Just gone. The back door was open a little, as if he were smoking out there, but he was nowhere in sight. The front door was still deadbolted, so I knew he had gone out the back. I called him on the phone. He said he went with a "friend" to get his work boots from his dad. I was shocked. I don't know why, but I guess we have this idea that if we can get the drugs out of the system, they will automatically become normal. Contrary to popular belief—the mental obsession is raging. I told him I didn't want his "friend" knowing my address. He told me, "That's why I walked out the back and down the street to meet him." Oh okay. See, this is why their behaviors make sense to them, even though most times we are left scratching our heads at what they do. I later found out it was his childhood friend that practically lived at my house growing up.

During his stay that week, I kept finding Mason with piles of coins near him. He said he'd been searching for older pennies and some type of quarter. He could spin a tale and easily make it believable. But the next day, when "the friend" brought him home, Mason had a bag of coin rollers. It hit me then that the son I knew had disappeared. The son who was once described by an old boss as "the hardest worker I know" seemed to have his moral compass facing south. He couldn't seem to overcome the increasing criminal mentality. Instead of getting a job (which would require a drug test), he foraged for money and items. His possessions were gone. Absolutely everything. So, he now resorted to eyeing others' property. Of course, this behavior made sense to him. He desperately needed money, now. Did he know he was lying? Yes. But the means to an end is foremost in their mind, I now know. *(And the end justifies the means- to them)*. At that time, I only felt disrespected and sad and mad. All the things.

I recall a conversation around that time about how he would NOT steal to fund his habit. To his credit, in all these years of addiction, these coins were literally one of a couple of things I ever suspected him of taking. It was so strange. This intelligent man, who once ran thousands of dollars a day through his business, was graveling to put pennies into brown coin wrappers. It was surreal and proved to me that addiction changes the brain into a desperate, gaunt, unsatisfied, hunting animal. So many families deal with so much more than this, I am grateful in a way, that Mason chose to isolate when he was deep, and I have to believe it was so as to not hurt us more. Contrary to what some may believe, I do not buy into the black and white thinking that they "choose" drugs over their kids and family. Even choosing drugs initially doesn't mean that we want terrible things to happen. People make choices every day that they never think will affect others. By throwing it back in his or her face, we are doing a great disservice to a soul who is just trying his best at any given time. I know, personally, when I've been accused of things after the fact– like taking today's information and applying it to yesterday's choices—it makes me feel like crap. I believe that addiction robs them of the ability to care for their kids and love them the way we want. To think they don't have guilt of not having their kids' arms around them, their wet kisses, a handmade Father's Day card. These things tear at a person's soul and it makes my heart hurt when I have seen the pain flash across my son's eyes while reading a text or watching a dad and kids on tv. There are no easy answers and I'm determined to not make any of these things any more difficult than they already are. Addiction is an ugly beast and both those addicted and those affected— are very tender souls whose love expands deeper than what is sometimes shown on the surface.

We are so accustomed to disguise ourselves to others, that in the end, we become disguised to ourselves. —François de La Rochefoucauld

Sour Grapes

May 11, 2020. This is a recorded conversation with Mason as he was leaving my house with my daughter to go to my other son's job site. The plan was for him to start a fresh new job after this third (short) detox. No rehab. Keep in mind he actually had not run his business or made significant legitimate legal money for seventeen months at this point.

>Me: *Being a businessman/entrepreneur-minded person at heart, doesn't it make you mad at all the money that's been made off innocent families over the years?*

>Mason: *Everybody benefits from drug sales. Drugs are part of the economy, and they always will be. Or [governments] would make them legal. The countries that have legalized them have dropped their economy completely. People love to make money on shit, just like coronavirus. They don't worry about who's suffering or not. They worry about themselves. People get killed over that shit. That's all there is to the drug trade. No one in it cares about anything else.*

>Me: *It's not fair though. This whole generation of kids is affected. It weakens societies.*

>Mason: *Fair is where you take pigs to win a ribbon. The kids might be better off. A girl I know grew up in a meth lab slinging dope for her mom, and now she won't have anything to do with it. She was court ordered to rehab at 21, had a baby, and now steers clear of anything drug related. She may not have had this early realization that saved the rest of her life.*

>*Mom, you need to focus on you. When I leave this time, are you going to focus on you? I know you want to write a book, so do it.*

>Me: *I don't know, Mason. I have an $8,000 bond on you. I have to pay that if you don't show up in court. How can I focus on myself? I can't afford that.*

>Mason: *I'm not going to go off the deep end again….*

He left and went to work with his brothers again. This was a miracle. Even after all the bad feelings from the last two years, all the misunderstandings, all the disappointments—the lost captain of the ship

121

was back, but someone else was captain now. I thought, "*It will be okay. They will work it out. Our family will finally heal. We will go on vacations again. WE WILL REBUILD.*"

I had almost eight hours of blessed freedom believing all that. The next night, my brazenly strong addicted son called me. He was crying. That was only the second time he had cried. The first was in July of 2018 when he called and said, "I can't save my marriage." This time he was in my other son's basement and said, "I'm not wanted here, and I don't know what to do." I assured him it would take time for everyone to trust again. He just needed to keep swallowing his pride and keep trying to get better. He just needed to learn how to work a regular job again and get used to working for someone else instead of being his own boss. It would all work out. I assured him that his brothers loved him. They could be a team again. It would just take time.

A huge family fight ensued. My youngest son felt deceived and dumped on, I assume. Mason felt like he was doing so well because, to him, rising early, working his long-lost trade, was a step forward, even if he had to eat a little pride by working *with* and *for* his former employees. Yes, he still had a huge amount of pride despite everything.

I frantically searched google for a liaison for businesses. Someone for them both to talk to. It was frustrating, to say the least. When I explained this scenario to my therapist (the third one that I finally tried), he was aghast at my involvement and my lack of boundaries. He said that all the contention and problems were their deal to work out. He said that I had nothing to do with what others perceive or feel as their truth. He said Luke has every right to be in control of his job site. I was unable to voice how this is different, because as all of us mothers know, our situation is *always* different. It's hard to explain the whole dynamic. It sometimes sounds like whatever the mother does is considered enabling. How could I explain all the "ya buts?" Ya, but Mason had given Luke many chances over the years. Ya, but this and ya, but that. Bottom line, which I would learn much later, is that people have a choice. It was Mason's choice in the past to help his brothers; they are under no obligation to help him, especially if it puts them at risk.

Sadly, the fallout with his brother sent Mason straight back into the arms of nowhere, and fast. He had nothing to his name. He was homeless, but in a different city than the last few years. Even though it was his homegrown area, he didn't know what to do. Since he wasn't willing to go to rehab, I was out of answers. (I had hurriedly set up a rehab in that city, also, which would be completely paid for. All he had to do was call, but he wouldn't. I begged the rehab center to call Mason. They wouldn't.)

He sent me a text on May 15, 2020, that said, *"Hey Mom. I love you. I don't know why they are doing all this, but we can't let it bother us. I will find a way out of this."* It was sad that he couldn't see things clearly, but it was also sad that he felt so rejected and unsupported. He was so lost. I was convinced that he must be ill with a brain disease that wouldn't let him believe he had it, or at least lied to him that he could fix everything without fixing *it*.

Luckily, he met a Mexican man who had worked for him years ago when Mason had given him an old truck. The guy fed him a Mexican dinner one night. He sent me a picture of the meal. I was so grateful, but he really needed a job and place to live so he wouldn't head south again.

I didn't hear a word from him after that, which sent me into another worrisome Facebook Messenger ordeal that lasted nineteen hours. Once again, I didn't know if he was okay. This time, it was definitely plausible that he wouldn't care if he "accidentally" died. He had burned his last job opportunity and bridge to his brothers. His family had finally rejected him after it took an immense amount of pride for him to admit failure and work for someone else.

That weekend, my husband took me out of town on a motorcycle trip. We sat by the rushing Colorado River eating lunch with the sourest grapes I've ever bought. We were in a cozy hotel by the Colorado National Monument. Liam was sound asleep when I woke up in a panic. I guess trying to pretend that I wasn't upset over the week's events had caught up to me. I started hyperventilating, crying, and gasping for air. I tried to keep quiet. I felt like my soul was bulging out my eyeballs. There was so much pressure in my head. I thought I would explode. I didn't care if I did. I just wanted this searing pain to end. I dropped to my knees by the worn green motel couch.

I pleaded, I begged. Then I silently cried. I had read somewhere in one of the Mom's prayer groups to imagine giving my son to Jesus at the bottom of the cross, with blood pouring all over him in the name of the atonement. I admit, I haven't been much of a religious person since my kids were teenagers, and I had given up going to church. But this unwelcome membership into the nightmarish club of addiction has sent me praying every time I feel powerless, which is daily. In moments like that, what did I have to lose?

So, in that little hotel room, I did the best I could with my "offering." I imagined the little baby back in that hospital room where he was born. I said, "God thank you for giving me this little nine-pound, five-ounce chunk of amazement and wonder, but I fear I have failed you. I'm "offering?" (That seemed weird, like Abraham offering Isaac on the altar); so now, I'm giving control back to you. Amen. Good night."

All the next day, I waited for the phone to ring. I didn't know what I expected, MAYBE just for everything to magically have worked out. But instead of relief at my deliverance to Jesus, I felt the most horrifying fear that my midnight prayer was telling God to kill him. All the other mothers who had "given it to GOD" appeared instantly better! What was wrong with my gift? Obviously, I had done it wrong. I had concluded that my middle-of-the-night panic attack was the actual moment Mason had died. I figured that my giving him to Jesus was me handing his physical body over to God for good. Then, like one hundred times before, Mason was back online by the time Liam and I left the mountain. That meant I could breathe again. There was hope.

Ironically, that week of Mother's Day 2020, was one of the hardest on my soul. So deeply seared in my pain and tears, I thought I would never recover.

You don't want to know the truth about [drugs].

Basically, Suboxone doesn't have any effect on me because I've tried to use it to stop too much. It's weird how tolerance builds up and I can't fix it. I'm the expert for me. It's about being smart about recovery. A less than 1% recovery rate. I'm not a sheep. I'm not going to go to Twelve Steps. That's just being told you were molested as a child and that's why you use drugs.

*Basically, right now it's a dependency or an addiction because it's hard when I have money, to keep my brain from saying that it's okay to spend $1,000 on drugs like I used to. A $100 amount of heroin is gone in, like, five minutes. It's not something that a poor guy can do unless he is robbing shit. What I'm doing is nothing more than someone taking a prescription in the morning. You're looking at it way differently from what it is. I don't shoot up and all that. My personality is all or nothing. To be honest, I need someone I can be honest with, yet have full control of finances, which is going to be hard. All I'm trying to do is get things running again and **stay level.***

This reminds me of one of my favorite shows, *House*--although I didn't think much of his pill-popping at the time:

*"Pills don't make me high-they make me **neutral.**"*

When Mason states, "What I'm doing is nothing more than taking a prescription," I believe he is begging for acceptance of his choice of self-soothing. Others may say he is trying to justify his use, but isn't that one and the same? We all get to choose our response to others' actions, and I pick door #3. Partly because I know any of us could have gone down that road. Would WE deserve or want the fury? When someone is angry at me, despite times that I was doing the best I could, I know it only sank me further into my pit of depression and discouragement. Yet I had no problem throwing occasional fury at Mason. I knew I had to tone it down in my fury if I wanted to maintain a connection.

Unchain yourself, my son, escape its hold! How long will you remain a slave of gold?
—Rumi, The Masnavi

PART THREE: SWITCHING DIRECTION

Anguished Freedom

On June 6, 2020, as I wrote this chapter, we were anticipating the bankruptcy hearing date. If my son did not attend, it was all wasted— my money, my nine months of work gathering all the info, my calling off the wolves who were rampant in my mailbox and on my doorstep. I cried every single night because my latest plan to keep him in treatment "just long enough to get through the financial mess" had failed. I didn't know where my son was. The lawyer was already calling and asking where certain vehicles were. How could I tell him that my son's safety might be on the line regarding any of these?

One summer day in June 2020, the gentle wind sent a faint whisper of understanding. I was watching *I Shot My Parents*. The documentary explains how Nathan Brooks shot his mom and dad allegedly after they made him clean the whole house one day. Both parents survived. The dad said, from what I recall, "There's heartache, there's sorrow, there's emotional pain that I can't begin to explain, and I don't know if I'm man enough to process it. So, the best way I can deal with it is to bottle it up and put it away, deal with it later. I don't have time to deal with it now. I don't want to deal with it now and IF I DID deal with it now, it could have repercussions, and I don't want to take those on yet. Maybe someday." [27]

I think this is how my son felt at this point. He was completely overwhelmed. A text he sent me on April 27, 2020, read, "I can't stand trying to deal with everything. It's an embarrassment."

This explains the "block" I kept thinking that he must be having in getting things done. Who wouldn't want to fix things? I would later learn so much about this. Unhealed people *can't* fix things instantly. Mental illness skews thinking. It puts them in a tunnel where the options look limited. Another breakthrough came the next day. I downloaded Jon

---

[27] https://www.amazon.com/Shot-My-Parents-Elizabeth-Brooks/dp/B07PRGTQB3

Vreeland's book *The Taste of Cigarettes*. At first, I thought I wouldn't get past the first few pages, since the needle part of addiction freaks me out to the core, even though I'm a nurse. Jon goes into vivid detail. But I was captivated because this was what my son had described and what I had personally seen the times he came home with cysts all over his arms and neck. I can truly say, with now- familiar, tear-soaked eyes, that this book was a game changer for me. Suddenly, everything my son had been trying to tell me made sense. All those times I had "helped" him, did he have any intention of quitting? Was he just going through the motions either to get out of jail or find an opportunity to make money in order to get back "out there?" Jon writes: *[28]

> *There comes a time in the junkie's life when he or she wants to quit, but for the life of them they cannot, and will not, **no** matter what's at stake. At one point, the junkie believes that living without dope is impossible—laughable even. Anything and anyone can be taken away, and it still won't fix the junkie's lust for boundless oblivion. In this mindset, with every shot the junkie takes, the junkie, somewhat furtively, craves an overdose or even a random act of violence that'll put them under without any sort of pain, like a stray bullet to the head. But the junkie is a nonviolent lover, who only wants a hug or a passionate friend like their road dog, not a bullet in the head, not an early grave like the junkie claims to adore in strings of melting words. The junkie is just a sentimental, selfish asshole.... We, the junkie, sell our soul to Mr. Black, and not because of our past, present or future, because heroin is a nasty black spell that wants to ruin us and does.* [29]

I knew, right then, the minute I turned off my Kindle, the stark reality of my son's situation. This addiction monster was not going to let the bankruptcy, the IRS debt, back child support, a mom's weekly

---

[28] To maintain the integrity of the original quote, I have left the term "junkie" in. This doesn't mean I condone labels that serve to keep people feeling trapped in that identity.

[29] https://www.amazon.com/dp/B079R3SPTZ/ref=dp-kindle-redirect?_encoding=UTF8andbtkr=1

pleading and begging videos, or the endless motivational quotes centered around addiction stop it. Not only did the drug have a contract on his life and, he, Mason, my precious child, was its willing puppet

Sadly, this author later lost his life, presumably to addiction. Repeatedly, on support group sites, a newbie will get on and ask the question, "How do I get my loved one to stop?" The answers almost always say, "They have to want it. Let them hit rock bottom." With the underlying premise being, "YOU HAVE TO FORCE THEM TO HIT ROCK BOTTOM BY STOPPING ALL ENABLING." I would try to embrace that theory over and over again with no luck. There are many recovery advocates who still insist that taking away any help and even emotional support is what changes people's behavior, simply because it worked for them. They say nothing about "holding space for the addict" or "meeting them where they are" or motivational interviewing, which simply means resisting the need to be right, understanding the patient's reasoning, listening with empathy, weighing out the benefits of recovery and empowering good decisions *until they decide they are ready to quit.* I would dive into the actual "non-evidence" that forcing someone to change actually has very poor success rates later, but for now, all I could do was learn how to hold space for my son. This entailed removing any judgment of his poor choices, not inflicting more pain and damage on the situation and not manipulating the outcome by trying to control him.

One night, around this same time, I was watching TV and was shaken with the similarities between Mason and I and the grown boy and mom in *Rectify* on Netflix. I mean, how could I deny a GOD at this point who was speaking straight away to me through Hollywood, of all places! I watched a scene over and over again with my now favorite actor, Aden Young. The story is about a guy who spent eighteen years in prison and was released to a nervous and worried mom who acted like someone I may know. It hit me with such magnitude that I rewound and recorded the segment. I may or may not have sent it to my son.

The son says to the mother (imagine a slow, southern, drone-like voice), *"You know why I didn't want to see you, Mother? Why don't I return your phone calls? Cause every time I look into your eyes, every time I—I hear your voice,*

I see and hear what I feel about myself. You are my confirmation. You have to let me go, mother, because no matter how badly you feel, or guilty or angry or sad or ashamed … It will not affect in any positive way what I am or what I will be, and especially what I might have been."

To which she says (as if that weren't enough for her to be silent, and yes, I relate), *"I can't abandon you, honey. I won't."*

He says, *"I'm not asking you to. I'm asking you to LET ME GO … to do what you've been wanting so* **desperately to do. To be free. Free of bondage.**"

"And what about your bondage, Danny?"

"It's not your problem," he says.

How I cried. Again. If this wasn't the dog damn blasted truth!

I was so confused. How would I let him go and yet hold on? I called it "anguished freedom," letting someone go, reluctantly, so YOU can be free from the need to be in charge of the outcome. When riding a horse, you can't control the horse but you are *guiding* it by holding the reins not too tightly and not too loosely. When I was single and going to West Coast Swing lessons, the hardest part of all the moves was learning the right amount of pressure to hold your partner's hands with, to provide support yet take direction from the lead. If you held on too tightly, he couldn't guide the direction of the spins, etc. If you were loosey-goosey, he had no control over the trajectory, and both would flail about like fish out of water.

In my quest for answers, I received this message from a recovered addict on one of the support sites. Keep in mind, before this experience, I wasn't necessarily a religious person. Addiction —as with any challenge —has a way of bringing you to your knees as a last resort- Sorry God, but I'm sure you're used to it. (Think of Burt Reynolds in the ocean scene at the end of *The End* -1978.)

Chris Bunton, a person in long term recovery who authored Made Free: Overcoming Addiction,[30] wrote this to me when my son was six weeks out of rehab and back in the fire:

---

[30] https://www.smashwords.com/books/view/936570

Addiction is a terrible thing, but God can help. I know you've probably heard that before, and I'm sure he has. God saved me and changed my life. But I had to be broken. Listen, your son is not going to listen to you. He has to figure it out on his own. You have to let God have His way with him. Pray for him, and I know you have. But when I was a drunk, I went through all of this. Homeless. Child support. Debts. I didn't care about any of it because I was POWERLESS TO FIX IT. I eventually went to prison, which we view as a bad thing. But it allowed me the escape, to get back on track. I had friends who helped me. BUT my mom was on my back constantly. In my mind, she became the face of the enemy that was ruining my life. It destroyed our relationship. And it has taken twenty years to get things back to normal. Please do not be the face of the enemy for your son. He needs you. My life would have gotten straightened out so much sooner if my mom had helped in the right ways. He knows he's a person with a substance use disorder, he knows he's in debt, and all of that. He knows he has failed. Let God have him. I'm not talking about tough love. I'm saying step back and listen to God. Love your son, and when God leads you to help him, then help him, but if you feel apprehension, then don't. Jail is rehab. When he gets locked down, be there for him. He will need you. Encourage him to use the time to better himself. I'm not saying you enable him or abandon him. I'm saying that you love him. And listen to God as he guides you. I'm telling you to walk on the middle ground. Balance. You need to settle it in your heart that you are fighting the devil for the life and soul of your son. And it is going to take a long time. It will be a hard road, and you will get tired. But forgive and follow God. Remember, the devil is not just trying to destroy your son. The devil is also trying to destroy you and the rest of your family and your son's kids. The only way to fight this battle is with God and spiritual warfare. Study everything you can about it. Study addiction. Tell your son to turn to God. Ask him to accept Jesus. This is a walk he must take with God."

You will get tired? I was already tired.

Change happens when the pain of holding on becomes greater than the fear of letting go. —Spencer Johnson

Wishbone Wishes

There's an ancient Roman belief that is one of my most cherished of traditions in my dysfunctional, sometimes bewildered, childhood. The breaking of the wishbone. It is done by cleaning off the wishbone from the breast of a whole chicken or turkey after you cook it. My brother and I couldn't wait for it to dry out for a few days so we could then fight over who got first pick at which side to hold. (there's a trick to holding it too) You both take a side, make a wish, don't tell the wish and BOTH pull at the same time. The one with the larger side will have their wish come true! The possibilities! Of course, I never remembered to see if my wish came true, and by the next chicken bone, I had forgotten my last wish. But hope alive, here was a new fresh bone!

So, with the bankruptcy hearing just days away, my daughter and I had just enjoyed a warm deli chicken. I excitedly cleaned off the wishbone and sat it on the stainless-steel sink to dry. Every day I checked it, to see if it was brittle enough. Finally, with anticipation, I asked her to break it with me. We did, and I won. A few days later, after not hearing from him for a week or so, I remembered a text screenshot my son showed me when he was last at my house. It was of a girl that had been a helpful friend to him, who was clean now. She was the "closet safe girl" that I had heard about from him during a drug bust where she was busted for a bunch of drugs that were in a closet safe at a house she was at with her boyfriend. I decided to do a search for her name on Facebook, and I messaged her to see if she knew where my son was. This was after zero communication from him for a week or two. She just happened to know that he was with her ex, and we conspired to get him to a phone on the day of the bankruptcy hearing so he could participate. This may not sound like a big deal to a normal person who has an appointment by phone or otherwise. With people in chaotic drug use, however, it's nearly impossible to get them to commit and follow through with ANYTHING. So, finding someone who was close to him, who was willing to conspire with me to help complete and finish out my involvement financially, was huge to me.

This was one phenomenon that was so hard for me to explain to people when I was trying to gather his documents while he was in rehab. Deadlines and hearings mean nothing to them, even if it means their life. THEIR LIFE! That's why it's so maddening to us.

I know the entire last chapter was about letting go, but people whose lives have fallen apart fairly quickly due to chaotic drug use face many challenges to get their life back. Even though it seems like they have it easy by avoiding responsibility, they are easily overwhelmed by life's normal stressors, especially after not doing them for months/years. Even the smallest tasks to get out of their mess seems impossible to them and the drug tells those engrained pathways to do the "easier" thing, which is to stay sick, isolate, and numb out. Numb out on their responsibilities, their health, their safety, and their future. Every time my son was detoxing or clean I would get a glimpse of his interactions with many people. "Sorry, I get overwhelmed easily, I just have to go day by day, I can't make any promises, I'm trying, I did what I could, No I wasn't trying to "spit in your face" by relapsing, I hardly understand it myself, I don't expect you to, I miss my kids, I don't know how to fix everything. I'm just going to keep working to pull out of this hole" along with lots and lots of "pleases" and "I don't know what else to do." This hard-core drug addict, graveling and begging to be shown some grace. When the *sorrys* weren't enough he slid right back into his isolation, proving over and over that positive connection is the key to encouraging human growth so they don't stay stuck in patterns of dysfunction and pain and frustration.

Brick walls, rejection, and criticism are hard for any of us to barge through on a good day and we all have to learn how to handle them. But I didn't realize the pain in the silence at this point. I had to just imagine him going in for surgery, or in a coma, during these times of confusion – then the silence made more sense. (I would find out to be very careful what to manifest). He was too weak and sick to make any calls, let alone make any responsible decisions. This is why he never returned my texts, see? Everyone has their idea of a timeline of recovery for someone else. I read it daily in the mom groups, "Well, he should have learned *by now*," or "Why doesn't he just do [X, Y, Z]?" or "If I were him, I would

135

NEVER be in that situation," or "I can't for the life of me figure out why …"

Of course, we can't. WE ARE NOT IN THEIR HEAD. As no one is in *our* head. And has had our unique experiences. What does **by now** mean anyway? Until brain transplants become a regular thing, we will continue to struggle with expectations and judgments about others. On my route to work every morning, there are about twenty bus stops that I pass. One day I saw this guy standing almost off the curb into the road and staring in the direction of the bus. He appeared anxious, trying to peer further than his eyes could see, bouncing higher as if to get the first glimpse of his *expectation*. I thought to myself, *Dude, the bus will come when it comes, and you bouncing out into the road isn't going to make it come faster.* That bus doesn't care about his anxiety or an appointment he might miss; it's just doing its thing the best it can, trucking along. Then it hit me. Yes, Samantha! Take your own advice. *You cannot control the BUS. OR OTHERS! The only thing you can control is* **your** *reaction and* **your** *experience and* **your** *desire for peace in* **your** *own heart, no matter how late the bus is.* Sure, you can look at your watch and say the bus **should** be here *by now,* but humans are complex creatures and will always disappoint someone, somewhere. There is no way they can't. ***Should-ing*** on them, as my *boundary* therapist used to say- doesn't help. We could say the same thing about people in a buffet. Watch people go back and forth to get a little of this, a little of that, then, oh, just a little bit more sauce. Now I have to have more of that, and less of something else. We sample and taste and use our absolute free will to satiate our appetites if even for a few hours with things that others would never sample. The rest of life is no different. We test out what we need at various times, sometimes oblivious to others' preferences and needs.

So here we are. He was in the hospital (in my mind). The repercussions of this "illness or surgery" would be massive **when** he got better. Unmanageable, even for an unaddicted person. Yes, He did it to himself. I understand that. But if my other son chose to get on his horse, knowing the risks, and he got bucked off and had a concussion or fell into a coma, I would do the same for him and help him recover with the least harm possible.

It's hard to define enabling when situations are so different for all of us. A one size fits all statement of, "Don't ever do anything for them," should be followed by, "that they wouldn't be able to do themselves (and I've added) if they were in the hospital deliriously sick." Because they are, right? Besides, compassion needs no justification. My eating disorder patients sometimes use cutting as a coping skill in treatment because they "can't" use their eating disorders behaviors while in treatment. (*Because we make them eat*). Although we take great care to protect them from themselves by searching for contraband and not allowing certain items like retractable pens and steel hair barrettes or elastics over 8 inches: they still find ways to harm themselves. When I see a long deep fingernail scratch or a series of them on their legs or arms–sometimes bleeding and raw; my first thought is "why?" then anger. "WHY would you do this to your young perfectly fine body!!?" but I can't say that. In fact, I have to not show too much attention, because some want and need to be sick in order to justify a variety of unhealthy beliefs. I can't blame and shame. I absolutely can't tell them what an idiot they are, or how unworthy they are to even be in treatment when we are all trying so hard to help them! Why would they throw all our effort and time in our face like that? I may have those thoughts, but it would be unethical and inhumane to say them. I must convey compassion with boundaries then take away what tool they are using– even if its fingernails– to protect them from themselves.

Loss of a Dream

The bankruptcy day hearing was so fraught with angst that I couldn't even go to work. I was so nervous that Safe Girl wouldn't be able to get hold of him or get him to hold still for long enough. Then, for two hours, I sat in a parking lot, while he waited on hold for almost two hours for his name to be called. I was texting the lawyer, who was also on hold, translating Mason's impatience to him, asking him if he knew when his turn would be. Panic set in many times, like when Mason said the lady whose phone he was using had to go to work and wanted it back, and he would have to call the number back when he found another phone. "NO, NO! You can't call back into a hearing for your massive, and I mean **massive,** debt"! Whiskey tango foxtrot! The brain process from this man who used to run three businesses, fly all over the country, and take care of all of us when we needed something, was shocking! *As if* I could still be shocked by the irrational, hijacked forebrain that lacked executive functioning. My boy. I knew he was in there somewhere.

When his name was called, it only lasted about ten minutes. They didn't ask anything about all the items we couldn't account for including the crashed truck acquiring fees in the impound lot. I could not believe this miracle. It had to be divine intervention.

Or wishbone wishes.

Mason's voice July 3, 2019

It's so unacceptable that people just want to feel good without there being a trauma behind it. There's not anything you can do to get an opiate high. There is NOTHING I CAN DO DIFFERENTLY IN MY LIFE THAT would give me that [high], and no one wants to admit that. That's why so many people don't succeed at recovery….

You're just like 90% of people who can't accept the truth that there are other things that affect people's lives badly. With the situation I was given, I was just trying to survive.

Survival. This is why I did all that I did to help him in those eighteen months. I knew that if I didn't, my son would be in so deep he would never climb out. As it was, even with saving hundreds of thousands of dollars in debt, he was already incredibly downtrodden. He still owed the IRS a lot of money and had many other debts that would take years to break even. The biggest loss was his signature positive personality traits: Drive and Ambition. With money and success being his main focus for so many years, he now had to face the fact that, not only didn't he have *any* of that, but he had lost everything else too. He was crushed. So crushed that he felt he couldn't climb out. He told me one day that at 35 he had less assets than a twelve-year-old. *The situation* that he speaks of is complex, and convoluted and won't be explored here but clarity and perspective is something that each person must do for their own peace.

Healing is not a miracle. It's a process that takes time.
—aguywhowrites

The Son I Once Knew

May 18, 2020: My daughter had sent me an article on a drug arrest, mostly to show me how badly the city my son was "living" in was becoming entrenched with drugs. Luckily, he wasn't in the town at that time. The article stated that a car was pulled over on a suspicious vehicle call and the occupants presented with slurred, delayed speech and drug paraphernalia. The article stated the car occupants had "gaunt, sallow looks to their faces" and "seemed nervous." Man, it hit close to home. Not two weeks before, my son had been living in his truck in that very city. It's not that big of a city to have a drug arrest happen every day, but often enough to have it in the local online news, apparently. The comments on the article were brutal. "Who keeps letting these lowlifes into our town? Go back home, you losers. Serves her right. Get a f-ng job." I remember sitting at work that day, thinking that before this monster drug had hypnotized my son to be a slave to it, I might have had those thoughts too, "Wow, those poor losers. Too bad. So sad. I'm sure glad my kids aren't...whatever...." I mean, I always had compassion for the underdog, knowing there was always a backstory to how people get to where they were, but I still had the impression/stigma/judgmental/look-down-my-nose attitude that they were somehow low IQ, poorly educated, or from dysfunctional, broken (for sure broken), and/or abusive homes. I sent the article to my son on Facebook Messenger. He put a "thumbs down" on it. I'm like, "I know, right?"

He said, "Damn. That sucks. I know who they are."

I thought my heart would drop out of my chest.

Not only was this lifestyle the one he was living, but **he knew these people**! My life at that moment, despite all the evidence I had had before that, changed my attitude (yet again) toward my son. I was shocked at how deep-in he must be. How he didn't look at that article and react the way the rest of us do and say what is happening? How can we protect the community? Our kids? He saw it as, "Damn. I wonder if they made bail." This was his life.

It was clear that his moral compass had sprung a navigational malfunction. Drugs have a way of doing that. There are criminals who break the law because they have a criminal mentality and there are people who become addicted who break the law to support their addiction. I drew a distinct line between the two. Others didn't see much difference. I mean the law is the law, right? John Phillips, founder of the Mamas and Papas and a lifelong drug addict, recalls that when he was a postman, he threw mail away because his mailbags were too heavy. As a graveyard plot salesman, he received down payments, pocketed the money, and never recorded the transactions. On one page of his memoir, Phillips reports how he skipped out on a $2,000 hotel bill. He writes, "My values were beginning to corrode under the prolonged influence of hard drugs."[31]

When Mason went to rehab, we decided to do the right thing and voluntarily turn his fifth-wheel trailer he had been living in, back into the bank. It was also so that he wouldn't have a place to return to when that setting was such a trigger. We managed to get permission from the scrap metal yard owner to go get his trailer. He was an ornery old man who drove around in his truck all day, looking for ways to make more money than he already had. He already received all the tailing sales from a steel plant that rented land on his property, which totaled $50,000 a month, plus rent from all the "little people" who stored their trailers and equipment there. I had written to him a few months before just to see what the stipulations were in my son's rental spot (which was raided when he went to jail), although I tried to avoid mentioning that part.

My son had called me one day, saying they had bulldozed all his stuff into a pile, ruining it. He said it was everything he had left from his business, almost $20,000 worth. It was all the items we had spent two days moving from the previous yard he had run his business from. He was devastated, but he had no truck and no money to do anything about it. After writing the letter, I received a mean and nasty one back from the yard owner's wife stating that if my son were any kind of man, he

---

[31] (Finkle, 1986:33) https://www.peele.net/lib/vision.html

would have gone and talked to them and made out a deal to get caught up on rent. She said she didn't know who he was, only that they had bulldozed his stuff out of there, including another camp trailer of his that he had let a guy live in. I am not kidding when I tell you I cried for three days over that letter. I even wrote a response, although I never mailed it because I knew it wouldn't matter. I had explained that my son had got in over his head and had lost his entire business and needed a lot of help. If she had zero compassion for that, what would a second letter do? There was nothing else to say. She stated that the trailer would be accruing penalties by sitting there or they would scrap it so he better decide what to do. Well, they couldn't scrap it because my son owed a lot of money on it. He had bought it new just two years before and had spent the last year pulling it around, trying to live in it since he had nowhere to go.

We paid the rich old man $800 to be able to get the trailer, cash of course, and he still tried to get more when Liam handed it to him. Liam had to fit his truck with a special hitch costing $200. The rich old man's side b-ch, also known as "little helper," burned off the wheel lock they had on it and sat there watching us while we hooked it up.

Finally, we got out of the hot hell hole of that yard and took it to the city landfill to see what we could clean out of it. They closed in one hour, which made this foreboding gloom all the stranger. When we pulled into the landfill, they asked what refuse we were discarding. I told them chairs and boxes because I was scared they would be worried about meth and not let us in. We acted like we were just remodeling it or something normal. We backed the trailer up to where the guy directed us to the landfill—the chair and box pile. As I donned my gloves, Liam hooked up the power so he could let the slide-outs extend. In the filtered light coming through the door, in the middle of a huge city dump on top of a hill, with the birds circling above and looking for something deliciously dirty to devour; we saw the tremendous task ahead of us. It was overwhelming.

The dust and dirt drifting over the items once meant to provide camping fun for families and friends now held a darkness that exuded the despair of people who had nowhere to go, who were just getting

142

through the day the best they could. These people weren't thinking of who took the effort to buy this trailer, who signed the papers, or who bought the insurance. These were people who had shrunk so far into their hidden, suffering souls that they couldn't see past their numbness. I looked at my husband of less than a month. What must he think? I couldn't speak. Neither of us could breathe. Suddenly, I was taken back to my childhood, going with my dad to pick up my brother's car (in which my brother had passed away). I never forgot that smell, the sense of malignity and despair.

Mason's year of pulling the trailer around, hiding it from repossession, not having money for utilities, and associating with that crowd had taken its toll on the trailer. But I also know that his friend had gone over a few days after he was arrested to lock it all up and said it was trashed by "the crowd." Without him there, they went crazy.

We didn't have time to be horrified. We had one hour of light left. We started chucking stuff out the door and into the landfill of others' trash. As we threw things out the door, the track hoe man would immediately push it off the hill into the ever-growing pile of refuse to be buried. As the remnants of my son's life as he knew it the last year flew into oblivion, I frantically tried to search through the four filing cabinets left over from his business office. I ended up with three large garbage bags of papers that I would spend the next few months going through. I was able to save a few of his childhood trophies and other mementos that made the entire experience worth it. I guess. They still sit in my garage, but at least they're not in that landfill pushed down the hill with all the other refuse; forever buried with others' remnants of their lives.

I stared at those trophies. My son, whose life before drugs revolved around camping and enjoying the mountains, was not even recognizable in that mess of a trailer except for the few memories that lay in a dirty, bent-up cardboard box.

We left just in time before closing and went to wash the trailer. We turned it into the credit union the next morning. I kept six pairs of my son's expensive Levi pants, even though they were about three sizes too big. He had lost eighty-five pounds in the nine-month descent into hell.

I wanted something of his life from marriage and the new house and all the things we wish for our kids. Those fancy pants were from that era. What a surreal experience.

One of the times my son was with me, I had taken a large rug to the car wash to spray it off, but to my dismay, a large wet rug weighs significantly more than a large dry rug and I was unable to even load it back in my car. As a man polishing up his sports car watched me struggle; I became angry and drove home to get my son to help me. He picked up that rug and swung it into the back seat like it was a dishrag. The guy was still there, so I made sure to glare at him as we passed him, but he didn't even look up. My son was saying, "Mom, you look crazy. Don't stare." Then a lady passed us. She wore a big hat and rode a funny bike sporting a large basket like Dorothy's grouchy neighbor rode in *The Wonderful Wizard of Oz,* right there in the middle of the city. He said, "See, Mom? You look crazier than her right now." We laughed. I felt the old-time warmth of our shared family humor. We could laugh about ourselves and others—about the irony of life. His humorous brain was still there. Such a relief.

On the way back home, with my soaking, heavy, shaggy rug in the back seat, I pulled onto a new area of the road. Construction crews had painted a wide circle around so you couldn't get into the turn lane until the last one hundred yards of the roundabout. I deliberately drove straight through the circle because it was such a dumb rule. I said, "I don't know why they don't want cars getting into the turn lane too soon. There's nothing interfering with doing it; look, see how I show them? I just drive right through it!"

He laughed and said, "Wow. That's your idea of breaking a rule?" and chuckled. He was right. My idea of risk was putting my coffee into the glazed glass coffee mugs deemed safe (I was sure they would explode) or waiting until I had one day left to change a password. We laughed again at the irony of how many laws he had actually broken by now and how silly it must seem to him. Then I deliberately let some silence in for a minute. Part of me was sad, in contrast. Part of me wanted him to see the contrast, without feeling like shit, of course, that this is what normal people feel guilty about, and how wide the gap had become.

I wanted so desperately for him to be healed without even being recovered yet.

The mood quickly changed when he actually saw a work truck from the company where he once worked. It was a sad moment from the past when he was so successful. But he didn't let it faze him. He went on to tell another story. He was always full of stories. Honestly, we could be anywhere, any town in the state, and he could find something entertaining to share. Once, in Dr. Suess's neighborhood of La Jolla, San Diego, he told me about coworkers from Hawaii who helped secure the beach that was disappearing into the sea at drastic rates. Yup. My enigmatic son always had a story to tell of a place, a person, or a workmate.

I wanted that son back. That funny son. That son who I had just got a glimpse of. Not the son with a trashed trailer. Not the son with sores on his arms. Not the son who couldn't see his kids. Although my son still had his personality, thank God, his moral compass and lifestyle that he accepted for himself seemed like a lost cause to me. This was a pivotal moment for me. The term "mourning your child while they are still alive" became my truth.

Detach

Anyone who has ever had to remove yourself emotionally from your child, even an adult child, knows the deep raw pain that rips through your gut, as if you are being forced apart physically. It must be a little easier to do if there's emotional abuse or violence going on–thank God I didn't have to deal with that; but it still shatters your heart.

This wasn't the first time I had to detach from a child. Remember my pageant girl? My first born? When she was fifteen, she started sluffing school and hanging with a different crowd. I made a counseling appointment and pulled her out of school. The counselor recommended a wilderness program to set her back on a good path, so we pulled together an insane amount of money (to us) and drove her to Arizona. She had a good experience although she won't always admit that. She came back and did okay for a minute, but when she started back with the same behaviors, I started spying on her. I would track down places she went which turned out to be partying houses, with police raids and the works. One time I couldn't find her and went to talk to the town police officer that I knew from my job. As he was asking me when the last time I saw her, a call came over his radio that they had found a body on Main Street by the bridge. I do not know to this day how I didn't pass out in the moment. I mean, this was a tiny town. Finding a body is rare enough, but at the exact time my daughter is missing? Luckily, she was safe. I sent her 65 miles away to live in a private religious university's dorms with a good friend that she had met at the wilderness program. She took her high school classes with packets and rode a bike to work at New York Burrito. I don't know at what point I finally detached. Even though she was a minor, I had to. It was driving me crazy to keep track of her every move.

I struggled with this because my kids were my life. I had this image of my family wherein I was trying to mold each of them into some kind of star, instead of just being present and letting them **BE**. I wanted them to toe the line as to the "Mormon way" of doing everything. I remember sitting in church one day and listening to a Mother's Day talk about how much influence a mom can have on her kids to do the right things and blah, blah, blah. The tears started rolling down my cheeks as I felt like I must have failed my family if that were true.

My daughter basically took it from there and lived independently from then on. She struggled a few more years but I will say that the girl who once said marriage was stupid, who said she would never become a nurse, who wouldn't adhere to any of my religious teachings or my demands to stop listening to music lyrics that promote swearing and violence, turned into a wonderful adult. She had legal charges from those years and was able to get those resolved to receive her nursing license. She married, had four kids, and worked her way into nursing. She later earned her Master of Science degree. She became the family's second mom and helped me with all the other kids, especially after my divorce.

HOPE! IT'S A GAME CHANGER!

So here I was again, almost twenty years later, with the next child in line that I needed to detach from. That weekend before my son left, he was sitting on my couch with one foot under his leg so it was facing in my direction. It caught my breath because it was so chapped and scarred. I asked him if he wanted lotion, and he said, embarrassingly, "No, they are used to it. I usually walk around on the hot asphalt barefoot, so they are hardened." Ugh. The life of being homeless is NOT good for mamas to hear. Interestingly, a mom's support group rejected this photo when I sent it in with a heartfelt post on our addicted kids, because they said it was too triggering.

I had bought him shoes this trip, so to my surprise, six weeks later, he sent me a picture of himself on a little wall at a construction site. It was a poor, blurry picture, but I swear he looked barefoot. He had on a long sleeve flannel shirt in the 105-degree heat. The text said, "I'm working for a concrete company and my first job is a cinder block wall. I've never ever done cinder block lol." I burst into tears seeing this man, who once ran cranes and trucks and equipment on many different job sites. At the height of his success, he had excavating, residential cement, fabrication power line, and framing companies. Here he was in the heat of the summer, possibly barefoot, in a hot shirt to cover his arms, being humbled by not knowing about cinder blocks. I waited for him to ask for money for shoes, but he never did. I think he just wanted me to be proud of him for working that day. Instead of nagging him that he could run his own cinder block company if he would just get clean and yada, yada, yada, I wrote, *"I'm so proud of you for trying so hard, it can't be easy for you. You are Loved. Even if it doesn't feel like it. I'm here for you when you are ready to say NO MORE & put your illness behind you. I luv you son."*

In between all the messiness, the "gaunt looking" police stops, the letters calling them less than a man, the emasculation, the snarkiness that you read in articles of crime and homelessness and addiction; there are real people suffering. People who still want to be shown dignity and concern. Moms and families wondering what to do. It might be our toughest lesson- to love when we don't receive any back. To pay for a phone for emergencies when we know we won't get a thank you or will just be asked again. To pray for someone's healing and mostly for our own.

One of his texts I read where he (was) actually begging someone specifically to please show him some dignity, "I don't think I'll be around much longer, but I love you" and was promptly given back the definition of dignity: *the state of quality of being worthy of honor or respect,* and was adamantly told, *"of which NONE of those describe him.* **Not at all!**" plus went on to describe him as just a junkie who is now useless to all the losers too. This kind of vitriol is common in people who have not healed from their trauma. They've been lied to or have been abandoned as children. They lash out to feel the burn sink in, so it will somehow equal the burn they feel inside. This pain cycle moves through generations in the form of toxic dysfunction. I would soon explore this more within the dynamic of a previous relationship of mine.

He had the same empty confusion in his eyes that I saw in my mirror every morning, that odd sort of denial that only seems to come when the world decides to jump the rails without warning you first. —Mira Grant

Empathy versus Enmeshment

When I was researching for this book, I struggled with what direction to go. There were so many options of books out there. Most of them were written by intellectual professionals who knew what they were talking about. What were my qualifications? Would anyone listen or care? Did they want another sad story about addiction? Did I dare mention God or a higher power? Or would it turn people off? First rule for every "product" is to know your audience and have a purpose. Well, I knew my audience. But what was my purpose? It wasn't to tell counselors and professionals how to do their jobs. It wasn't to tell people with chaotic substance use disorder to please get help. They are NOT reading books, I guaran-damn-tee it!

148

Nope, my audience was people like me—moms, dads, spouses, siblings, grandparents who were deep in their pain. Those who felt powerless. Those whose stories I read day after day of watching their loved ones "disintegrating before their eyes" just like my medical director had told me. My audience was/is innocent little kids who one day were up in the seat of a backhoe with their hard-working funny dad and the next minute he hasn't come home for days/months/years. Despite their dad living close by in the camper, they can't go talk to him. They don't have the ability to see how it might hurt them more to see him that way. But is it worse to have him absent?

He wanted to have it all. The drug told him he could have it all. The drug helped him get through the hard times before. He admitted on my recordings of him that it was his coping mechanism. When he didn't know how to handle a problem, when it seemed he was up against brick wall after brick wall, the drug told him to come on over to the smooth side. The smooth side of numbness, of energy, of bliss. Or to get some much-needed rest from always being the man to get everything done. No rest for the top dog if you are wearing yourself to the bone. The man who always has a solution for everyone. For everyone but himself. He once said that the oxy helped him have more energy and the heroin helped him sleep. It was a slippery slide of just getting by one more day, in which he always said to himself, "I'll take care of it later." Never was there a more correct meme for my son than the one that says, "If you don't take time for your wellness, you will be forced to make time for your illness." Unknown of how truly difficult the future would be, I told him that thing, many times during those secretive years where he was always going like an energizer bunny.

I remember in the beginning of this journey; before we knew what was in store, my other sons and I were soaking in our favorite lake on a hot summer day. Gliding along in kayaks, we reached a little island in the middle of the lake. My younger son, Luke, listening to some tunes, said to me, "See mom, this is what Mason needs to do once in a while, instead of always working. This is why I refuse to work on weekends."

So now, here we were, four years later, the drug seemed to be his escape again. Unable to deal with losing everything, there was his old friend to comfort him. Why not? The trauma bonds created by that lifestyle is hard for a non-hijacked brain to understand why they can't just see that the *root* of the problem is actually the *solution* to a different problem. If trauma wasn't the original problem it is now. Trying to navigate through an addict's chaos-strewn path feels impossible. As hard as it is for us, I can't imagine how it feels to be so discombobulated that you can't figure out how to jump off the hamster wheel.

On one of my long road trips to look for my son after not hearing from him, I ran out of minutes on my phone plan for some reason. This had not happened in years, but a glitch at work had me using my own internet service all day long for months. I couldn't believe how complicated my life became on that trip. I was hours from home and couldn't access anything. My email wouldn't work as I was trying to arrange things. I was actually stopping at places to use their Wi-Fi, but then my phone provider had me on safety mode and I couldn't get it off. I was exasperated. I thought, *is this what my son faces daily? And then I berate him for not getting this and that done?* All the while, I was trying to take care of physical needs of food and logistics and safety. We take for granted all of our conveniences that we become accustomed to, then we wonder why others less fortunate (at the moment) can't do the same.

When I went to nursing school, we had to go to the state psychiatric hospital to do a rotation. Part of that was wearing headphones which repeated voices over and over again, while we performed a series of simple tasks such as a simple math problem or picking a verb out of a paragraph. Then we had to have a dialogue with the peer next to us without breaking the cadence and tone of the conversation. It was one of the most excruciating things I have attempted. I literally could not keep it on for more than a minute. I secretly turned down the volume as far as I could. I just could not deal with it.

The words were to mimic what a schizophrenic hears, such as, "You are so stupid. You're not worth anything. You must do something to fix it. See that person over there? They are a spawn; you must destroy them to save yourself. Go, go, go, go YOU COWARD GO!" This sounds like demonic language, but it's the type of havoc that drugs and some mental illnesses have on the brain. It's their job, if you will. Thank heavens for medication that can stop these voices in schizophrenia. Yet the lies that unprescribed drugs seem to tell a person's brain in order to get them in complete obedience. You can't have it both ways by having drugs for relief of pain and the horror of mental illness and not have the possibility of them being abused and misused, leading to dependence or the very least: obsession.

So, where's the balance between having compassion for a person with a substance use disorder and not becoming so called "codependent?" Where does empathy stop and enmeshment begin? I had to learn.

Brianne McWilliams, an expert on attachment styles, states:

> *"Empathy is the art of stepping into the shoes of another person, looking at the world from their perspective, and feeling the way that person feels. Unhealthy enmeshment enters into the picture when this empathic person starts with thinking that they need to agree, support, and feel the others' emotions and* **meet their needs without the person even articulating their needs.** *That's not empathy, it's enmeshment because it dismisses the individuality of the other person, and perceives any boundary, disagreement, or contrast between the two as unempathetic, or an abandonment of the relationship.*
>
> *When your sense of self IS dependent on others, you are primarily preoccupied with getting others to do and FEEL what YOU want them to do and feel, so you can feel the way you want to feel about yourself.*
>
> *Thus, people pleasing is actually quite selfish: 'I want you to feel good, so I can feel good about myself making you feel good. So, I feel better already! So, I can feel better about myself.' We see this happen all the time: 'You're sad? Here, have a cookie/ hug/ advice/ pill/ gadget to make it go away. It'll make you feel better…' (so I don't have to suffer your sadness anymore). We tend to project our own inner conflict outwards onto the people closest to us. Why? It is easier than confronting it within ourselves.[32]*

This is huge, because since we didn't *cause* the addiction (and we must ultimately come to that conclusion because of the free will of others); we absolutely need to find ways to become as healthy as possible

---

[32] https://brianamacwilliam.com/anxious-avoidant-relationship/

during the chaos. "If only they would......." becomes our mantra as we become addicted to that *one thing*, we *think* will solve all our problems. Problems that were probably there–albeit, they may have been hidden even before the current addiction crisis, are moved out of view as we seek this ultimate goal of having the other person behave as we want them to. I agree this is easier for those who don't necessarily *need to* practice unconditional love.

As a mother of five very different—and stubborn—children, I spent many years trying to push my views and needs onto each of them. It's as if my mother card gave me the Oz of the world wisdom for everyone's life. I agree that Mothers have fantastic intuition and use it to keep their little kids safe but with addiction and other twisted scenarios; our thoughts and feelings become skewed. My two children who struggle the most, are very much foremost in my mind as the two that I didn't give my best self to while they were growing up; but like my third (or fourth) counselor told me, "You have to work through any guilt that you may have caused the addiction before you can feel peace as to the outcome-whatever that may be."

Enmeshment is common with maternal bonds. Hanan Parvez gives an example in his book *PsychMechanics*:

> ... *a son going through a breakup experiences depression. His mother also feels depressed. Because she's enmeshed with her son, she feels it's her responsibility to rescue him from his negative emotions.*
>
> *There's a subtle but important difference between providing healthy support to your child and fighting life's battles for your child. The former is an example of a healthy, cohesive family, and the latter, of enmeshment.*
>
> *Over-interference, constant criticism, helicopter parenting, possessiveness, rescuing, treating as a child, and discouraging autonomy are all signs of an enmeshed family pattern.*[33]

I don't necessarily want to rescue my son from his negative feelings but I do feel bad for him at times. I want him to feel more joy than pain–what Mom wouldn't? And yes, I admit to wanting to get him back a normal life with life's normal battles—those he can

---

[33] https://www.psychmechanics.com/enmeshment/

do himself. I try to empower him with strength and courage and not emasculate him. I know his capabilities and strengths.

Ian Short's summation of Roman Krznaric's book *Empathy* states the following:

> *Empathy relates to sympathy and compassion, but it doesn't have the same meaning as these words because they don't involve attempting to understand emotions from someone else's point of view. Opposites to empathy are introspection and narcissism—looking inward rather than outward.*[33]

Ian further states that we have to practice having empathy if we want to obtain it as a personality characteristic:

> *It is impossible to know exactly what it feels like to be a hedgehog. But what I ask people to do is to change their perspective. Literally. Get down at hedgehog level, get nose-to-nose with a hedgehog and then look at the world from this position. This will give you an insight into the complications we have thrown in the path of hedgehogs. Whether it is the cars on the road that not only threaten extinction ... we get to see those anthropogenic threats all the more clearly. But for me the most important thing is the contact of the eyes – looking at a hedgehog looking at me—eyes meeting and there being this almost intangible spark of wildness....*[34]

I admit that I have zero clue what it's like to live on the fly without security of home and car and job. I would be a sniveling mess, if I didn't have my safety net of my home and car and daily routine where I can be totally myself and safe.

I do believe some people are incapable of empathy, that is, being able to feel others' pain or even imagine their viewpoints. After my divorce, I was in a relationship which opened my eyes to survival in the midst of those who refuse to heal. He tried desperately to separate me from the bond with my children, even though *his* daughter was *his* main

---

34

http://www.open.ac.uk/blogs/is/?p=450#:~:text=Empathy%20is%20the%20art%20of,understanding%20to%20guide%20your%20actions.

treasure. He spent massive amounts of energy trying to break me in order to maintain control. He hated that I continued to find brightness no matter what anyone had done. He tried to shame me into hiding my intuition, my discernment, and my endless quest for beauty.

He was an energy drainer who caused everyone to limit their interactions with him, yet he could not understand why "everyone" backed away or was *so damn rude*. Any idea, thought, book, positive affirmation, happy person, or goal of anyone else was ridiculous. Any original thought or feeling of my own became a spark for fuel to argue and push me into bewilderment, where I must be wrong. He despised the saying: *Life isn't about waiting for the storm to pass, it's about dancing in the rain.*

Looking back, it reminds me of the old Mario game where you jump hoops, dodge bullets, climb mountains, die 1000 deaths and you finally make it to the end: serving up a heaping of "here I am— here's your orange juice!"; Only to have him say that it's too sweet, or too much pulp. Sooner or later, your efforts will slow down and then stop, to which he retorts, "See? I was right all along, you are pathetic!"

It took me sitting in my car with a razor to my wrists, while he lay soundly sleeping, to realize I was dying inside. There was no amount of money, love, companionship, words, sex, or compromise that would ever satisfy him. The goalpost to (my) happiness or (his) contentment was forever being moved. Immersed in this confusion and gaslighting, I would have taken anything possible to numb my shattered soul. I literally left with whatever could fit into my little Rav 4 stuffed to the ceiling, even the passenger seat. Christina Perry's "Jar of Hearts" is the haunting song that captures that time in my life.

I mention this because there are people like this who get caught in addiction, and there are those who aren't addicted who are like this, incapable of empathy, of deep connecting love, or of unconditional anything. There are people who literally can't hide their glee when someone else is bleeding or at their lowest. They have an agenda, or at least a story- and nothing will get in the way of its ending. More contact with them just provides more ammo. They are able to warp perceptions to make you look like the antagonist. Building up the strength to leave these relationships takes time because the gaps when things are coasting along are so immensely peaceful that we just want to breathe.

Hurt people are usually unable to help others. In that case, it's survival of the fittest, which usually creates toxicity. In my most painful moments of turning inward, I couldn't possibly have enough emotional energy to see anything but my own misery. Back then while trying to please my ex, and now trying to survive this addiction. Although my son is usually pretty grateful and hardly ever demanded anything from me; my emotional energy was still caught up in trying to get some traction and stay ahead of the addiction monster.

Everyone is in such a different place that sometimes it's almost impossible to get past the strong emotions, insecurities, and deeply ingrained pain in order to lean into empathy for others. I certainly didn't have the capacity to understand why others felt the way they did. As a young mom, I was clueless to what others were doing, because my plate was so full. We just *can't know* what it takes for others to get through the day.

It takes a certain vulnerability to be able to open up and see others' perspectives. Maybe that's why some men remain "seemingly" unphased so as to not open themselves up to the work and effort required to have empathy. After all, if we are *all* crying and sad, who's gonna go fry up the bacon? Someone needs to remain functional, as Liam told me many times about the silent sufferers of addiction, like the moms who have to reserve all their emotional energy for their kids. Like the wives who can't be drawn into the chaos. Like the grandparents, who just can't understand any of this-and do what they do best—just love and encourage but want no details!

As for having unconditional love FOR these rigid people, you can accept them for who they are without being their emotional punching bag. In my case, the one thing that my ex knew I cared about more than anything, my children, was always being used against me. I think that is almost the cruelest thing humans do to each other. Children should never be used as pawns, prizes, or scapegoats.

In *Fully Human Fully Alive*, author John Powell states, "Rigid People cannot live comfortably with doubt. They need to complete their

155

pictures in a hurry. So, they put together only a few of the pieces in a small and tight pattern. These few pieces are all they need. More pieces would only confuse them.... [They] are like detectives who take the first scraps of evidence discovered and immediately come to a definite and unshakable conclusion about the mystery they are trying to solve."[35]

In my 'toxic' ex's case, he was taught early on that people who were supposed to love and take care of him would ALWAYS disappoint, so he had to take people down first in order to avoid that pain ever again. His lens in life was pain and abandonment, yet he did the very things he despised. There were no boundaries between cruelty and love, because to him love *meant* being cruel and nasty at times especially when he felt threatened. That feeling felt natural to him. Usually these people are unable to see how they are making a situation worse. I have even done it myself–and sworn to high heaven that I was doing the absolute only and *right* thing. And it may have been the right thing at the time. But cruelty is never warranted in an already cruel situation. Hurting others to make ourselves feel better is just wrong. I would learn that just like the addicted can't suddenly make themselves stop, neither can those affected suddenly stop their learned behaviors of reacting to pain and perceived abandonment.

I think it can be hard for mothers of SUD peeps to separate empathy from enmeshment. My main struggle, besides finding these boundaries, was to project this motherly empathy onto others involved in my addicted loved one's life. I wanted people to care EXACTLY as I did. It sounds crazy, but I was adamant in that quest, and it put a wedge in my relationships. I had to learn basic boundary lines. Remember (at least I think I mentioned it); my role as a child was to keep my parents from fighting and hating each other. Even in the last days of their lives, I was trying to elicit empathy from my mom toward my dad's emphysema. She insisted he was faking it to get attention. I mean, he was down to eighty pounds at his point. He was using his inhalers constantly and struggling to walk daily. Emphysema patients spend all their energy breathing; eating takes too much lung power and energy. My mom, bless her heart

---

[35] https://www.amazon.com/Fully-human-fully-alive-through/dp/0913592773

and rest her soul, as one of fourteen kids growing up, never had her emotional (and at times, physical) needs met, so although she could be a loving mother and grandma, she struggled with compassion for others, or at least for those who with whom she had unhealed conflict.

At this point in my experience, the popular belief I was finding was that any behavior toward supporting them emotionally or physically was considered codependency. I would soon come to believe that the ONLY link between codependency, empathy, and enmeshment as they relate to addiction is with boundaries, particularly "having trouble setting and keeping boundaries." During the intervention, my youngest son, Luke and Liam tried to tell me how enmeshed I was becoming with Mason's addiction. Basically, they were saying, "Mason is ALL YOU THINK ABOUT!" But, just like the blindness of the addicted one during chaotic use, I couldn't see any of that at the time. My other people were healthy and able to function. They had to. They had families to take care of. My boy was in trouble, and yes, I was obsessed with it, there was no doubt. Luke only wanted a little recognition for how he pulled out of the sinking ship of the business failure and started his own company. This was HUGE for him. He had struggled for years with his own problems, and here he was picking up the slack and succeeding! Just like Mason had done. But Mason got all the glory when he did it. Luke was getting nothing from his mama because I was always off trying to pull one of her ducklings out of the drain on a stormy day. Plus, all the days were stormy.

At the intervention, Liam's testimony of his experience is a heartbreaker for all spouses and siblings. They are the hidden sufferers. The silent ache of wanting to be seen, heard, and loved with even half the magnitude that the prodigal son receives, is devastating. If only he had only known how much worse it was going to get, he might have rethought this "dream girl" (me) he had found.

At the end of the day, addiction is not about others' opinions or beliefs of someone's intent, motive, or character. It's about the condition of the human spirit, body, and mind. All of us. We all do matter in this, but we seem to be the most fit to lead the way, so it's about loving those who suffer and supporting them to move toward a life of joy. It's creating connection and communication so that when those precious windows of opportunity arise, we can show them some direction, not inflict more pain or pressure on them *or us* with our *unhealedness*. It can be hard to realize that our expectations and judgements can be manipulation, also, *EVEN IF OUR INTENTIONS ARE NOBLE*. Of course, we learn boundaries for our safety and peace of mind, but within true, caring boundaries there is no room for unneeded cruelty or disdain. We have to break free from these conditioned responses that keep the cycle of dysfunction and disconnection going. For *everyone's sake*.

There are two ways of spreading light: to be the candle or the mirror that reflects it.
—Edith Wharton

ADD in a Nutshell

There was a Reddit discussion that posed this question, "People who shoved their school papers in their backpacks with no binder/folder etc., where are you?" Among the 21,000 responses, these three were right next to each other.

"Still taking risks and losing."

"I'm a risk analyst, and it all started with me realizing the time spent getting the folder out simply wasn't worth the effort."

"European quality manager for an aerospace multinational. Because dealing with slightly crumpled notes is nothing that I take in my stride daily."[36]

"Absentmindedness; distractibility; inability to control physical impulses; inability to follow physical directions; interrupting, childish, emotional outbursts; bumping into things; dropping things; nearly impossible to learn from their experience; poor impulse control." [37]

These are all characteristics of the ADD brain according to Gabor Maté's newest book, *Scattered Minds.* How many of those do our addicts possess? The inability to see the value of time and future, no concept of self-regulation, having the rage of a screaming infant, making poor or quick decisions because they just want to move past the uncomfortable moment. These are all because of an inability to regulate emotion, not because of willpower or trying to spite or hurt us. THE PATHWAYS and RECEPTORS AND EVEN BLOOD VESSELS that regulate those things are missing or decreased in the ADD brain and when you add what the actual drug use does to these areas, it's a wonder the person in chaotic addiction can even function. Don't get me wrong. I know it takes great strength and fortitude to be in that world of survival, just like I mentioned in the beginning chapters, but the correlation into "never getting it right" has to have some effect. How these kids are responded

---

36

https://www.reddit.com/r/AskReddit/comments/eutai7/people_who_shoved_thei r_school_papers_in_their/

[37] https://drgabormate.com/book/scattered-minds/

to when they stuff their papers in their backpack and don't pick up their things, has to contribute to shame stacking.

With seven billion synapses in the brain, there's bound to be a few that trigger (or don't trigger) according to our earliest emotional conditioning. Dr. Maté says that the orbital frontal cortex (OFC) is responsible for visual and spatial orientation, attention span, and **what to pick out to focus on.** It regulates emotional information and *impulse control.* It also records and stores the emotional effects of experiences. The way these things are imprinted on the OFC in the early years is what we tend to follow the rest of our lives. If we yell at someone in traffic, we are sometimes surprised at how enraged we become. That's a good example of retelling a story of our early interactions with our caregivers. The car/a person/an object became the target for our deep rage that we didn't even know existed. The need to fulfill that part of our past where we didn't feel "relevant." Or heard. or understood. People who have been injured in the OFC area of the brain display the same habits as those listed above, the same characteristics of ADD. With ADD, it's not damage, it's that those circuits just **did not develop**. Dr. Maté states that these mis-wired ADD circuits in the prefrontal cortex are *as much of an effect of unhelpful circumstances as the plaque-clogged arteries of atherosclerotic coronary disease.*

So, the reward system and impulse control are not regulated. The neurotransmitters are decreased in ADD patients so they can't feel pleasure as easily, without flooding the brain with massive amounts such as caffeine, and stimulants. Why are those areas lacking in ADHD patients?

Dr Mate infers that one reason might be poor verbal and non-verbal interaction between mom and baby in the first few years. Even in well-taken care of babies, the baby picks up on the mother's distractibility or unconscious emotional states. Apparently, it's easier to fool an adult with forced emotion (staged smile) than a baby. So, if I was focused on my daughter while just going through the motions with the baby, it actually decreases the dopamine receptors to the frontal area of the baby's brain, causing damage to those receptors. I saw myself on my home videos: My seemingly ornery gaze (resting bitch face), my

160

monotone voice, and my depressed movements and actions. It was a misalignment in my actions. Dr. Maté calls this "attunement." It's kind of like filling someone's emotional bucket with good things. Yes, they receive endorphins with other happy interactions, but the tenseness of a mom who is not fully engaged with her baby still takes more away from that bucket than it adds- in my opinion. Dr. Maté states that most ADD patients have admitted to having depressed or stressed mothers. They admit to not feeling attached and a feeling that no one truly understands them.

You do better when you know better. I was young and unskilled, with a depressive demeanor and poor communication skills. When I did get angry, I projected it to convey the false narrative of, "If only you would do this, then I could feel this way." I didn't understand that my own anger and emotions were **mine**, not my child's or anyone else's. Placing the responsibility of **my rage** or **my frustration** on my children (or husband), was not helpful. My son exhibited classic ADD behaviors, which, of course, led to a lot of exacerbation and frustration toward him. This led to a childhood of trying to learn ways to comfort those feelings without knowing how. I know this because I keep meticulous daily journals of events and MY FEELINGS.

I think most kids (and adults) these days accomplish this self-comfort by endlessly burying themselves in social media or TV, but a kid, back in the 1980s and 1990s didn't have that. When someone, anyone really, is constantly getting stuff "wrong" it creates a lot of internal anxiety as to what's wrong with them because they don't have the knowledge of why they may be lacking in certain areas. They only know the shame of always being the kid who is reprimanded at school and at home. Some kids turn this into being the class clown. Some turn into the school bully, but whatever role they turn their characteristics into, their internal piggy bank is keeping a record of all the endorphins that are provided by either the attention, or the side benefits of being "different," despite the overall damage being caused.

In 2019, Dr. Maté stated that all addictions—alcohol or drugs, sex addiction, internet addiction, gambling or shopping—are attempts to regulate our internal emotional states because we're not comfortable, and that discomfort originates in childhood.[38] Despite my son's adamant stance that he wasn't abused and had no childhood trauma, I do believe his ADD, and all the behaviors and feedback that go along with that, played a huge role in the start of his addiction. Not even mentioning the trauma that they actually go through in the lifestyle, especially in the correctional system.

This inability to regulate emotional states is fascinating to me, because it always seemed like my son had poor self-discipline and self-regulation. The ability to "check himself" to see if he was getting too this way or too that way seemed to be non-existent. What's worse, is that I didn't seem to have the tools to help him. I just wanted strict compliance with the behavior that made *My* life run smoothly. This may have led to the ADD patients' overwhelming core belief that they are "not okay." Whatever feeling they're having must be changed and changed quickly. I've battled that in myself, struggling to understand that my feelings are okay.

GIVING SOMEONE –OURSELVES INCLUDED– PERMISSION TO FEEL IS A GREAT GIFT.

The sensitive ADD brain becomes easily frustrated with failure, tends to blame someone else when things go wrong, and usually, excessively blames itself. People with ADD may be incessantly argumentative with others, rigidly rejecting what others have to say about their work or behavior and may have trouble with authority figures. Gabor calls this "counter will." They need to achieve in order to feel good about themselves. Many ADHD kids are extremely sensitive, which explains their inability to accept their emotional state in varying situations, causing them to "cover them up" with work, shopping, or substances.

---

[38] https://californiahealthline.org/news/addiction-rooted-in-childhood-trauma-says-prominent-specialist/

Abusing body and soul with harmful chemicals is a huge marker of low self-esteem. The inability to say no is the biggest jump into addiction. Dr. Maté calls ADD "underdeveloped emotional intelligence."

Harvard Medical school agrees as follows:

> *Many people consider addiction to be a problem of personal weakness, initiated for self-gratification and continued because of an unwillingness or lack of sufficient willpower to stop. However, within the medical and scientific communities, the notion that pleasure-seeking exclusively drives addiction has fallen by the wayside. Clinicians and scientists alike now think that many people engage in potentially addictive activities to escape discomfort—both physical and emotional. People typically engage in psychoactive experiences to feel good and to feel better. The roots of addiction reside in activities associated with sensation seeking and self-medication.*[39]

I remember at Mason's preschool graduation when he stood shyly next to his teacher in his little white polo shirt with blue stripes. She read his bio about what he wants to be when he grows up. "Mason doesn't want to grow up because there are too many choices." Even at that young tender age, his brain was twirling and twisting. Although Mason never took on much of the victim mentality like a lot of substance users, I believe he was embarrassed by some of his actions and behaviors and suffered deeply and silently with his losses.

Luckily, in spite of the ADD tendencies, my son grew up with some great role models who helped guide some of that distraction into activities of the great outdoors. His dad and his grandpas were hardworking, solid, dedicated men. I believe that helped Mason grow into a determined, responsible, funny, kind, heart-of-gold man. He believed in people and gave the shirt off his back to anyone. He helped people with cars, new tires, money, and rides to work. He took his workers to rehab and gave them second and third chances. He was a special breed. Overconfident? Yes. Even cocky at times? Yes. Pushing every boundary possible? Yes. But he worked hard and provided things

---

[39] https://www.health.harvard.edu/blog/what-is-addiction-2-2017061914490

for us and his own family that most guys never achieve. He took many trips to Jamaica, Cabo, and San Diego with his wife and some with our family. He went deep sea fishing many times. He was privileged to finally be able to have all the toys, hobbies, and vehicles that he wanted after many years of struggling. He is the image of the entrepreneur's endless search for things just out of reach to the average person. "It's in my DNA," he always said about anything he did that was remotely odd or different.

Even if that little preschool grad couldn't choose what he wanted to "be," as an adult, he knew how to buckle down and sharpen his drive when needed, but he certainly didn't have "an addict" on his list. That's why labels such as that are not helpful. That's not *who they are*.

Michael G. Dash's book *Chasing the High* explains a bit of the chaos of addiction, "I was reckless and never thought of consequence, completely living in another reality at the time."[40] Michael explains the connection between the addictive personalities' obsession with money by the addict's basing every single decision on money. This was my son. Even, (and more so) in deep addiction, Mason chased money with fervor. Michael's motto, "Let's get shit done so I can make money," could have been Mason's motto. I feel like those with such a drive sometimes don't have a stop button as they search for more "things." Is it a void? Or is it just the human drive for purpose? Whatever you call it, addiction was ready and waiting to fill that need. Some people have more ambition than others, but I believe the ADHD tendencies, plus having a "red" personality, were like hot lava just waiting to spill. That's why simply detoxing or getting off the drugs isn't the total solution but just the beginning. When the core problem isn't addressed, there will always be another "solution" to fill the void.

As an adult, my son was like a hurricane when he swept into a room. We would always say he was a force to be reckoned with, a tornado of chaos. For years, it worked in his favor because he was doing good things with that hurricane force, and he had a lot of helpers to pick up

---

[40] https://www.amazon.com/Chasing-High-Entrepreneurs-Addiction-Lawsuits-ebook/dp/B07RMJY13D

the pieces. The forward motion, the momentum, was impressive most times, and the chaos left in his path was quirky and endearing and written off as just a side effect of his personality. Since he was onto the next (good) project, people would just shake their heads and fix what he dropped. As the addiction progressed, there were fewer people there to pick up the pieces, and the money wasn't covering up the aftermath. Suddenly, my son's actions were wide open for judgment and negative consequences.

When he was in one of his short hospital detoxes (his *only* detox-only visit), he said the housekeeper came in the room and yelled at him for the condition of the room and floor. I can imagine what it looked like, with candy wrappers and magazines on the floor. He argued with her, I'm sure sarcastically saying, "Well, isn't that what you came in to do?" That did not go over well. Normally, my son was respectful and personable to people, but in withdrawal mode, like anyone who is sick, he was crabby and miserable.

After his first home detox, we were rushing to get in the car to make the four-hour drive to meet a court date. I was waiting in the car for him while he was on the back deck smoking. He rushed through the house and out the front door. When I returned home four days later, I noticed the back door was left slightly ajar. Soon after, I was sitting on my couch and saw some dirt around the floor of my big potted plant. Suddenly I saw a little face sticking out of it. IT WAS A MOUSE! I never have mice! They must have come in while we were gone. It took me quite a while to capture this little hobo mouse family. My own rats of NIMH.

It's silly, in a way, to be surprised at Mason's intense hyperfocus on substances. We all know the ADHD kid who can play a video game for hours. As 'normal' healthy adults, we practice balance almost every day in our lives of work, play, kids, etc., which is moderation in all things. But when the prefrontal cortex is jacked up with massive amounts of dopamine, the brain has no brakes to stop to create that balance. Then you have the prefrontal damaged ADD cortex that is dysregulated with decision making and poor self-control. So, when someone says to an addicted person, "pull yourself together," they don't understand how they are functioning in their reptile brain (survival), and they are doing the best they can.

Nicole Labor states in her book *The Addictoholic Deconstructed,* "Addiction is a broken pleasure sense in the reward system. This part of the disease is not unlike cancer…. Cancer cells produce at a faster than normal rate and/or that organ or organ system is unable to break down or eliminate old cells fast enough to keep up with the production [of the bad cells] [IN addiction that] the reward system becomes dysfunctional." She (or someone she knows) calls this pleasure deafness. With prolonged drug use, the dumping of dopamine into the brain becomes the ONLY coping skill. She states what I have seen with my own eyes, "Stress leads to [more] addiction, which leads to more stress."[41]

As I explored this, I wondered if it's not that they don't understand that continuing to use drugs is a bad choice, because we all get the frying egg thing. Maybe it's that the prefrontal cortex is not functioning enough to CHANGE THEIR BEHAVIORS by supplying them with REASONS STRONG enough to overcome the bad habits they have acquired.

What would be *reasons strong enough* for each person? If their pre-addiction environment sucked, then they figure why not stay "comfortable and safe" in their trauma-bonded addiction. In their state of mind, their behaviors make sense to them. Even behaviors that aren't addiction-related are hard to explain to others but feel perfectly justified to the one doing them. One day I watched *The Kindergarten Teacher* on Netflix, and even though it's a little creepy and even borders on borderline psychosis, I could see how someone's obsession may look on the outside to others. All the while, the person feels completely justified in their actions. Even with the end goal being somewhat honorable, the female character crosses so many boundaries, it's cringe-producing.

As for the Reddit question at the beginning of this chapter shows, having ADD or being unorganized or addicted to chaos is not a future predictor of success or failure. I wish I would have realized there's never

---

[41] https://www.abebooks.com/9780578580524/Addictoholic-Deconstructed-irreverently-quick-dirty-0578580527/plp

a reason to be cruel or diminish someone's worth because they don't behave in the way we want them to in order to make us feel more comfortable. In the Netflix movie *The Alpinist*, character Marc's friend stated, "If a free climber falls and dies, everyone thinks you're an idiot, a risk taker, a daredevil. But if you succeed, everybody celebrates you as a big hero. But the reality is, you're the same person either way."

This is how I feel about Mason. I was so conflicted in thinking that he is wonderful as long as he's pulling in the money and following society's ideals and making everyone happy. Yet despise him when he has fallen into patterns and behaviors that seem like survival to him but are typical behaviors from the armpits of society. It really made me dig deep into what actually constitutes the worth of a human. As a parent, I used to do the "proud parent moment" on Facebook a lot, thinking I was just displaying gratitude for my family, but we all know it's an ego boost when your kids are doing well. Now I see that I can't take credit for the good things my kids do if I am struggling to prove this addiction wasn't my fault. There were so many thoughts to work through.

It isn't the mountains ahead to climb that wear you out; it's the pebble in your shoe. —Muhammad Ali

PART FOUR: LEARNING

Connection

I found out that life after you learn to start "letting go" is still exhausting. You are still caught in the battle of deciding what is too much, even though your mom heart is pulling you toward helping, especially if your child is still deep in addiction. And homeless, jobless, carless. This was when everyone had stopped mentioning Mason; when I was just supposed to pretend I had only two sons—I suppose. I was back to "working on my own recovery" with counseling, Zoom meetings for Nar-Anon, and many audible books. I awoke at 4:00 AM in extreme anxiety. I hadn't heard from him in a while. It was straight back to the life I describe in the first chapter, "Messenger Goodbye." I sent him a text that said, "Please be ok," followed by a voice message five hours later to please get somewhere safe to someone who could help him. I floated through the day in a dreaded daze. I couldn't shake the feeling of doom. Between seeing patients, I prayed all day, "Just please be alive. Please be alive." To the people at work with their trivial (to me) small talk, I wanted to scream, "MY SON IS A HEROIN USER AND HE MIGHT BE DEAD TODAY! Again."

I came home for lunch between jobs and was sobbing in panic. My youngest daughter never asked what was wrong, but I'm sure she knew it was about "him," the elephant in the room. I pulled myself together and took off for my other job. On the freeway in the never-ending, busy construction zone in between two semis, my eyes filling up with stinging tears, I screamed at God, "Please, please send him someone who will help him since he refuses to help himself. Then send me a sign of that person helping him because I have an eight-hour shift to get through, and I need peace!"

One hour later, my phone rang. It was my son. I couldn't talk at work, but I then received the text, "I'm okay mom." As casually as ever. Just like every time before. The old familiar relief mixed with anger came flooding over me.

"But you are not okay, son! You've been hijacked into thinking you're okay. What will the ransom be this time, Mr. Drug Demon Monster, who pierced my son's brain like a voodoo doll? First his mind, then his body, then his life? Fuxxxx you. I'm not bowing down to you. My brain is NOT going to believe your twisted lies!!"

In those moments, I was always glad I kept my feelings to myself, because telling someone the same story of how I didn't know whether my son was alive or dead was just crying wolf. Thirty-seven minutes later, I got a text, "I'm going to jail on those warrants."

He spent five days there, and it was my first real attempt at tough, loving detachment or whatever you want to call it. I mean, I was out of ideas anyway, so it wasn't that hard. Even though he hadn't had any new charges in ten months after that first year of the court system, I found myself thinking, "Am I (and he) so complacent now with going to jail that it's not a surprise?" I did write to the public defender to please put into place what I had previously "mentioned" which was in my many letters and emails to the courts, "Please withdraw the bond option and order treatment." They did neither, and he was released. I received this text from my jailbird boy:

Hey mom, they let me out and I just want you to know I'm going to be okay. I'm going to do some work in scenic Arizona and try to rebuild. I'm nine days clean with one minor hiccup Tuesday about three minutes before I got arrested. I'm done running, your son will be back soon, this is something you're just going to have to put in my hands so pray for me mom this is so hard I'm sorry for everything I'VE done and notice **the I'VE is in caps** *lol love you thank you for never giving up.*

Lordy. Scenic Arizona? Between that and the pictures of himself he sent me the next few days, all my resolve was gone. I cried for three days straight. I hadn't seen him in five months. My once buff, stocky, six-foot, 240-pound son looked like a little old man who had not eaten in a month. One of the pictures was him looking directly into the camera, his eyes pleading with me. But I couldn't focus on his eyes. The pain, the pleading? Was it longing for acceptance? Or just Connection? I

172

bypassed his eyes and focused on his arms. I, of course, had to torture myself by pulling up his old pictures and making a split screen to see the drastic difference that the toll of drugs had taken on his body. I sent them to my daughter, and she was so upset she had to leave work. After weeks of not mentioning what he should or shouldn't do, I sent him the split screens with my concerns about him not being able to see how much he was dwindling away. After my husband pointed it out, I told him to please notice all that in all of his *before* pictures, he was connecting with people, and in all the *after* pictures, he was alone and isolated. That ended the good rapport we'd had for days. He said, "As soon as my image looks better, I can talk to you about all this." Dang it, I had closed the open communication that I had worked so hard at building by NOT focusing on his addiction as defining him. What he was really telling me with those pictures were, "Can you still love me in spite of what I do? Am I still accepted as a person despite what you say I've become?" He was showing me how nice the house he was living in was. He said it was a remodeled trap house. But I didn't focus on the word remodeled, I focused on the word trap. He said he was lucky to have come upon that deal or he would be in the streets. I knew that was true. But all I could focus on was what *wasn't*. I decided that I had to put aside my inner anguish of sadness seeping out of every interaction and figure out how to meet him more where he was at. I had to figure out a different way of being.

It had been so long since we talked about anything else that I decided to focus on other subjects. I had to think about what his qualities were before addiction. HUMOR! That was his signature personality trait. I signed up for all the funny meme Facebook groups I could and just started sending those to him. He actually even "liked" some. I can count on one hand the things he has 'liked" on Facebook since he started in 2018. He was always a big critic of social media previous to this saga.

Boundaries

My favorite spiritual guru Matt Kahn explains that when we are raised as caretakers or rescuers, we are constantly shifting what we are for other people, either to be an ally, or when their ego gets triggered, the victim who puts their needs before our own. This blurs boundaries and causes you to lose the caring for yourself which then causes resentment because it's not reciprocated. The inner freedom comes when you become your own caretaker and are not swayed by events and situations out of your control.[42] I've read that if you want reciprocation, it's a business arrangement not a relationship.

I desperately needed to learn about my role and function in this journey so I could survive emotionally and keep my other relationships intact. In *Addicted to Misery*, Robert Becker describes Stephen Karpman's Drama Triangle. It describes the roles people play in relationships and even the kind of people we look for to be involved with. I found this fascinating when I was single and dating because there is such a cat and mouse dynamic playing out in those scenarios. If they like you too much, it's a turn off, but if they don't like you enough you get all weird and insecure, wondering what's wrong with you or worse, you start pursuing them. In longer term relationships, we fall into these roles also. There's always a rescuer, a perpetrator, and a victim. We all move around in this triangle at times with different people, but in certain situations, such as an abusive dynamic or an addiction dynamic, we pretty much land on one particular role, despite what our personalities have been in the past. In order to find some sort of peace we have to explore family dynamics and the role we play when someone is sober so we can be ready to not fall back into those patterns.

Basically, and for a variety of reasons, rescuers seek out and find people to rescue. They "never feel satisfied or fulfilled unless they are able to rid the victim of his problems." Victims look for people to feel sorry for them. They use the sympathy of others as a survival tactic. They

---

[42] https://tickets.brightstarevents.com/event/angel-academy-11-becomingyourhigherself

want to stay in the victim role. Victims "NEED to be the ones suffering *the most*" and often as martyrs. The rescuers derive "their self-worth from the outcome, so when it doesn't go as planned (which it never will-because you truly can't control another human), the rescuer feels defeated and inadequate."[43]

Why do people yearn to feel in control of another person especially in times of stress or trauma? Is it to have a better feeling of control of ourselves? We are so complex that we are constantly readjusting and re-evaluating, so it makes sense to try to control things and people outside of ourselves. The role that others play in our life story changes with situations and stress, so it may seem like we are constantly seeking this power.

Some of my eating disorder patients have many comorbidities, just like SUD patients. Since they can't control their food behaviors, they find something they CAN control whether it be severe OCD rituals, cutting, and other self-harm. They are trying to numb the pain of whatever is causing their body dysmorphia and replace it with something they can control. To the healthy brain, it seems ridiculous to pile more harm on top of the current problems. But like I have mentioned many times, we don't live in an ideal world where everyone performs *accordingly.*

What is *accordingly* anyway? When I had been single for a few years and Facebook was in full swing with adults, my coworker said to me one day, "Why do you post so much on Facebook?"

I said, "How often would you like me to post so that it's not too much? What would make *you* feel more comfortable?"

He said, "It's just not a good look. It makes you seem needy and insecure."

"What if I am needy and insecure right now?"

"Well, that's not going to help you find a man."

Okay. He may have made a good point in theory, but what is "acceptable" is really all about perspective. My son told me that a lot of

---

[43] https://www.amazon.com/Addicted-Misery-Other-Side-Co-Dependency/dp/1558740295

this book is inaccurate (according to his experience), but he's not going to interfere with my story because it's *my perspective,* and that's what MY book is about.

Letting people live their truth and experience their truth is giving grace. Holding space is one way to do that, but not at your own emotional expense, of course.

When I went back to nursing school at the ripe age of forty, I had a professor with a big wart on the end of his nose. I'm not even kidding. The entire first few days of class had me completely focused on why, at forty-something years old, he didn't see the need to have it removed. I wondered if anyone ever told him, "Hey, you know…." Surely, he knew. Thank God no one in class asked him, but it really was like an elephant in the room. I soon found that when I quit worrying about his life (and his nose), I could actually start learning.

We truly don't know about someone's intent, despite how it may look. When I go to work in the morning, I have to do a quick three-lane change after the stoplights at the onramp. I put my blinker on as soon as my light turns green so I can alert the fast-moving lane that comes upon me quickly. As I maneuver through each lane, I may be cussing or pleading out loud for other cars to slow down or speed up so I can make my move. When I get to my desired lane, however, I am done with my quest, but once in a while my blinker stays on (mostly because my mind has moved elsewhere and I'm okay until the next exit). To oncoming cars, though, I am still intent on moving to the last lane. I'm oblivious to their antics of, "C'mon already. Get in if you want!!" or other road rage ramblings.

Two minutes earlier, I was the one muttering. Do we ever learn to consistently give others grace, whether knowing their true intentions or not? Can we agree that maybe, just maybe, they aren't the evil thing we thought they were? I believe this balance of empathy, grace, and boundaries is the key to supporting those in addiction and also the others who love them too. How many times have we wished Karma on someone because of what we perceive of their actions towards us? I think Karma is dangerous. It's like getting a ding in your windshield. You can go chase down the truck that did it and fight about it, but truly you don't have any proof, and furthermore, what if *you* deserved it? We would need lots of colored string diagrams to follow who deserves what. To receive grace we must practice offering it.

Sometimes society isolates people who are in pain into good old-fashioned shame. We're interconnected for a reason; we need one another and a perspective outside of our own in order to see the limitations of our own.
—James Robertson

Mile Markers

When I married my husband, he taught me about mile markers. In my state, there are green posts along the edge of the interstate that represent another mile from the border of the state. If you are ever lost you can subtract that number and at least know that you are that far from the border. The mile markers can also help you to know which direction you are traveling by paying attention to whether they are increasing or decreasing. If the interstate you are on is an odd number and the numbers are increasing, then you are going north. I never paid attention to the relevance of those posts. In Spring of 2021, my husband and I got caught in a flash flood storm in Texas. Texans must be used to them because the roads are built with huge dips to let the water pass. The trouble is you don't know how deep it is except for they do have gauges that look like mile markers that measure the depth of the water. They seemed inaccurate to me though because the bottom measurement started too high. I had to wonder how deep the water was before the first measurement. The poor visibility and danger of the flash flood we were in left us stranded underneath a huge power line in a torrential rain and hailstorm for almost an hour. It's one of the few times in my life that I feared I may die either by a lightning strike off a power line or being swished off the road and drowned.

When the rain cleared long enough to venture out, we thought we were in the clear, as google told us the quickest way back to our hotel while avoiding the moving storm was to make a left. We soon found out that google maps didn't know about the flooded road which we didn't dare cross through with our rental vehicle. So back we went to the danger zone to go the long way around. We soon found another road that veered along the outside of the storm. With the mile markers and storm clouds as our guide, we were relieved to be on our way. As we drove along in silence, reliving the terrifying experience in our own minds, my eyes peered at the sky beside us as I witnessed a full rainbow seemingly traveling beside us. Tears came to my eyes as I knew we were on the safe path home. It followed us for quite a while as if to guide us back to the hotel. I realized that even with all the tools and technology, sometimes all we have to do is look up and find the rainbow. We later learned that two LDS missionaries died in that storm.

In my journey with my son, I found myself lost on the side of the road and clinging to the mile markers in the most harrowing storm of my life. The rising waters threatening my safety and my son's. I lived for each mile marker to safety. Just as a brand-new mom religiously writes down every new tooth appearance and milestone, I would measure success from court date to court dates.

With babies you are celebrating a tiny life progressing in monumental increments! Soon, the milestones start going too fast, and you want to go back to that toothless grin. I remember crying the last time I breastfed my babies, knowing I was losing that special moment of bonding and Motherhood. Now, I found myself back to watching that little boy walking timidly from the center of the room to the couch.

If I could just get him to the next court date, he'd be on his way. If he could just get back his license, he could get a steady job. Being the perpetual optimist he is, he believed that too, despite not being able to follow through.

As my gut-wrenching anxiety of the missed milestones started stacking up, such as him not calling in to court dates; I knew I had to quit opening up the baby book. I quit reading the hundreds of pages of names and dates and crimes on the court calendar. I quit checking the booking report. I had to turn off every news feed in his area because I was petrified of seeing any crime or drug bust and even more scared of reading the hurtful comments underneath. I turned off messenger live. Sometimes, I put his conversation thread on "ignore" so that I could control when I looked at it and not get PTSD if I saw a message.

So, the mile marker became one great big: *If only he would get to rehab again.* That became the mantra for all things success. That would surely solve everything. The first was just a sham. A good enough second one would interrupt the cycle long enough for him to want to change his life. I would learn later that rehab is just another tool, like jail is, yes, to interrupt the cycle of scrounging for money, finding drugs, and "staying well". Rinse, repeat. But it's only a part of the tools needed for THEM to change the patterns of THEIR LIFE, in order to see life without drugs as the better option. Give them a porkchop to look forward to— instead of just a bone.

> *Life will bring you pain all by itself. Your responsibility is to create joy.*
> —Milton Erickson

Purpose

People see things through the lens of their own experience. One look at their social media profile, can give a good glimpse of what lens people use. My lens for years consisted of: "You should ALL care about addiction–you just should, like I do!!!" (As I stomp with my feet with my pigtails swinging.) Those who haven't lost a brother and don't have a son in chaotic use, would shushhh right on by. You can't make someone care. But we all keep trying because it's our **cause.** And someone we love is our **why.** It's like religion or politics. If religion has failed someone before, they resist it, and spend time debunking it for others.

We think we are doing others a service by educating them on these very personalized issues that work or haven't worked for us. There are times, however, when people need certain things to get by. For instance, when you feel completely lost and broken, that you've completely failed your family and can't even see the point of living another day, you tend to lean toward a higher power. Even if you can't wrap your head around an actual "heavenly being," then having some "purpose" to help pick you up is a saving grace. For years, I tried to raise my kids with some sort of foundation of religion that included service, history, context, purpose of life, etc., but it didn't seem to carry into their teenage years. Let's face it; at your wits' end, who hasn't said, "Thy will be done, God. I'm done?" Okay, a lot of people probably haven't said that. But I did. I had to. I was shriveling up, almost unable to function at work and home.

Every single day, I would pray for a shield of armor around my son. I believe that he was saved many times. The stories he has told, sometimes nonchalantly, of near misses and things that saved him from continued problems are chalked up to only divine intervention. Some are simpler, like hocking his guns the week before he was pulled over, saving him from a felony charge with drugs. Walking away from a guy in jail, who was waiting in line behind him on the phone. He was asking him if his sister was single and what she looked like and other inappropriate crap, when all he wanted to do was punch him. He said he would have had an assault charge in jail. My son was vomiting sick with withdrawals and didn't care if he got the charge at that time, but he did care about some guy being disrespectful to his sister. A few days later, a man came up to him in jail and put his hand on Mason's chest and said, "Feel this, this is what matters. I was saved from jumping off a bridge once by a stranger who did this to me." This saved him from another assault charge. Other miracles, like deciding to leave a house minutes before the cops raided it, guns drawn. They stopped and talked to him, a guy walking down the street, middle of the night, barefoot and let him go. More serious ones too, like having a gun to his head and running away, calling his ex-wife and telling her this was it; that he was going to be shot and just wanted to say he loved everyone. Overdosing, blue lips, rushing to the hospital and pulling into the ER parking lot, his friend giving him a shot of meth to wake him up. Being successful in digging a bullet out of his leg which is his story to tell, not mine.

I believe that these and many other moments in my quest for my son's recovery and healing were much more than coincidences. I firmly believe that without them or some sort of guardian angel, these things wouldn't have happened the way they did. Our interventionist told us that when you start doing the right things, more right things follow, and the momentum builds. We found this to be true.

When we were stopped or hit a brick wall or did not have cooperation due to others' free will or the adversary's evil ways, things would come to a screeching halt, and it took twice as long to get that momentum built back up. Such is life, but being in the groove with a higher power sure helps facilitate that momentum. Randomly finding an interventionist within days of my son being arrested was a perfect opportunity. His public defender texting me at 10:00 p.m. to say he was on board and had put the order into the judge, which NEVER happens on a Friday, was amazing. The entire intervention being pulled off with coordinating plane schedules was a miracle. Getting my son to finally meet with the bankruptcy lawyer, even though he didn't even have shoes on, was incredible and saved him hundreds of thousands of dollars in judgments.

I kept by my bedside Pamela Lanhart's book Praying Our Loved One Home. I drew extreme comfort in those pages, feeling deep in my heart that it was true that God does NOT want us to live in the darkness of addiction. Even if you don't believe in a higher power, the words are soothing to a parent who is wondering, "Why?" Her words calmed my troubled soul and heart. I believe in the written word having power. Why else do the great motivators tell you to write your manifestations and goals down? Despite the somewhat sad title of this book, I have notebooks full of manifestations, master intentions, and the 55 x 5 rule, which is writing your desire down 55 times for five days in a row. All of my passwords were changed to a positive, hopeful word regarding my son's future with his continually changing age as the numbers. When Mason still had a mailing address, I mailed him a twenty-eight-page "story" of his bright future with specific details of how he used his few "bad" years to help others. I painted a chalkboard wall in my bathroom with positive messages on it. I wrote "Who the Son sets free is free indeed" over and over again.

We are mothers. We love deeply. We are made to give life, to keep things alive and thriving. We admire and nurture beauty. We water and feed everything in our paths. Even if you are not a mother of a person with a substance use disorder, you likely know the pain addiction causes. God did not order a path of destruction to teach you a lesson. He did not say that a Mother's Day barbeque gone wrong should tear a family apart forever. He doesn't want families ripped apart because of lying and cheating and financial collapse and ruin. He doesn't want constables coming to the door and handing the mom of a son or daughter a court subpoena while she bursts into tears. He doesn't want to see his child writhing in pain and sweat, with no money, no possessions, and his supposed "friends" in their droned-out state of mind not coherent enough to help him. He never wants a precious daughter to use her sacred body in order to survive another day. He doesn't condone abuse or lying or complete disregard for human life and property, yet his wayward children do those things under the influence of substances.

We, the believers, the sufferers, the nurturers, must be the ones to shed light on darkness. Addiction is at the very least, a learned disorder of the brain. It's not about willpower, strength of character, or simply quitting. These drugs are powerful. They are not an aspirin that you can just decide not to take one day. Yes, you can decide to quit them. You can decide to do whatever it takes to never go back to that vortex of hell, but it's just not as simple as one day deciding to go to Walmart instead of Kmart to shop. Easy, since Kmart hardly exists anymore. It's more like the minute you decide, every single Kmart that ever existed is suddenly right in front of you flashing its blue light specials. We can be the ones to show them the way. We can be like the alchemist's most famous quote by Ralph Waldo Emerson, "Once you make a decision, the universe conspires to make it happen."

This is why alchemy exists," the boy said. "So that everyone will search for his treasure, find it, and then want to be better than he was in his former life. Lead will play its role until the world has no further need for lead; and then lead will have to turn itself into gold. That's what alchemists do. They show that, when we strive to become better than we are, everything around us becomes better too. —Paulo Coelho, *The Alchemist*

We can lead them to a support network to help them battle this evil. You can believe Ezekial 37 and Lauren Daigle, that dry bones can come back to life. Your loved one can be shown that they are worth saving, that recovery is possible. We cannot contribute to the sheer cruelty that is sometimes shown to not only those in active addiction but those in early recovery too. Dehumanizing them with malice only perpetuates the shame they may carry deep down. Lamaya Outcalt wrote this in one of the addiction support groups. He gave me permission to use it.

This life, man this life of mine has been a f-ng whirlwind. Highest highs, lowest lows and Every. Thing. Else. Do you know what it feels like to think your only option is to plunge a needle deep into your vein? In that moment it's the only thing that will release you from the darkest thoughts you could imagine? I do! Do you know what it feels like to go home every night? Only your home is a bush, and you're sleeping on gravel and pine needles and whatever else decides to crawl into bed with you? I do! Do you know what it feels like to have no other escape, your only option becomes the suicidal ideation bombarding your feeble mind? I do!

Do you know what it feels like to one day wake up and be saved from all this? To have that triggering event your life needed once again begins to heal itself? I do! Do you know the emotions that flood in when you finally defeat all those demons and you connect with the great spirit, the universe, your higher power? I do! This is the face of someone who fell, who fell hard to the bottom and clawed his way out. The face of a warrior who won't accept defeat because he knows what the other side looks like and now fights against it. This is for me! For every time I fell and told myself it was impossible to go on. This is for every time those voices rocked me and wrecked me. This is for those who told us we'd never recover. This is the face of recovery. —Lamaya Outcalt

The bottom line is that the war on drugs has failed. Sorry, Nancy Reagan. You made a nice effort, but things have changed since the eighties. Until we can enlist the engagement and commitment of society as a whole to combat this problem, just like they did for COVID-19, this problem will only get worse. I don't have the answers to how we finally win, but I hope books like this can help dispel the myth that those addicted are dispensable lost causes. Those kinds of comments hurt families of addicts deeply because, as I have illuminated, the pain involved in the ripple effect of addiction cannot be quantified. Some may argue that these people should pay for their choices. They will. Our court system is designed for that. But what isn't needed is for ANYONE to play God before that fact by withholding life-saving measures like Narcan all because of a judgment on what that person has done in that moment of his or her life. None of us want to be judged by our worst moments. This brings me to my last plea. WE are the ones who can lead the way to make change. WE are the ones who can make a difference. WE have to be the ones to fight evil with good. WE have to be the alchemists and be the light in the face of darkness. Without letting the arguments of disease versus choice, enabling versus tough love, and MAT versus abstinence divide us.

When you become comfortable with uncertainty, infinite possibilities open up in your life. — Eckhart Tolle

Unfinished

So, I had finally given in and joined Nar-anon. I did thirty meetings in thirty days. I joined CRAFT and THRIVE and Parents Helping Parents meetings. I started listening to K-Love Christian radio because the political climate was so draining and negative at that time. I was trying to find my balance between the tough love, "blocking my child" like some of the moms had to do to obtain peace and showing my son the power he had deep inside him to pull out. His legal cases were mounting, but I HAD to learn to trust that everything would work out. I couldn't keep getting on his court Zoom cases and having the judge tell me I couldn't speak for my son, which may have happened once.

I hardly missed a day without messaging my son that I loved him, that he was stronger than he thought, or what he is labeled. I said that he deserved to have a happy life again. I told him his life was only half over, and he had time to rebuild. That he still had time to be a dad again and go fishing and camping again. He rarely answered me, but he was reading them.

One Friday I awoke teary-eyed again, which happened most days when I would dream of my kids or pass by their pictures on my wall or on my phone. I had talked to my middle son the week before for four hours about addiction and the spiritual state of the world. He had mentioned how good my older son had been on the job projects, how fast he completed them, but always left the job sites *messy,* so someone always had to come *clean up.* It was a much-needed conversation on the pathway to healing for both of us.

The saying that a mom is only as happy as her saddest child is true, no matter their ages. Our family had been through such changes that we had all retreated to our corners of the boxing ring for months. I had been organizing some albums on social media and Google photos and the whole "pretend like he's in a coma, or on a long vacation" just doesn't work when I see that innocent little face before all this started. I swear I feel his pain. I feel his frustration. It aches into my soul like no one can know or understand. It doesn't matter what he's done to me. In those moments, I am so sorrowful for his little kids that they don't get to know the man he truly is. I feel his losses. How hard it must be to know you lost everything you worked for. That your family is disappointed in you, and no one is talking about it. To know you've lost two or more years of your kids' lives, that you can't even support them anymore. All the things a man values and bases his worth on. I can imagine the feeling of just giving up. Why try? Especially if my worth was so tied up in success. Who am I even without any of that? God, it just pains me to think of him having those thoughts and then numbing them out because they are too overwhelming to fix.

I started to think of a video I saw a few months ago about a series called *The Chosen*. The director, Dallas Jenkins, was quoting a song called "Faithful Now" by Vertical Worship.[44] I remembered the passion in his eyes as he was reciting the lyrics and I remembered it said something about prison walls, which was becoming a touchy subject for me.

Mountains moving, giants falling, prison walls shaking. As he sang the words, the thunder ripped above and poured rain onto him and his selfie stick. It was a powerful video of having faith that things would work out.

I remembered his passion; I remembered him breaking down, wondering where they were going to film the next season with COVID running things amuck. So now that I was relying more on spiritual survival to get me through this, I wanted to find that spiritual passion. I looked up his follow-up video about the location of the next season of *The Chosen*.

Stay with me here.

The Chosen Miracle

After that thundering first video, he had immediately received permission to film on a huge outdoor set-in rural Utah depicting the ancient city of Jerusalem. That set was the scene of The Piano Guys'

[44] https://www.youtube.com/watch?v=9YexUJ2WHik

Christmas video "O Come, O Come, Emmanuel."[45] It was a beautiful song and the site of the movie set interested me because I had been there a few times on my rockhounding trips and never saw anything like it out there. I was curious to see it. As I watched another one of their videos, I recognized a song sung by Lauren Daigle that played on K-Love called "You Say."[46] I was shocked to see it was filmed in my son's town 400 miles away. Remember? That town that used to be our family's paradise. In fact, it was at a beautiful state park, right behind my son's now lost, custom-built house he had built himself, at the height of his success. His backyard was the incredible scenery in that video. I gasped at the beauty of it all, mixed in with sadness. As I listened to the perfect sonata, I said the words along with their music. It was then I realized the words to the song.

I keep fighting voices in my mind that say I'm not enough
Every single lie that tells me I will never measure up
Am I more than just the sum of every high and every low?
Remind me once again just who I am,
because I need to know, ooh oh
You say I am loved when I can't feel a thing
You say I am strong when I think I am weak
And You say I am held when I am falling short
And when I don't belong, oh, you say I am Yours
And I believe (I), oh, I believe (I)
What You say of me (I)
I believe
The only thing that matters now is everything You think of me
In You I find my worth, in You I find my identity, ooh oh
47 USED WITH PERMISSION 48

Voices? Sum of my HIGHS? I am loved? CAN'T FEEL? I am strong? *Falling short?* The song uses everything I had been telling my son. It was everything that I felt HE MUST BE FEELING. I'm not putting words in his mouth, but this was too much coincidence. But it wasn't over. Bear with me.

As I scrolled down to the comments, below their introspective virtual sing-along, the Piano Guy, cellist Steven Sharp Nelson, wrote this the following (used with permission):

*Okay. Vulnerable time. I had an emotional experience atop the **half-built building** you see near the end. It was so beautiful to play cello there. As we were playing this song over and over again while we filmed, I thought about its meaning. I thought about where I was in my life emotionally. I expect a lot from myself. I always have. Often, I expect too much. I admit it. And when I don't reach the zenith of those expectations, I can be hard on myself. If ever there was **incarceration** for self-abuse perpetrators, I'd be prisoner of the month. As I was thinking about how much I still need to **build** in my life, a strong impression came to me. Has that ever happened to you? When you feel an impulse that prompts thoughts that don't feel like "normal thoughts." They feel weightier, with more perspective or profundity than the average passing notion -- the same way a good bridge elevates a song by throwing you from a repetitive verse and chorus regimen. These are thoughts that teach you rather than learn from you.*

*I had such a moment. They don't come that often, but when they do I try my best to listen and learn. The impressions convinced me to look at my life from the top of a **half-built** building. Figuratively and literally. I began to think that maybe I spend too much of my life in the bottom floors of my life's construction project -- that I fuss over **the mess of my jobsite**, I fret over the lack of finishes -- the ugly marred subflooring or the exposed metal framing. I berate myself for being way behind in the building process. I was taught that I needed to ascend more often to the top floor. Where there's a view of how far I've come, how high part of my building has reached. And most importantly, where there's an incredible view of the sunset, reminding me that **tomorrow is another day** and that I should **keep building one day at a time**. I totally embarrassed myself as I shed tears, trying to describe these "elevated* *thoughts" to the site's supervisor after we had finished filming and I was thanking him for the opportunity they had given us to give visual meaning to the music.*

*So, I guess for me, and perhaps for anyone listening, that could be a takeaway. You don't have to live your life on floor one. Or floor two or three. Or on any floor that isn't yet completed. It will get there one day. And so will you. Don't worry that the building next door is at floor ten. Just take a trip to your top however often you need and watch the sun set on all that you've strived to accomplish. Remember that there is Someone who built that sunset for you. And He doesn't care **how high your building is**, just that you're willing to keep building. And He says you're **plenty high enough** for Him to see.*[48]

Despite the ironic references to *high*, I sent all of this to my son, with the excited message, "You're HIGH ENOUGH! He says you're high enough! You're not done building! You're gonna be okay. God has literally saved you over and over again. And you don't have to be a *prisoner* on the *first floor of life*. He doesn't care how *messy your jobsite is*!"

This whole sort of spiritual scavenger hunt left me with no doubt that God was sending me a message to calm my soul. Just two days before, I had begged again for peace. After listening to another two-and-a-half-hour Nar-Anon meeting, one of the moms had said her son was wasting away, losing weight, and she told him he was killing himself and she was not going to watch it! I had burst into tears and begged God to help me find peace with whatever happened because I COULD NOT LOSE HIM. Oh, the sheer pain of the thought of it. Over and over again, I experienced that raw, aching, endless pain. I needed relief. That day's deep dive into my son's journey, intertwined with my worst fears, helped me see I had zero control over what happened. I also had zero control over my son having these spiritual breakthroughs like I desperately wanted him to. In fact, my son didn't appear to be feeling anything.

The night of my middle son's four-hour phone call, my boys' childhood friend and coworker hung himself. He had struggled with drug use but had recovered. Everyone thought he was doing well. He stopped to talk to my boys just that day, and nothing seemed wrong. I was scared to tell my addicted son about it because I feared the shock would incite him to do the same thing. Then I remembered, *He can't feel pain right now.* If he could, he wouldn't be a person using mind-altering substances. He would be in recovery trying to fix stuff.

We all know from the early days of Tony Robbins that energy goes where attention flows. Yes, my attention was flowing. I needed focus. I needed help from a higher power because nothing was working. The Chosen Director Dallas Jenkins calls these moments "Red Sea Moments." Or actually it was his wife Amanda who coined the term. Dallas described it as "moments where you get to a certain point that you've done everything you can think of and there's nothing else you can do. Like Moses needing someone's help holding up his arms so the battle can be won."

"When your evidence for potential success is just multiple examples of failure."[49]

And just like our interventionist stated when he slept in late on the big day of the intervention, "I guess I needed that;" Dallas stated: "If *I* continue to need to learn that lesson—it's okay being in this place of surrender, desperation and helplessness... there's no better place to be than that."[50]

And boy, was I ever helpless. I needed help and to get that help, I had to find a way to get to that place of surrender. I had to surrender ZERO control over every aspect of my son's actions and trajectory. I had to give up the idea of pushing control over my son to have these spiritual breakthroughs like I kept having, even though I wanted more than anything for him to experience that shift. But, it appeared, my son wasn't feeling anything (I can't feel a thing) or at least wasn't communicating anything, so these moments were for ME!! Why couldn't I just take the gift? The gift of freedom for myself without worrying about him receiving the gift of freedom. I wanted to buy my son's redemption. I still had so much to learn about a person's own salvation. It can't be bought and sold again at a goodwill store. It's

---

[49] https://www.youtube.com/watch?v=77Id2H3PfKAandt=3557s minute 49
[50] https://www.youtube.com/watch?v=77Id2H3PfKAandt=3557s

already been paid for. But it's a very personal and private journey. We can't save another.

I wish the following words were mine. They could be. They are mostly. But I want to give credit where credit is due. Roxy is another mom of a person with a substance use disorder.

One day my beautiful boy will remember how amazing he was before heroin stole his soul. The way to achieve this is by showing them compassion and respect. They need understanding and compassion to show they are worth taking back their life, their health. Mostly, they need hope. Because when they are caught in that cycle of destruction, the last thing they see is hope. Addiction is bad enough when controlling one person, don't let it control two. They didn't anticipate how their life would turn out, how many people they hurt, or how much they would lose. They are still human and still needing to be loved, heard, and seen. — Roxy Britt

This is my own tribute to my beautiful boy that she inspired me to write in 2020:

*One day my boy will realize how loved he always was. He will forget the frustrations of his childhood, of always getting it wrong, not seeming to be as organized and detailed as everyone wanted. He will forget the furrowed brows and harsh "why can't you just...." voices. He will forget the teacher's disapproving marks. Screw school, then. Who needs it? I'll do it my way. He'll forget the endless quest for money, for control of his mind and body. He will forget the endless explanations and defensiveness. He will forget the disappointment, the shame. He will forget how he risked everything, every day just to please that puppet master. He will forget the lost, desperate face staring back at him in the mirror and the endless search for daily survival. Now, life renewed- he will only know HOPE, being fulfilled for the first time in a long time. Years of denying his own truth finally ends when he accepts himself—fully and completely. All the sadness and shame will be feathers in the wind. He will see the sky for the first time in years. **He will feel the warmth of the sun on his tanned face.** He will thank God for the glory of freedom. Freedom from the chains that held him captive for so long. He will finally revel in the honor that he deserves,* *finally free from the battles that this life tried to crush him with. He will love fully and completely, embracing life with true joy.*

How true these words would become. As Liam read these words years later, he said, "Wow, that was pure inspiration on your part."

Go inwards. Find your inner space, and suddenly, you will find an explosion of light, of beauty, of ecstasy -as if suddenly thousands of roses have blossomed within you and you are full of their fragrance. —Osho

Forgiveness

What do all these things have in common with forgiveness?

Soap
Goats with pool noodles on their horns
Non-slip shoes
Sunscreen
Carrying snacks for diabetics
Baby stair gates
Fire screens
Egg white breakfast sandwich
Cigarette filters
Stop signs
Condoms
Swimming pool covers
Snow spikes
Canes
Walkers
Fire extinguisher
Nightlights
Insect repellent
Window locks
Steel toe shoes
Hard hats
Goggles
Drinking water between martinis
Designated drivers
Bartenders
Lower alcohol content

These items are all accepted harm reduction measures that society puts in place to help people stay safe and prevent further harm. In fact in some jobs they are mandatory for employees. My belief has come to accept and welcome harm reduction after many years of thinking abstinence is the only answer. The argument is that we are condoning drug use with needle exchange, safe consumption sites, fentanyl testing strips and even Narcan. Harm reduction for drugs is a whole other discussion.

In any case why wouldn't we want to reduce the pain and turmoil with addiction—ours and theirs?

Question after question would be asked: "How could they do this to me? Why are they so mean? " Why don't they care what they are doing to all of us?" How do you forgive for all those transgressions?.

Forgiveness fits into these harm reduction measures for us and for the perpetrator, because getting rid of our anger and spite and bitterness prevents further victimizing of ourselves. When we relive the agony of trauma or what someone has done to us, over and over again, we are re-victimizing ourselves again and again. Offering forgiveness prevents further harm by offering forgiveness to others or even to ourselves; helps us release that cycle of resentment and pain. It doesn't downplay or justify the crime but by offering our grace to the offender, in fact it just may be the ticket to their asking for their own atonement and salvation for their sins leading to a resolution of their deeply embedded shame and guilt that is almost always at the heart of hurtful and self-defeating behavior.

Forgiveness and unconditional love ARE harm reduction because they stop the cycle of buried pain and resentment. Being free from these shackles help future generations avoid repeating patterns of addiction and other conditions that result from unresolved pain and trauma.

I know this might be easier for some than others. After all, addiction creates a feeling of powerlessness. Anger gives the illusion of power because it *feels* like you are doing *something*. Same theory as 'washing your hands of something'. It feels powerful in an otherwise powerless situation.

Some parents and spouses experience severe violence with their person during active use. Many have restraining orders on their own children. How do you forgive someone who has–or still is–threatened, (ing) you? It's so hard to have empathy, let alone forgiveness, during these times.

I believe time and active effort is the key.

People are in such different places resulting from their experience. A wife who's been left to raise the kids isn't going to have the same level of forgiveness as a sibling who wasn't affected quite as much.

What everyone does have in common though, is the feelings of hurt and betrayal that the person in addiction failed the relationship. All of their relationships. But how can one person be responsible for all of these issues? I was beginning to see that someone in addiction, who can't even take care of themselves, isn't able to keep any type of functional relationship with others, giving them what they require. Every day on the Mom support sites; I read how their child or spouse took off and won't answer them or outright leave them for another person. Of course, even people not addicted do these things. Some questions are not answerable. We hear over and over again that OUR reaction to things is the key.

People in chaotic addiction often disappear for days, weeks, months. The feelings of abandonment are real plus not knowing if your child is okay, brings out all sorts of emotions of anger, fear and despair.

At this time, I was on four to five addict recovery sites because I wanted to glean any information on how their brains work in these scenarios. I wanted to find out how I could best help facilitate his recovery and rebonding of relationships by knowing what he's thinking-if anything.

One day I did a very informal poll.. I asked: ***"When you were in active addiction, what thoughts did you have when you isolate from family or abandon those who need you?***

These were my results.
- They're better off without me- 39
- They'll know I'm high and we'll just end up fighting 36

197

- I have to force myself to not think about them- 33
- My drug of choice keeps me in full throttle for its attention- 32
- Time is misleading. I told myself I'll take care of it tomorrow-31
- I'm too far gone so it doesn't matter if they're worried or hurt -26
- I don't want to have to answer to them or have them see me destroying myself- 10
- My family is dysfunctional and I can't deal with them-9
- I hurt knowing I was hurting them and it drove me further away-9

Guess what question got ZERO ANSWERS in all 4 groups?: *"I don't care about them or love them anymore."* Yet how many kids or moms or wives think that very thing, day after day, year after year?
Some of those who answered stated that while in active addiction their mind is their worst enemy. Some said they wanted to spare their loved ones- especially their children- from seeing them in that way. They stated that they used substances to numb how they felt and that if they were to feel fully about all they had caused or done, it would eat them alive. So the isolation, the detachment, the seemingly lack of caring is really a defense/coping mechanism that serves to help preserve their sanity, in a way.

My friend Shianne stated: "I'm finally realizing how expensive my trauma [in addiction] was for me, How expensive it's been to stay standing in it like a prisoner. My moments of feeling the desire to self-sabotage are brief now. Safety is something I've always longed for but to be honest, it felt yucky when I found it."

So even though I had spent so much time ruminating on my own pain and discomfort and suffering almost daily, the more I discovered that most chaotic use behavior was really not intended to hurt others. It wasn't done in spite or on purpose. Of course there are many drug psychosis behaviors that cause drama and violence. But also the person might have been abusive and basically an asshole even before the drug takes over all moral and empathic pathways in order to obtain the drug.

As I read through the pain and turmoil of the support groups, it struck me that there's no way all of these relationships were going just dandy, when the addiction flared up. Just like the SUD person could be a jerk before addiction, so can their friends and family. Family dynamics and problems with control, jealousy, insecurities, unfaithfulness, death of a child or other problems can be quickly forgotten when addiction takes front and center. Since the consequences and behaviors of addiction are full on for everyone to see, it quickly becomes the scapegoat for every problem the family may have had.

Even though I never have had good communication and emotional coping skills; I finally learned that someone has to be the healthy one. This is why action and movement are so important in those times when we can't seem to reach our loved one. Going to classes at smart recovery or Pals will help us learn how to communicate effectively and reduce unneeded suffering and stop the toxic interactions that seem to happen. We can model how people work through problems and handle conflict resolution. Handling stress and showing how to have emotionally healthy communication is the key to successful business and personal relationships. And what a grand opportunity addiction gives for that! Over and over again.

In Letting Go, Rugged Love for Wayward Souls, the authors write: "If you have ever loved a prodigal, you know what it feels like to be sinned against. A wayward soul stays afloat by cutting away the ballast of concern for other people's feelings and interests. And when they do, things get pretty nasty"...." how do you keep from collapsing under the weight of resentment? Rugged love forgives. Often. Not to keep peace, or appease prodigals, but because it sees its own greater debt to God wiped clean." The Bible makes it clear that forgiveness is a two-way street, meaning if we want to receive forgiveness from God, we must be willing to pass it along to others. (Matthew 6:14-15; Luke 17:3-4).

Forgiveness is foreign to me. I wasn't taught it, and I've never truly practiced it.

During this journey, I had to read The Prodigal Son over and over again. I had to forgive my son over and over again. I had to look into his eyes—usually in his pictures—and say, "I know you're in there and you're hurting and I miss you with all my heart. I know you can't be what I want you to be right now, and I forgive that. Because my love for you can't be dependent on what I get back." That's how a mom loves. She doesn't just give her kids a set amount of time or chances, because chances aren't about success or accomplishment, they are about love. My son taught me the meaning of unconditional love. I also learned about Agape love, which is the highest form of love, and wrote about it in my blog.

Addiction gives so many opportunities to learn about the true value of a person's soul and how far the soul will reach to find love and acceptance. Even if "they started it". The anger I felt at drugs, the drug world, my son, the Columbian cocaine pipeline- that probably paved the way for heroin and fentanyl and anything else I could blame was stagnating me back into my victim mentality that I had fought hard to overcome over the years.

Robert Ricciardelli states how much worse it makes our lives when we live with anger and resentment.

"Engaging in the blame game is a waste of time. No matter what someone may have done, how much fault you find with another, and regardless of how much you want to blame them, it still does not change you. When you are looking for external reasons to explain your unhappiness or frustration you may look for others to blame. While this keeps the focus off of you, the real problem remains to be a destructive poison within you. You may succeed in making another feel guilty about something by blaming or shaming them, but you will not succeed in discovering and then changing whatever it is about you that is making you unhappy. Do not do the blame game, it does not work. Look within, talk to God, discover what the real issues are. As you move to forgiveness, releasing, and healing, the peace of God will reign in your heart once more".[51]

One of my favorite motivational guys Joe Dispenza said this:

"If you're stuck in an emotion, it's probably some negative emotion from your past." (Such as resentment and fear.) *"When you can't think greater than you feel"*. He states if you're stuck in your past then you're still telling the story of your past and you're not telling the story of your future"*[52]

---

[51] https://www.patheos.com/blogs/robertricciardelli/ricciardelli/the-dangers-of-playing-the-blame-game-by-robert-ricciardelli/

[52] https://www.youtube.com/watch?v=QwrkOWUt5Mg

It may take years but I believe almost everyone can achieve a level of forgiveness that helps with the anger and disappointment of addiction and all the trauma surrounding it. What's important is that we work in our own lanes, our own traumas and not project those traumas onto others, while they're fighting their own demons too.

There's no shame in needing to step back to protect ourselves from our loved one or those surrounding them.

When I found myself the most frustrated, the most hateful, the most controlling, I knew that I needed to step back and work on myself. My boundaries, my triggers, my insecurities and my expectations. Once in a while I will find one of my old self-videos of my reddened swollen face, begging my son, God, anyone to please help me. Please help my family. I was so very angry. I would go from yelling at my son to begging him and God to please stop! Just STOP! I would call into work knowing that I wouldn't quit crying for hours. I would isolate myself in my own misery and guilt, wanting anything outside of myself to save me and my family. It took years to realize that it wasn't all about me. I mean I was all I had, so I had to take care of myself, but others were NOT going to help fix me. I desperately HAD to find the right coping skills, the safe people and just the right amount of prayers to help calm my aching heart. Peace beyond understanding.

"Even when everything screams out that we should give up and the situation seems hopeless, we need to remember that apart from God, we are all hopelessly lost."[53]

"Hurt people really do hurt people. and unless we climb up into the hallways of their minds, we will never fully understand where all the brokenness is coming from. and why, in the justification of their own weary hearts, they would heap their pain upon another. But I have gathered this much. That sometimes love is so inconceivably absent. That sometimes sadness is so tremendously heavy. That sometimes trauma and loneliness and grief and unsilenced demons are passed down from generation to generation and the only way that they can trick themselves into coping, is to project the burden onto anyone who stands in the path of self-reflection and healing. and

---

[53] https://www.amazon.com/Letting-Go-Rugged-Wayward-Souls-ebook/dp/B01CXDN6XO

sometimes that someone will be you. know that they are fighting a battle. and your only responsibility is to choose whether you need to invest in offering peace or if it's time for burning bridges —Ullie Kaye, used with permission

I was determined not to make anyone else's experience more painful, and certainly not to place unneeded suffering on my son as he was trying to maneuver this darkness. Building bridges was my goal. Even if we didn't all end up at the same place.

"If you wish to be a warrior, prepare to be broken. If you wish to be an explorer, prepare to get lost. If you wish to be a lover, prepare to be both." ~Daniel Saint

Lost in Las Vegas

February 17, 2021, at 9:48 AM, I randomly texted my son this quote, "In case no one told you today: You're beautiful, You Are loved. You're needed. You're alive for a reason. You're stronger than you think, you're going to get through this. I'm glad you're alive. Don't give up." I hadn't heard from him since February 13 and was getting nervous, although I could see that he had read my messages.

Finally, at 3:30 PM, he responded that he had been stuck in Las Vegas for two days without eating or drinking anything after his "friends" were arrested. He said he just needed some money, or a room, or a bus ride home, but he didn't have any ID and only one shoe. He was at Santa Fe Station Hotel and Casino, and it was cold outside. but since he wasn't gambling, he had to keep walking around pretending he would gamble, but he figured he was about to get kicked out. I knew I wasn't going to give him money or a room in my name. He texted me pictures of the fast-food places there, so I ordered food for him. I offered to Uber him to the shelter, where he could stay until 6:30 AM (when the bus would leave). He was afraid the shelters would check his warrants so it literally took hours to convince him that he needed to get somewhere safe. I had called the shelters and asked if they checked warrants, and they assured me no. He asked me to let him get twenty dollars back from his hamburger I had ordered so he could put a few pennies in the slot machines every hour. That way he could stay inside.

I declined that idea, mostly because of all the "no money" advice I had read about as the "only way" to get them to the gift of desperation. After a few calls, I found out the Courtyard Homeless Resource Center would give him a bus ticket home if he stayed there. He said, "no, I have warrants with seven federal felonies." This was NOT true; they were not federal, but I learned later that if someone has felonies in another state, then the arresting state is obligated to charge the person and send him back. One of the phone calls I had made was to a guy who works with the homeless in Vegas. I found him through Jen Elizabeth, founder of Resurrektion of Me (The Sidewalk Project) on Instagram. Jen said the man would try to send someone to Mason, but only if my son called him. I gave my son the number, but he was too untrusting. He thought I was setting him up to go to treatment. He wasn't wrong. I may have mentioned a couple of rehabs, including one in Bullhead City, Arizona that a lady in a support group had recommended.

Mason texted me again, "Mom, I'm at the 7-11 on Rancho and Craig. I'm freezing to death, I only have one shoe, I wouldn't ask you for help if it wasn't like I'm going to die tonight. I am so f-ng cold right now. Can you please just give me an Uber to the Cannery or somewhere by the freeway and I can probably find someone I know or at least hang out there until they kick me out. I have only 4% battery, so if you don't hear from me, I'll be between here and home."

I said, "Please ask the clerk if you can use his phone."

He said, "Mom, this is Vegas. People die every day. No one cares." Boy was this ever a true statement as I would soon find out. After two Ubers, I got him to the Cannery, where he said he missed his last possible "ride." He then said, "I should have stolen that 7-Eleven clerk's jacket that was on the chair so I could make it the rest of the night outside."

I couldn't believe it. When I told him to go ask the hotel clerk if they had any shoes or a charger someone had left, he stated, "If I ask to borrow something at the front desk, they will know I don't have a room

203

and kick me the F out. They DO NOT WANT TO HELP people here. THEY just want your money."

I begged and pleaded with him to stop this madness. That isn't enough? I scream-texted him, "GET HELP! Not temporary help, not an UBER, NOT A CHARGER, NOT A FEW BUCKS!! Permanent help! Don't live in a constant state of chaos!!!" I was so mad by this point. Even writing this out, I feel the frustration, the desperation rising up inside me. My gut is churning just thinking about it. I told him that he needed to just surrender right now, go to a shelter, and let someone help him! This went on for hours. I did not sleep. My son said he hadn't slept in three nights, and when he drifted off to sleep outside, his fingers were numb when he woke up. The temperature was forty degrees that night, cold for Vegas and what he was used to also. I made literally dozens of calls to agencies for assistance. One representative was very abrasive, contradicting the organization's goal to battle the opioid crisis in Vegas. They questioned every word I said. It was as if I was on trial or that they had never witnessed an addict's behavior. I could not believe the lack of support. Every other place I called wanted to get him help.

At 01:09 AM, Mason messaged me, "So thank you for your help, Mom. You tried. I should have just tried to get you to send money to a card of some kind, but my phone is going to be off now, and hopefully I will find an empty building or something or a piece of glass, so I can slit my wrist cuz I'm done with this shit." Finally, after an hour of this sort of talk and me sending quotes such as "This is not how your story is going to end" he agreed to go to the rescue mission and sleep, so I arranged an Uber. However, upon arrival, it was closed up and not accepting new patients. I didn't know that and didn't hear from him for almost an hour. I then received a blurry picture of a dark alley and he said he almost got jumped in the dark and was now running to the Golden Nugget. I then said I was done, that he had one more chance. It was either the bus to come home (his home on the streets, four hours away from me) or Crossroads, a rehab just eight miles from him.

He responded, "Please keep in mind that wherever you send me right now, I'm not sleeping inside of it. I'm not giving my name so they can send it to the cops. I'm sleeping outside somewhere. I'm going to go find that bridge and get some sleep. I really don't care if I die tonight. I really don't. I just need some sleep, that's all." Then a few minutes later, he said, "I should have just taken a car and I wouldn't have had to walk. Then I'd be home quick."

"That's great," I said. "Add grand theft auto to your problems."

Finally, "Just get me an Uber Mom, so I can sleep in the car. I want to go as far away as possible so I can sleep."

I sent another Uber at 5:17 for him to go to the bus station, but when he was picked up at 5:20, the Uber driver handed me the phone because Mason wanted to switch his ride and go to the airport because the Greyhound station wouldn't allow him to be there sleeping until 8:00 AM. The uber driver dropped him off, and he must have sat down to sleep because he called his ex-wife at 6:52 and said he was sorry it had to end like this, but he wasn't going to make it through the night. He told her he couldn't move his fingers anymore, his lips were blue, and he was going to freeze to death. And that he loved her.

She couldn't get him to tell her where he was. She couldn't get hold of me and called Haven in a panic. She filed a missing persons case with the Las Vegas Police while I managed to file one through my home police department. I called the Uber driver to see exactly where he dropped Mason off. He called me back and said it wasn't that cold down there and Mason would be fine. I hung up on him because he was in his warm car all night with BOTH shoes on.

I called my husband at work and said we had to head to Vegas. He came right home knowing I hadn't slept all night, and wondering if we were going to identify a body. We threw a bag of clothes together and headed south.

My son had a missing person's report from two states, along with five warrants for drug possession. All the while he lay sleeping somewhere close to the airport shuttle station because next thing I know, a police officer is calling me asking if I bought Mason a shuttle ticket because otherwise, due to Covid, he couldn't stay in the station. I said I had and said I would send him a screenshot of the ticket. My son ended up not even using the ticket. He "got a ride home from someone." It was over. Just like that. This real experience reminded me of my dream

205

just six months before of being lost in Vegas myself. It was so odd that I would dream of being lost there only to have it come to fruition with my son. Talk about grabbing onto the rope with both hands in the quicksand! This is the life they pull you into. It's so easy to be sucked into the quicksand if you don't create a lifeline and healthy boundaries. I don't regret trying to keep him safe and alive, but by this time I was exhausted. It took three Uber rides, two pricey meals, and one unused bus ticket. My emotions were reeling along with Liam, Haven, and the worried mother of my grandchildren. My daughter said, "When I dropped my kids off at school that morning, I thought, *My brother is dead, and* I have *to act like normal because nobody cares.* I was thinking this is all insane. You just can't explain this shit to normal people."

I said, "Welcome to my life almost every single day the last two years."

Sometimes our lives have to be completely shaken up, changed, and rearranged to relocate us to the place we are meant to be.
——Unknown

A State of Unbliss

The movie *Bliss*, starring Owen Wilson as the main character Greg, offers an intense look into what it's like to be in an alternative world and seemingly unable to break free. Greg, while on the verge of a mental breakdown due to prescription use and life's heavy stressors, becomes enamored with a mysterious homeless woman and is thrown into a world of depravity and secret powers but ONLY when consuming magic "crystals." Meanwhile, his daughter never gives up trying to pull him back. The scene of him seeing her on the TV monitor as he shows zero emotion is so telling of our loved ones who appear not to care about their own children enough to break free. Some key quotes from Greg are, *"It's hard to figure out what's real, like it's all a big trick,"* to which he repeats in true brainwashing style, *"My past life will fade away. I just need more blue crystals."* In another scene, he states how all the turmoil is worth it because, "It's all so beautiful, cops coming, us running, everyone playing their part and you never know what will happen. One minute we are laughing and the next we can't afford a sandwich." His daughter eventually tells him that he will have to choose between the two worlds. His version of his previous world was not going well, so the illusion of this new, although traumatic world-even if it means the loss of his daughter, has him transfixed.

I believe that in the chaotic lifestyle of addiction, they become obsessed with the thrill of the risk; but I believe it's still in the context of motivation for survival. Of making the "best" of what is. Osho states:

"Man ordinarily lives in loneliness. To avoid loneliness, he creates all kinds of relationships, friendships, organizations, political parties, religions and what not. But the basic thing is that he is very much afraid of being lonely. Loneliness is a black hole, a darkness, a frightening negative state almost like death … as if you are being swallowed by death itself. To avoid it, you run out and fall into anybody, just to hold somebody's hand, to feel that you are not lonely… Nothing hurts more than loneliness."[54]-Osho

I'm not saying that every person who becomes addicted is lonely, I'm just saying that humans are creatures of habit and connoisseurs of pleasure, so the more they perform a habit, the more pleasurable THE ACT of it becomes. Staying in that cloud of safety. The chase. I know the chase, the drive, the desire for risk– is hugely embedded in my son. The actual process of needing more and more drugs to obtain a high is only a part of the life.

The terms Addicted to Chaos, or Addictive Personality come to mind as I write this, but also the torment of on the surface KNOWING you are doing wrong, abandoning your kids, not paying your bills, yet somehow feeling comfortable in it! How guilt producing is that? Is this where a lot of the stigma comes in? Thinking that they are enjoying that life, enjoying "screwing people over," hurting everyone. As I state many times, I believe that for one: they don't fully understand the impact they have on people while their brain is still hijacked, and two: If and when they do realize the damage they have caused, the pain and embarrassment and inability to fix it all, is too much which I believe this is the reason for many relapses.

When my son was "lost" in Las Vegas all night and sure he was going to freeze to death; he told me to stop sending pictures of his kids, that he "couldn't look at them, I'm nothing to them." Without the bonding moments of seeing them grow up, I firmly believe he had to develop a distance from them by detaching, in order to keep the pain away. Otherwise, it would destroy a person with any kind of heart. The hopelessness of that lifestyle, when every attempted effort doesn't seem to get them back on track; their desire and motivation are sunk as low as the titanic. So, the squirrel wheel continues. A state of un-bliss, disguised as bliss.

---

[54] https://www.goodreads.com/quotes/1423381-man-ordinarily-lives-in-loneliness-to-avoid-loneliness-he-creates#:~:text=To%20avoid%20loneliness%2C%20he%20creates,much%20afraid%20of%20being%20lonely.

PART FIVE: RESOLUTION

Correcting the Correctional System

As I work with eating disorder patients, I notice the similarities between addiction and purging, binging, and cutting. These behaviors are symptoms of a greater problem-one in which they can't control. When they engage in them, they feel a sense of control and relief. They feel an eerie sense of numbness after vomiting, which is so comforting to them, that it becomes addictive. They literally lose their hunger cues due to changes in the hypothalamus. Even as their thoughts become further skewed due to the underlying thought disorder of body dysmorphia and a malnourished brain, they become more capable of hiding their disorder– sometimes for years. By the time we get them in treatment; they truly believe they can't fit through the door to the kitchen or sometimes they will try to scratch their skin off their arms and bellies as we start the refeeding process and they see a little "puffiness." Food is their enemy yet we force them to be exposed to it. If they don't partake, we put a feeding tube in. We don't kick them out and tell them to come back when they have fixed their problem and can eat. It may not be a great comparison, but my point is, they face the same stigma of "Why don't you just eat?" as our addicts get with "Why don't you just quit?" Yet they are not shamed or punished into compliance. And just like removing the drugs doesn't "cure" addiction; adding weight to the anorexic doesn't "cure anorexia." Positive coping skills are taught along with counseling of the core issues. I've heard many times that one of the failures of drug and alcohol rehabs is they target behaviors, not core issues. Eating disorder patients return to treatment many times and they are rarely, if ever, shamed for needing more support like addicts are.

My son was facing three felonies, nine misdemeanors from his years in addiction. Basically three years of back charges all grouped into one. I feel like the charges could have read, "Operating in a reptile brain which has zero room for rational thinking, gauging consequences, and empathy for others." I'm not condoning any law breaking, I just think that it's the only disease which the patient is charged with behaviors relating to the symptoms. A society that glamorizes alcohol until that fine line when someone can't control it, at which time they are suddenly a criminal and looked down upon. Then, if we do somehow convince others to have a little compassion for the addicted brain and its challenges, it's quickly demolished if they cross that line of selling. Now they are suddenly akin to a violent criminal. They should suddenly know better. We could say there's all these invisible "crossing the lines" like lying, stealing, or selling, are just unforgivable-but the fact is, if they aren't in recovery, or working a regular job (which requires abstinence from substances immediately) then these things are almost a natural progression of the disease. A society that would never arrest a diabetic patient for buying donuts, or a gambler for touching a slot machine yet they criminalize addicts. Yes, my son made poor decision after poor decision to get him there, just like others make poor food choices or poor sex choices. Luckily, those situations are not illegal or everyone's sins would be known.

One day, while listening in on a zoom hearing, waiting for my son's name to be called, I heard the previous case of an inmate who got thrown in solitary confinement for handing a magazine to another inmate. Maybe he threw it or swore at him, I'm not sure, I only heard the judge say, "I get mad a hundred times a day and I don't lash out at other people or I would get myself in a lot of trouble. You have to learn a better way of thinking."

I agree. They do. They need new skills, new habits. They need HELP. Not to be shoved in a room like Napoleon was to St. Helena where he declared as he was sent away; "For what infamous treatment are we reserved?"

Many studies are beginning to show that people with addictions, just like any other human being, respond better to being treated with respect and dignity rather than being cast out and shamed. Pierre Tristam stated it well in his article, "Addiction Is Not a Crime. The Drug War Is." He states there are approximately seven million people incarcerated, on parole or probation with non-violent crimes. "Treatment works better when cut off from all these threats and penalties."

As many people have stated, "we are not going to arrest our way out of this crisis." But I might add that it's surely a great business for all the agencies involved, so why would they want to stop criminalizing it?

While my son was in jail, he was charged a thirty-day sentence for contempt of court for missing an ORS hearing. He was denied a clergy visit, had zero counseling, and was in severe withdrawals. He was also charged with possession while in jail. I'm not condoning any of these charges but I am condoning treating people in pain with dignity and respect. Imagine being immediately cut off from what was literally keeping you" well" (As my son calls it) for months, years even and being told to suck it up just because you were arrested. We would never tell a diabetes sufferer that they ate one too many brownies so they'll just have to deal with the consequences of high blood sugar, no insulin for them. I know it may be an unfair comparison but as a nurse, I was trained to care for people no matter what their choices were. Although, I will say that when an eating disorder patient self-harms, they do get "punished" in the form of self-reflection, a session with their therapist to do a "weapons removal," and program phase drop which means loss of privileges. Since they have lost the ability to understand or control their own self-sabotaging behaviors, they are "guided" into exploring how to begin to recover–not just told to or else. They are walked through their behaviors such as over-exercise or constantly standing and stretching because their body tells them they cannot stop moving in order to burn calories, so this was arrest number four.

Since medical staff at Purgatory wasn't allowed to return calls, I made sure that I left a couple of messages to them the previous week about his tendency to develop Rhabdomyolysis during withdrawals.

My state had turned down a house bill for detox in jails in 2019 so I had no way of knowing what their policy was. Without a MAT policy, the system somehow makes it seem okay to treat withdrawal symptoms with nothing but electrolytes twice a day, EVEN IF they immediately vomit them up and have to wait until the next time they are due.

This was the longest he had stayed in jail so far. Since the extra charges for using in jail had sent him to "the hole" I had no way of communicating with him to prepare for the next hearing. At the first hearing, he had waived his right to an attorney, but now he had 3 new complicated charges added on with no way to defend himself since he had already waived his right. Plus, at the previous hearing, he did not represent himself adequately in the two minutes he was given to answer a question.

It was at this time that we decided he may need a lawyer instead of a public defender. We wanted to be able to communicate effectively with counsel in order to get him the best outcome. Things were looking serious between the criminal case and the civil case. He was looking at possibly 9 years in prison. Keeping him locked up with no adequate communication at this point was only going to make things worse and leave him at their mercy, being unable to start paying his debts and/or getting treatment for his addiction. We found basically the cheapest lawyer we could but he was one whom I thought I could communicate with after talking on the phone a few times with him.

Body Language

At the first hearing with council, my son was shuffled to the zoom camera in leg chains and handcuffs. The camera was above him and the phone on the wall beside him. He had to maneuver the phone between cuffed hands, look up high at the camera and try to keep the anklet bars from rubbing into his huge cankles. For 10 seconds my son was allowed to speak; just responding to the judges' questions. His lawyer told me after, "I just don't know about him, his body language says, 'Just get me out of here.'"

Um, okay.

Basically, the judge told him he needed to complete a 30-day addiction program then he could start his 30-day sentence. My son was like what? He thought at the time, "So you want me to leave then come back here? Who would want to do that?" So yes, my son was irritable. He was in isolation, uninformed, uncounseled as far as working out a deal, and still feeling yucky. Even though he was on the end of acute physical signs of withdrawals, his brain was still in a complete state of chemical incompetence and confusion that doesn't regulate until at least

4-6 months. It's the brain's way of getting them to do anything to comply with its needs even after most people think they shouldn't need anything because they are not vomiting or shaking. The withdrawal symptoms of insomnia, mood swings, and loss of appetite can last several weeks. All while craving sweets and liquid.

But no one in the correctional system has time for that. Even though they are not doctors or medical professionals we still have to listen to them diagnose our loved ones as "should be better by now," or, "you should have thought of this before using drugs" or "He should have better body language."

A family member wrote me this:

> So now, just because you have been arrested for a drug charge, don't mind the other charges you have also committed to feed your habit, theft, whatever, but now just because you have a drug charge you get a posh hookup to gently wean?? Now everyone committing crimes will just plead that they are addicted to get a seat in the nice zone.

I was crushed. But at that point, I wasn't going to let anyone stop me from advocating for my son. At the seven-day mark on a Friday, I wrote to the sheriff at the jail again. "I would like a well check done on my son. I haven't heard from him for 7 days. Voicemails go unanswered and written messages say he isn't available. He needs to fill the requirements of the court and we are unable to do that without communication. Clergy has been denied. I have a power of attorney agreement and would like a call back please. Thank you." The response Monday was, "Did you get your questions answered regarding your son?"

Me, "No, I still haven't heard anything. I just wrote to the DA because of his hearing coming up on the 20th. Without him being allowed messages we have no way to prepare. I arranged a clergy visit for tomorrow. I really hope he will be allowed in.

"He is currently in a detox section; He is allowed phone calls as well as attorney and clergy visits." (Clergy was denied the next day). I sent a new message," He was not allowed the clergy visit due to being in lock down. Were we given the wrong info?" "He is not on lock down, but due to his detox, he is currently being held in medical observation. As soon as he is cleared to come off of medical lockdown, clergy will be allowed." "Ok, thanks. In preparation for Tuesday's hearing, he needs to call this number- can you give it to him?"

I'm sure he pretended to take down the info.

Mason spent 23 days in "isolation/medical detox/solitary" on that 47-day visit. It was frustrating to try to communicate regarding his cases and his health status. Yes, I may have gone overboard with worry and helicoptering. Yes, I may have written to the ACLU. And yes, I may have asked for the county commissioner in charge of jails when he was released on a Saturday afternoon with nowhere to go and no plan except to return to court Monday morning. (My request went unanswered).

Believe it or not and yes, call me crazy, but during that tortuous and worrisome time of not knowing if he was sick in withdrawals or had bailed out suddenly or was being hidden due to misbehavior; there were two bodies on the news that had been found. One by the lake where my son frequented and one in a car trunk just up my street. The news said the one by the lake was an "assumed heart attack" and the one in the trunk said, "no foul play." I panicked both times thinking that corrupt prison people, who grew tired of my antics, made my son disappear outside of the jail.

I started thinking, "Am I just being a worried MOM?" I started looking into solitary confinement for isolation for non-violent crimes and inmates.

Corey J. Brinson, a policy Associate with the Legal Action Center in New York in a letter to the Committee on Criminal Justice stated that his experience in solitary confinement was worse than being in war. "...That experience of living in a cell, which was the size of a large closet, with no clock, lights that went off at midnight, no privacy for sleeping, showering, and being fed through a slot in my cell door was psychological torture. You can tell a lot about a country by how it treats the people it incarcerates. Placing people in solitary confinement for any period of extended time is immoral, unethical, and it should be unlawful. People need meaningful social interactions with other people to

216

maintain their mental health. People in prison are already isolated from society. They are already isolated from their communities and their families. And when they are placed in solitary confinement, they have been essentially buried alive."

He also stated that New York's animal cruelty laws are stronger than the jail laws, "If an animal is worthy of good and wholesome air, then should not a human being, who is subjected to the confines and cruelty of living in a closet for extended periods of time, being granted the same freedoms as an animal? We cannot countenance a law that treats people worse than we treat animals....... Solitary confinement damages the mental health of the people subjected to its cruel and unusual punishment. When we damage the people in solitary confinement's mental health, we damage their opportunities, we damage their families, and we therefore damage their communities.

Robin Zabeigalski writes this in *The Tempest*:

> *Alcoholics and addicts are not criminals, they are sick people who need treatment. We shouldn't be focused on locking them up, we should be focused on changing our healthcare system so they can get the help they need. And we should be working on our own understanding of addiction so we can approach addicts with compassion instead of judgment. Doing this will change the state of addiction in this country and prevent thousands of deaths.*

There are still many people who believe that jail is the only cure for addiction. Because they know someone who seemingly got better while incarcerated, they assume it's the answer for every addict. In reality, most addicts use the minute they get out despite how long they served. Many die due to overdose at that time also.

I began to notice how every jail visit turned my son into more of a gangster. I saw the light slowly go out of his eyes. Years later, Callen told me that even when Mason was clean it was like talking to a version of his big brother that he hadn't met yet.

After his first arrest, he got on the family Facebook thread and said, "I'm really sorry I embarrassed all of you." No one responded but me. I think everyone was truly still in shock that it had come to this point. Little did we know how worse it would get and how he would apologize less and less.

Even when substance free or semi-substance free in jail; I saw his spirit being crushed by homogenous punishment meant to scare and intimidate a human soul into never wanting to go back. Without proper treatment, someone can't be scared straight. It just interrupts the process for a while, which sometimes is needed, but not to the extent that jails do (or don't do) for a struggling person. Johan Hari, in his book *Chasing the Scream*, visited the Arizona chain gang camp under Sheriff Joe Arpaio where he saw "tent City" where the dogs live in air-conditioned tents but the prisoners don't. In 2012, when he visited, the statistics for the number of people incarcerated for drug offenses in the US was more than the number from all other crimes combined in the Western European nations. The justice department estimates that 216,000 people are raped in these prisons every year. As journalist Christopher Glazek and many others have pointed out, the United States may be the first society in human history where more men have been raped than women. Does this sound like a healing environment to "cure addiction.?" This is on top of the fact that, in the aftermath of prison, people struggle to find housing, jobs, and public services because the general public wants them to pay over and over for their crimes.

The Snake's Venom

I carefully made my way up the steep rocky mountainside. It was a hot June day in the desert just a few hours from my house. My husband was ahead of me with the pic and hammer. That's right, a pickaxe and hammer. I'm sure we were a sight to see. He wore equipment, and I wore shorts, hiking boots, and black plastic bags that stuck to my sweaty legs. Despite being deathly afraid of snakes, I had forgotten to wear pants, so as a nurse, I figured the plastic was akin to wearing gloves and could take the sting out of a rattlesnake bite. Needle sticks can be less dangerous if they go through plastic into your skin versus prick without a barrier.

We were into rockhounding that summer. We searched the deserts and mountains for precious gems like topaz or amethyst or just plain old pretty rocks such as chert or agate. We were there to find some quartz crystals or more specifically, smokey quartz. It was found in long sparkly veins that ran through the slick, hard, granite rock. The quartz wasn't quite as hard, so it could be pried out with some effort. The rattlesnakes loved to hide in the eaves of the rocks to find shade from the blistering sun. They also didn't like their shady spot invaded, and would strike out if surprised, so I started my usual whistling-as-I-walked method, keeping my sunglasses off and watching 180 degrees in all directions.

Normally when out rockhounding, I start to feel the fresh air encapsulate my being, and I embrace the freedom of having nowhere to go and nothing to do. The focus of looking for rocks while noticing the landscape and the beautiful clouds wafting across the blue sky is mesmerizing. It's similar to riding on a motorcycle. The focal point of the scene plays out in front while the world and all its problems are oblivious in the background. Today, however, besides being afraid of snakes, I was in a gut-churning turmoil. My son had been in jail for forty-seven days, his longest stint so far. It had been a rollercoaster ride of solitary confinement, searches for rehabs, and lawyers' antics. So, little did I know, that the minute the thirty days expired, they would let him out, without even a hearing of what rehab we had found or anything. The day was a Saturday, I had been communicating with my son via the jail messaging system for a couple of weeks and had some wonderful conversations. He had been reading a lot and seemed to have his head clearing up. That morning he had read my message but didn't respond, and when I sent another one, a flashing message came up that said, "This inmate is released. This conversation has ended."

My body froze in fear. *NOOO!!!! This can't be happening!! He cannot just GET OUT!!!* I wanted to scream! I was determined to not ruin my husband and I's Day of rockhounding, so I swallowed the lump in my throat and squelched the tears forming behind my flushed face. As I switched to Facebook messenger, I told my son to PLEASE, PLEASE GO SOMEWHERE SAFE!! I knew the high risk of overdose right out of jail. I knew he didn't have anywhere to go except right back into the same environment that he got sick in. In a flurry of messages, I told his friend to please not let him overdose, and please give him a ride to the clinic, first thing Monday morning for an injection. (Yes, I had talked to them and verified his insurance which was 'paused' while in jail- a fact that I wasn't aware of- which caused a lot of problems finding a rehab to be released to. I later learned that our state has a special insurance plan for those in jail, homeless and in rehab).

I had visualized this day in my fantasy of expectations as a ride to rehab with a stop on the way to an addiction doctor with whom I had been communicating. He would give Mason Vivitrol or Sublocade. I had envisioned finally seeing my son after thirteen months with his fresh, jail weight-lifted, non-scrawny, non-homeless body, and new outlook on life. Despite my pleas, I knew he wouldn't make it until Monday without using. The process of detoxing and waiting seven to ten days for the injection would be impossible now. Releasing a hard-core chaotic user on a Saturday afternoon with no stable housing, no job, no car, no bank account, no support system, and no meds for the cravings is a HUGE crack in the system. Then expecting the addict to show up Monday morning bright-eyed and bushy-tailed, ready to solve all their legal problems with a great attitude is insane.

Something had to change. If my sick, out-of-control, hijacked, irresponsible son wasn't going to change, then I was going to change the system. I immediately looked up the area state senator. I penned out a descriptive letter of what I thought could improve the system such as a mandatory seventy-two discharge "leverage house," where they can acclimate from jail and be guided toward recovery and housing solutions. I later received a long response about everything that the state was doing to combat the drug war such as a recent traffic bust which confiscated so many pounds of meth. So basically, what the last 50 years of the war on drugs have failed to solve. Those drugs will be replaced in no time, driving the price up and increasing the risk that they'll be cut with more deadly crap to make them even more profitable for the bigwigs who never get caught.

I was defeated once again.

Who would listen?

Who would help?

I had exhausted all my money, ideas, and energy. Like millions of heartbreaking people suffering the same feelings, I felt alone. Where would this end? Would my boy be one who is in the meetings telling his amazing recovery story? Or would I be placing balloons on his grave? The only one who knew the answer to that wasn't talking. My God, my sole Savior I had begged and pleaded with for years for this "problem" to be resolved, was as silent as that hot, dusty, snake-ridden desert. I could still hear my rustling plastic bags in the wind as I waited for the snake's venom to strike out of nowhere. The sharp fangs holding deadly poison were nothing compared to the piercing heaviness in my heart. I wanted to lie down and drown in the dust of my sorrowful misery. Would this actually be my final last goodbye?

Incapable of being a blacksmith, you blame the metal. —Khmer Proverb

Lawyers. They get a bad rap. Now I see why. The problem with hiring a lawyer is you somehow think that they will solve all your problems. The images on TV of lawyers conversing with their clients and coming up with plans and deals are misleading. Those are million-dollar cases. Or at least $100,000 cases.

I failed to get the proper procedure of what our lawyer would do. I thought that if only I explained enough, he would be completely on my son's side and be his advocate no matter what. I thought he would immediately go see my son in jail before hearings and make a plan. When I saw that wasn't happening, I sent a couple emails a few days apart. (I really tried to restrain myself from telling the lawyers how to do their jobs.) Finally, after a few weeks, the lawyer sent "his kids" to jail. They were legal aides, I assume.

Mason was still in withdrawal. His version of that first visit is that they shoved a paper in front of him and said, "Sign this. It's your get out of jail free card."

My son asked, "What charges am I signing?"

They said that they hadn't received discovery yet. My son was mad that they didn't know of his charges, so he felt they couldn't be helpful as to arranging a plea. He wouldn't sign something that he didn't understand. I'm convinced that between that visit, the "body language" hearing, and possibly my over-involved communication, my son's lawyer decided that he didn't like him or wrote him off as another worthless addict. This happened despite the lawyer once saying, "I don't know what to do with him," when the judge ordered rehab.

It's okay. I do know what to do with him. I've been researching rehabs for over a year. I just NEED YOU TO GO VISIT HIM and give him this info to call since they won't allow him communication.

We had hired the lawyer two weeks into Mason's first arrest of 2021, the one when he spent forty-seven days incarcerated. I was feverishly trying to arrange a rehab, as the judge had mentioned to "find a program." Out of twenty-six rehabs in my state that I had previously checked on, many of them now wouldn't fit the criteria we needed. Some had changed insurance providers and didn't take Mason's policy. Others required long stays, to which Mason would not comply. Plus, we couldn't afford them at a co-pay of $ 2,000-$6,000 per month. Still others wouldn't take people directly from jail. I fell into the trap of possibly bagging the free state insurance and getting a commercial policy, because as long as you paid it by midnight of the end of the month, coverage would start the next day. I found out, luckily before signing up, that there may be a huge percentage left over that they don't cover. For instance, it might be an 80/20 policy, which left an even bigger amount than the Medicaid co-pays they were charging. The system is convoluted and hard to maneuver. Also, the person is sometimes resistant to treatment, especially when he is unable to smoke or if there's a long blackout period (which is daunting to an addict).

For court, Mason almost didn't call in until his sister helped him get the numbers right. When they called his name she explained to the court that he was having problems dialing in. When he was ordered to go to court support services the next day, it was a gut-wrenching, hour-by-hour cat and mouse game of me trying to not bug him to go and him saying, "Mom, you can't keep checking up on me and acting like I've done something wrong. It's not a big deal. I didn't sign up for a Level 5 while in jail so they can require me to go. I'm going to Vegas to see my buddy who they are pulling off life support." I couldn't believe it! Or could I? I knew this would happen! The situation really was setting him up for failure. To expect an unhealed, untreated brain to suddenly become responsible and rational, EVEN if it would avoid negative consequences, is basically the definition of addiction.

It took six weeks for him to be arrested again on new warrants for not complying. Liam and I had just spent a great weekend in the vacation town where Mason was incarcerated, not seeing him but seeing his kids and going four-wheeling with them and their mom. During the four-hour trip home, I received a call from my detoxing, jailed, sick son who was angry. He stated that his life was over and he was going to go hang himself. I froze in fear. I didn't know what to do or who to call! I tried calling the medical staff on previous visits. They had never answered before, but that Sunday night the nurse answered! I told her what Mason had said and that he needed medical attention. She said she would check on him. I was able to stay in contact with her for the next few days, which had never happened before. She was concerned about him and even talked of transferring him to the hospital. He finally started feeling better. He was kept in a medical unit for a week without any communication or lawyer visits. The only way I found out was by emailing the jail because Mason had hearing dates coming that he was unprepared to attend. He was at their mercy. Mindset is important for any human, and he found ways to tolerate jail. As long as he had his commissary radio for $8 and a bag of chips or coffee, he settled into some semblance of safety, as well as someone can while in jail. Below are a few pearls of wisdom he sent me on the jail messaging system. I will always cherish these.

"You can regain everything you lost, except wasted time."

My response: "I've been thinking about camping. How cool it would be to take K and G [his kids] camping. I can't even imagine that. I can't stop thinking about it. Yet I'm here and I can't see that ever happening. FML."

"Thanks for staying with me, idk how you did it."

My response: "You're welcome. I hate seeing you depressed, but just let it move through you. You have a beautiful future full of joy. Your kids need you, they need you to teach them how to roast marshmallows and tell them stories of deer and elk and camping and of your grandpa."

"I don't mean that I don't have a future, just a different one. I've lost my freedom for at least four years. I don't know what to do with that. But it doesn't matter what I do."

My response: "Yes, you will. You are an old soul and have such breadth and depth that you were a perfect target. You are a fighter and a gentle soul all in one. You still have great things to do. You are so loved, even if it doesn't feel like it. There's a little girl and a little boy who you are going to make so happy real soon. All these feelings you're having are real and raw. It's hard to process them.

Just give yourself permission to feel them so you can create the space for hope, joy, and true happiness."

"I haven't eaten or slept all weekend. Everyone around has food. I can't ask for anything. I'd rather suffer, I don't know why. The loud Hyenas were yelling all night and put me in a bad mood."

My response: "Son, these conversations show me how hard it must be to live in your head without being able to find relief. I think you have always struggled with overwhelming bursts of confusion where your brain is flooded with ideas, just like [the girl] who ran in front of the semi and left five little kids. Except you dealt with it in a different way, either with anger or deep sadness. You self-medicated and are being punished for it. Yesterday was proof of how you suffer. You can get help once you're out of here. You just need to find a better way to live life on life's terms. This is exactly what Gabor Mate talks about when he says, 'Don't ask why the addiction, ask why the pain?'"

"Have a good day. I'm going to be in the best shape ever. I'm working out with guys that came from the state pen. One is a monster and can do 300 burpees in an hour. It took me two and now I can't move, but I didn't die."

My response: "Your insight when you are forced to slow down is amazing."

"I'm finally having a good weekend. I work out 3 hours a day and haven't been eating anything bad! Except I did read on one of the bags of food, 'Not suitable for human consumption.'"

"I read a cool piece in a Steven King book last night. I couldn't sleep cuz they raided our block at 2 a.m. and C boy got rolled to block A. 'When the power of love is greater than the love of power the world will know peace.' Jimmy Hendrix."

I replied, "Oh no, Poor Cboy, I somehow like him already. Pain, I'm sure his PTSD is untreated so he self-treats it, giving him more trauma. What do you think Hendrix meant by that? He was in the 60s, 70s, right?"

"Love of power, universally. People seem to feed off power like Hitler for instance. But the need for power will probably never be outweighed by anything.

"It's a better day today. I stayed up all night writing and listening to music. The small things like music make things so much better. My buddy Cboy was walking around yesterday all cheery with his swastika tattoos. I said to him, 'You are so happy, you're pissing me off, why are you so happy?' He said, 'What's not to love, I have everything I need, I can work out anytime I want. I have coffee, music, and hey I'm not on drugs and can think clearly. Some of these Badaxxx are down for twelve years, I have 180 days.' So Mom, it got me thinking: Little things, if you appreciate them, the rest falls in line. There is no complicated blueprint to being happy. Success doesn't make you happy. Being happy makes you successful."

This jail visit, he was in trouble for not complying with court support services after being let out last time. The funny thing is that the night before his hearing, I finally got a hold of the plea deal that was being offered for the possession charges. I received it by writing to the district attorney because Mason's lawyer had not sent it despite several requests. These conditions were the same as the previous jail stay. He was basically pleading guilty to almost all the felonies instead of the usual dropping of some. It was dated May 2022 before we hired the lawyer. Furthermore, Mason contemplated what he would be signing up for (since it did involve his life and freedom from now on). The lawyer told me he hadn't "looked at his charges yet." Keep in mind this is three months after hiring him, with a six-week break when Mason was out of jail. Mason was becoming increasingly frustrated at sitting in jail with no plan or counsel. So, imagine my frustration, after requesting some sort of communication and clarification on what the plea entailed, when I received the following email:

I had it all set up and there would not have been a felony plea but he did not report and follow the rules and the law. Now he is back in jail and wants everything to go back the way it was. He wants the Judge to let him out of jail and see if he complies with the rules and the law. He was given a change to have all the charges reduced or dismissed if he simply obeyed the rules and followed the law. He did not do that and so everything sucks and it's the law and the rules' fault. Do you support that?

I immediately felt like a character out of Johann Hari's book Chasing the Scream: Hari states of his own experience with addicted loved ones:

I had been taught how to respond, by my government, and by my culture- when you find yourself in this situation. It is with a war. We all know the script: it is etched onto your subconscious, like the correct direction to look when you cross the street. Treat drug users and addicts as criminals. Repress them. Shame them. Coerce them into stopping. This is the prevailing view in almost every country in the world.[55]

But I didn't say that. I said nothing. How could I explain that I supported none of this, that I didn't sign up for any of this, and that most days, I just wanted to die?

Instead I thought of what Gabor Mate told Johann while sitting in a Greek restaurant over dinner. "If I had to design a system that was intended to keep people addicted, I'd design exactly the system we have now, I'd attack people and ostracize them." He has seen that the more you stress people, the more they're going to use. The more you de-stress people, the less they're going to use.

And the big finale from his teaching is, "IF negative consequences led people to transformation, then I wouldn't have a single patient left." He continued, "Because they've experienced every negative consequence in the book. Being jailed, being beaten up, being traumatized. Being hurt. HIV. Hepatitis C. Poverty."

All of these issues cost society even more money. And yes, it's easy to say, "They just need to do the right thing-quit using drugs and follow the laws." But if we applied that analogy to every issue with human nature, life would be an episode of Pleasantville where everything is exactly perfect. We would all live in rolling green Teletubby hills full of fun and laughter. Is that what you want, Mr. Lawyer? Do you want televisions on everyone's bellies? That vision makes me laugh now, but I was hurt and angry that the person who was supposed to have our backs and defend his rights was going right along with societal views

---

[55] https://chasingthescream.com/

that punishment and force automatically leads to abstinence. Of course, Mason should have complied. But at what point was he magically cured during those forty-seven days? At what point did you become a responsible, practical, full brain functioning member of society? Taking away the drugs does not make an addiction gone. He had zero classes or counseling in jail. No, I wasn't making excuses for him, I was the maddest as anyone that he did not simply walk in a door and do the right thing and sign up for pre-trial probation. But I also feel like it's a bit like telling a person in a wheelchair that they better figure out how to get up and walk in that door by tomorrow at 5 or else! No wheelchairs allowed!

I emailed the entire law firm that I wanted a phone call today after not hearing from them Friday. I explained that he's on suicide watch and only has lawyer privileges. I was told that they had no plans to meet with him before Thursday's hearing. I took a deep breath and said, 'So you don't think an addict locked up confused and depressed should have any knowledge of the "plan" for the hearing Thursday or what his options are? Do you not think mindset and hope are vital to someone's actions?"

He, the senior lawyer, responded with, "He won't do what I tell him to do anyway. He's already proven that by not showing up at court support services."

I said "Yes sir, I'm aware his frontal lobe is trashed. I'm aware he acts irresponsibly and irrationally, if he didn't, he wouldn't be an addict. But he's not going to suddenly heal and do everything correct without treatment. He still has a right to know that you are working in his best interests and fighting for his rights." I then said, "You and your lawyer son have not even met him. You sent the kids [legal aides] to meet him."

He said, "Well, my son usually does that stuff, but he's in court until August 29. So, I will call down to the jail for him. I will do that for him since he's so busy."

I said, "Well that's nice of you " to which he replied, "Well, he's my son. I'll do anything for him."

I said, "EXACTLY!!!! I feel the same way."

If I had the conversation to do over I would calmly explain how executive function is compromised in the addictive brain. Planning, remembering details, moral compass issues and impulsiveness are all compromised. Sure, I would still be accused of making excuses for him but at least I would feel better in advocating for those who keep disappointing people with their inability to follow through and complete tasks.

There comes a point where we need to stop just pulling people out of the river. We need to go upstream and find out why they're falling in. —Desmond

Shame, Blame, and Other Bonding Moments

In some of my most intense moments of dealing with my struggling son (like the freeway meltdown), the anger that I felt was incredulous and shocking to me. I was surprised at how much rage I could manifest. Just like Gabor Maté's example of yelling in traffic is just us telling our stories of a raging baby who feels abandoned; my rage may have brought to light deep emotional wounds of my mom ignoring me when she sunk into her silent moods. The powerlessness and pain of loss can completely deplete a person if they don't find ways to cope. It also sheds light to the power addiction and the adversary has to take prisoners–especially when we fail to understand and implement boundaries.

Learning to do this with kindness instead of fury takes practice.

Pam Lanhard of Thrive, Family Addiction Support Facebook group, stated, "You can't be effective without connection." This goes hand in hand with Johann Hari's "Addiction is the opposite of connection."

On the website Goldsmith Media Group, Paul Goldsmith quoted Johann Hari, in his book, Chasing the Scream: The First and Last Days of the War on Drugs. Hari studied drug addiction around the world and summarized the underlying source of the epidemic, "Human beings have an innate need to bond and connect. When we are happy and healthy, we will bond with the people around us. But when we can't because we're traumatized, isolated or beaten down by life, we will bond with something that gives us some sense of relief. It might be checking our smartphones constantly or it might be pornography. It might be gambling, etc. but we will bond with something because that is our human nature. The path out of unhealthy bonding is to form healthy bonds to be connected to people who you want to be present with. Addiction is just one symptom of the crisis of disconnection that's happening all around us. We all feel it.

Jane Nelsen writes, "Where did we ever get the crazy idea that in order to make children do better, first we have to make them feel worse?

Think of the last time you felt humiliated or treated unfairly. Did you feel like cooperating or doing better?"[56]

After that disastrous first home detox, we didn't have anything arranged and didn't know the first thing about applying for Medicaid or rehab. We naively thought he could just fix his life with the absence of drugs and were shocked when he couldn't. I wrote him this long text when that didn't happen:

> *Yesterday I CRIED for 6 STRAIGHT HOURS!*
>
> *It's scary to see you so out of control. I know you can't see it but it affects my whole day- my WHOLE life -to see you like this. I'm the last one you have! You lose my support and you're screwed. You don't have the resources to follow through on all the irons in the fire you're trying to clean up.*
>
> *I keep trying to help and you keep using me because you make decisions that aren't helping YOU or ME. I haven't been paid back ANY of the almost $10k that I've paid to get you functioning better.*
>
> *But more than that, I haven't seen you be humble and sorry and WANT TO DO WHATEVER it TAKES to get HEALTHY again. Now you don't even want the Vivitrol injections anymore. All that work me and your sister did. to get it free. You don't even want to apply to be cleared of all that debt. You are still just chasing money backwards like before getting detoxed. This Thursday is court (at 1:30 DO NOT FORGET!!!!) It was your last chance to get a lawyer. They will now set up for trial for your charges. You've been given 7 months leeway for those charges. Your time has run out on that. Clearing your brain and staying alive is paramount right now. Your ADD brain is on fire right now whether it's from the clearing out of all the drugs or the adding them back in. Whatever you are doing isn't working. Your brain isn't healed enough to be in that environment making those decisions.*
>
> *Scavenging and selling all your stuff on Facebook is embarrassing. All that work we did two weeks ago and it's just getting stolen, EVEN THOUGH that $500 I gave you was supposed to cover the whole month of rent for $20k in*

[56] https://www.goodreads.com/quotes/18441-where-did-we-ever-get-the-crazy-idea-that-in#:~:text=Learn%20more)-,%E2%80%9CWhere%20did%20we%20ever%20get%20the%20crazy%20idea%20t hat%20in,felt%20humiliated%20or%20treated%20unfairly.

equipment!!! I'm not stupid It's time to cut the Bullshit. We are losing ground at this point. There is a better way to do this. You need to make changes. Every single day. I cry and cry. It affects every relationship I have and my job every single day.

You HAVE to step through doors that have been OPENED for YOU. Quit being bullheaded and trying to do things your way.

Oh, how that makes my heart hurt. I've learned so much since then. All that could have been whittled down to, "You're ruining my life, you're stupid, you must do what I say, I don't care how you feel. Your feelings don't matter. You've ruined EVERYONE'S life. My pain and inconvenience are all that matters. THIS is what YOU need to do with YOUR life!"

It's no wonder that so many relapses occur with this kind of anger and hatred thrown on a raw brain that is still months, even years away, from being healed. Not only are they dealing with all their thoughts and feelings without anything to cover them up, but they have the impossible task of meeting every single person's expectation for their recovery and fixing all this damage that is being flung at them. The thought of living with all these expectations and anger and blame is just too much for some. They want the safety of no pain again. To us this might seem weak, but anyone who's ever been in a conflicted relationship knows that you can't be responsible for someone else's emotions and happiness on a good day, outside of addiction's tidal wave. Now times that by five people or ten people. Everyone who has an opinion on how your recovery should look and feel TO THEM. Ultimatums seem to be useless to the addicted brain because they've already lost so much. At a certain point in their addiction, they learn to fear nothing, because they have nothing, and have usually lost everything- including their self-respect.

The Freedom Model for Addiction describes shame this way, "Drowning in shame can be the most influential secondary reason people develop a strong preference for substance use. Such shame develops because of the social views that there's something wrong with people who prefer heavy, or even mild, use of substances that are big taboos (such as heroin and cocaine). When users believe their use has made them into a monster and permanently stained them and they've taken on an 'addict identity,' they may believe they have passed the point of no return. This makes continued use *appear* to be the only option." [57]

Brene Brown describes shame as being lethal. She defines it as the "intensely painful feeling that we are unworthy of love and belonging."[58] I believe shame grows exponentially in addiction. Secrecy is the petri dish of shame. The stigma of addiction and the punishment inflicted on someone who can't manage their disease pushes them deeper into secrecy and the lifestyle that furthers the pain and disease of addiction, including hep C, HIV, criminal behavior, and a poisoned drug supply. When my son was released from "The Hole" in jail for using while incarcerated (since they don't provide anything for withdrawal symptoms except electrolytes); I sent him this message:

> *Ya know, I'm sorry that the correctional system still thinks locking someone up alone, who's suffering and not managing in life, for 21 days, bringing him out for court only to berate and shame him—actually works. I'm sorry that you are hurting or scared or ashamed or that you feel running is the only answer.*
>
> *I hope you will soon find your true self and know that you are not your mistakes. I hope you will find your higher power. One who loves you even more than I do. Can you imagine? Enough to give you free agency on earth like I sometimes can't; but his deepest desire is that you will come back to the fold. To be the honorable self-respected man you were meant to be. No matter who says differently, or what conditions you are in, know that you are loved and honored for your journey here on earth.*

So, I had to learn to save my advice and be ready for when he hit a wall. and those windows of opportunity opened up. Literally once, he actually did hit a wall of rocks in the median and wrecked his "home." Only then did I feel ready to offer an option *(let's do a quick medical detox)*,

---

[57] https://www.amazon.com/Freedom-Model-Addictions-Treatment-Recovery-ebook/dp/B077MFMV4M

[58] https://www.youtube.com/watch?v=GEBjNv5M784

explain the benefit of that option *(it will* **buy you some time** *to figure out what to do and where to go)*, and tell him what I would do to help it happen *(I'll drive the four hours to get you and take you to detox if you'd like)*. Addicts have zero sense of time. Tomorrow is too much for them to think about.

My son always had a "yeah, but" excuse. He always just needed one more tank of gas, one more registration. At first, before I knew how bad it was going to get and his business was sliding, I was clueless about what was reasonable., partly due to his perpetual optimism. Yes, some may call it manipulation, but he had the talent to turn $2000 into $4000 in the past, why would this temporary "setback" be any different? As he fell deeper and deeper into his addiction, he would need $200, $300, $400 for this or that, or just for a hotel room, and yes I did pay for it— on a credit card, of course. I paid for nine days in a cheap vacation rental on the edge of town after the first detox when I didn't realize that a one-time detox isn't enough. When Rylee went to pick him up from there, she literally dropped her big brother off onto the street in town. We were heartbroken, but we didn't know what else to do. This girl, her hero, big brother. The girl who drove an hour in the desert to bring him electrolytes when he was having severe muscle spasms. The girl who then lay in the other bed the rest of the night to make sure he and his labradoodle were okay. Almost every single picture taken of her as a baby is with him holding her. He was her protector. Just two years before that he had paid her rent for almost a whole year in a three-bedroom house so she could live alone when she turned 18. He was one of her last male figures in her life who she saw slowly slipping away. I can't imagine what she was feeling while driving away. This is not what families do. It all felt so wrong.

Making Lemonade

As I was navigating letting go, holding on, loving better; and while my therapist was telling me how blurred my boundaries with everyone was; I was listening to Matt Kahn one day speak of becoming your higher self. Boy did I need that. I did NOT like that person in those red-faced, crying, threatening, ultimatum videos. I wanted the serene, caring mom who lovingly drew a line in the sand with pink fluffy spray paint and skipped down the warm beachfront with bare feet and my flowered wrap-around skirt. Keep in mind, you do NOT have to believe in a higher power to believe that there is a better version of yourself.

Matt Kahn stated, "If you are dreading an interaction with a loved one, ask your higher self to help you be that person you want who is full of wisdom and radiance. Ask for help in bridging that gap between the two versions of yourself. If your loved one wants you to listen, but they are demanding that attention through their ego {and through their disease]; [you can] say, *"I see that you are in so much pain and feeling unsafe in your reality (even if you're not aware of it) that I am going to take space from you so you can just be with yourself and I don't have to be who you project your feelings on......"*[59]

He admits that we are not obligated to be their best friend or their emotional punching bag but can honor their presence and their desire to involve you in their moment. I would soon learn that sometimes that requires giving yourself time to get your composure in order to respond with loving boundaries.

Matt continues (and this is pretty deep so skip it if you're not into looking at the bigger picture of why in tarnation we are going through this madness), "All of us in our core being, are innocent, and through the eyes of love, everything is just a set up for a greater transformative moment. The more you call on this higher self, the more you can play your true role and see how capable {you are} of living through this experience."[60]

Getting to a place of seeing how these dreadful experiences might actually help me was rough. I was determined to not stoop to the level of the hijacked brain that stirs up OUR inner crazies! I learned that if we don't resolve our pain with it, we risk furthering and deepening the trauma. We also risk destination happiness. We say constantly, "If only... If only he would ask for help." Then we give him some resources

---

[59] https://mattkahn.org/shop-angel-academy/
[60] https://www.youtube.com/watch?v=Lv9g8HEG0P4

and he actually calls, then we pray, please let him qualify, let him get in, let him stay thirty days, let him stay sixty days, let him get into sober living. It goes on and on. I see it on mommas posts every day. "My daughter gets out in five days and I'm terrified she's going to use again." Oh how many times I would think, *"Just be happy she's gone that far, I would give anything to have my son be getting out in 5 days…."*

It was looking like, as Moms, we are never satisfied. We want life. WE want happiness, for them and us. We want what we want and that is always changing. And that's okay. I just knew that I had to find a way to have peace and gratitude along the way, regardless of outcome.

This is the premise that The Secret, Abraham Hicks, and many other philosophies going back to Dale Carnegie's, "How to Stop Worrying and Start Living" are based on. They ALL state that in order to get to the place we want to be to FIND THAT FEELING first then everything else will fall into alignment. Otherwise, it is a never-ending search to fill a hole of contentment and safety.

Fear

Don Miguel Ruiz states in *"Beyond Fear: A tilted Guide to Freedom and Joy,* "THE GREATEST FEAR, subsuming all other fears, is fear of loss or death… Fear is the normal result of our domestication in childhood. Fear is the root of the reality we usually perceive around us. Fear is the source of disease, of war, and an alienation from the joy that is our birthright." [61]

I think we would agree that the entire undertone to this book and my journey has been fear. As I searched into each dark crevice of confusion and pain, I had to face this fear a little at a time. I had to come to terms with first that my son might be addicted to pills. Then the fear of his marriage ending-, then his business. The stark horror of your child in jail the first time, then again and again. I always felt like I was a slow learner but this was ridiculous. In therapy this could be called exposure therapy. Slowly exposing the person to what they fear most so. It didn't

---

[61] https://www.anunlikelystory.com/book/9781641607742

matter what milestones were reached or what occurred out of my control, the base emotion was always fear. And not just of losing him in the same manner I lost my brother, my hero as a young child. It was the fear of my family crumbling. It was more than I could comprehend yet it was happening in slow but real time right in front of me complete with dramatic sad music to cement the seriousness and play right into my horrors. And of course, the squeaky wheel gets the grease, so the more you buy into that mode, the more that is returned to you. Then we tend to transfer that fear to the one struggling.

In a post I wrote on my blog called "Arachnophobia," I stated that when I talk to my son in fear mode, it just creates defensiveness on his part. He just doesn't see or feel the fear. I mean, let's be realistic. If he did, he probably wouldn't be in that mess. Addicts are not weak people. I think this is part of their resistance to recovery. They just can't be given an "ultimatum" or threatened with consequences. My son is a debater at heart, so imagine with such a monster of substance use added on, he wins the argument every time, EVEN if he's wrong.

In *Beyond Fear*, Ruiz states the Toltec tradition that humans, like planet earth, have two parts: the nagual and the tonal. "When we refer to a person as a nagual, we mean that the person has a strong characteristic energy which creates a direct connection between the nagual and the tonal. The nagual can split emotions from actions. The nagual is born with a strong will and is not paralyzed by fear. A human who is not born as a nagual is often played by fear."

My son told me many times to stop worrying about him. I took that to mean, leave me alone so my addiction can have me all to itself, which may be true but I also think he did not want the responsibility of having to calm all my fears and be responsible for all my emotions. That's just too much for one person to bear. And I'm only one of the people he had to bear all that on. I know it's easy to say, and I am guilty of saying it and believing it too. "If only they would stop using then everything would be fine." But life would show me that that's just not a true statement. Drugs are a symptom of a problem. There's a reason they started and there's a reason they continue to choose them over regular life. Disease or not, they will always choose what feels better to them at the time, which I will soon discover—empowering. The following could be written by my son. He has made these statements several times to me.

> *Dearest Parent,*
>
> *Please notice where your fear takes you. You have me dead already waiting for that call. You see images of me dead. But I'm not there. Even if my physical body has passed or if I'm homeless and can't be reached, break free of your fear and imaginations. Please remember my goodness and my life. I live elsewhere, and always in your heart. Look for me there. Look for me in the good, in the living. Look for me and honor me with your life. I cannot do this for you.*
>
> *Please tell me you love me, and what you're willing to tolerate, or not. I eventually hear you say no. And just repeat it or don't answer the phone. This is helping me. When you repeat what's not working for either of us, it just keeps not working. Just be clear with your love and your boundaries. I need this. It helps me with my own fear, and helps you take care of your own. I cannot do this for you.*
>
> *I actually want your love. I want you to love me as I am whether I live or die. Trying to fix me is beyond your control and obsessing on this will kill your chance at any peace. It's your fear that makes you do that. And you make me responsible for it. I'm under the influence of drugs. Drugs have their way. You must choose a different way when I cannot. I love you and I cannot express it right now. Just trust in that love, even though it's silent and difficult to see. Please remove this pressure from me that I have to get fixed and take care of your happiness. I really cannot handle it. Please seek your own recovery. I cannot do this for you.*
>
> *Live your life so I don't have to feel the shame of taking it from you. I did not take your life from you. I don't have that power. So please don't give it to me, or to drugs for that matter. I don't want that for you either. God gave me a life and a death, same for you. If and when I can choose differently, I will. Will you? Show me the way. If I ever recover, I'll need you to be clear and strong. Healing is possible for me, and for you. You be the one. I can't do this for you either, and please don't wait for me. God has plans for me, and God has plans for you. Staying in pain is not His plan for you. I know it's not God's plan to have me addicted but God is going to use my life in ways we both cannot imagine.*

Find every way to live and inspire peace and joy in this life. I cannot do this for you.

I know you love me very much. I love you back. Nothing can destroy that. I will be with you always. God created me as love, and you are too. It is indestructible. Remember this and you will remember me well. And this love can break through your fears. Know I love you even when it doesn't look or sound like that. Know this, but I can't do this for you.

Forever, Your Child, and God's. —Author Unknown[62]

I returned this sentiment many times back to him by saying, "Son, you are loved deeply, even if it doesn't feel like it. People just don't know what to do and what to say, so it comes out in their pain and discomfort of feeling powerless. You are missed immensely and loved deeply." The discomfort of not knowing where someone is and what they're doing is deeply painful. I was starting to see that the experience was the same for him. I was getting peeks into the pain of his soul—*even if he didn't show it by his actions.*

"Words kill, words give life; they're either poison or fruit—you choose."
—Proverbs 18:21 MS

---

[62] https://www.capitaldistrictrecoverycenter.org/post/helping-myself-is-the-best-thing-i-can-do-to-help-them

Empowering Change—The Freedom Model

I sat on the cold steel folding chairs in the echoey tall cinder block gymnasium. The sunlight drifted through the top windows of the large room onto the fading ripped basketball hoops that were folded up against the wall. I kept whispering and giving the evil shh finger-to-mouth sign to my other three little kids as we awaited the main program for D.A.R.E. I watched my ten-year-old son walk to the microphone in his white T-shirt with the red and blue D.A.R.E. logo on the front. He had his paper clenched tightly in his hands as the girls his age towered over him. He was the only boy picked by the teachers to read his essay out loud as one of the "best."

With one shy sweeping smile to the crowd, he adjusted the microphone as if he was an old pro. He started reading his essay to the class of fifth grade parents and grandparents. I re-watched the home movie of this moment with loving compassion for this little boy who seemed so similar to the other kids there. In that moment he was a precious innocent child who would be searching and navigating his way through the stress and strain of daily life with the least amount of discomfort possible. In that moment, he had the best intentions for his life and those who loved him. In that moment all my love for my 30 something struggling son came rushing back with a warmth like I had never felt. I wanted him to know that it was okay. Whatever he felt then and now was OK. I wanted to reach back through time and send him a back to the future hug, forging a secret bond of strength and hope of what he would face.

In March 1998, The Baldwin Institute presented a public statement regarding their findings on D.A.R.E. consistent with the University of Illinois review of the D.A.R.E. program stating, "There appears to be no reliable short-term, long-term, early adolescent, or young adult positive outcomes associated with receiving the D.A.R.E. intervention." They were not alone. "The University of Illinois is not the first organization to report poor results by D.A.R.E. Probably the most telling report of the damage that is being done by D.A.R.E. was reported

240

in the National Household Survey on Drug Abuse for the Health and Human Resources Department in 1996. This survey reported that teen (12- to 17-years-old) drug use rose more than 100% from 1992 to 1995. These teenagers would have been exposed to the D.A.R.E. program during the 1980s. The evidence is clear: During the time of D.A.R.E. 's most rapid growth, the results it achieved five, six, and seven years later were the worst in more than a decade. Moreover, it is probable that D.A.R.E. actually contributed to the increase in drug use during that time.

To my surprise, some twenty-five years after that D.A.R.E. program, I came across a book called The Freedom Model, which was written by the same Baldwin Institute people who did the D.A.R.E. study. This book echoed EXACTLY what my son had always preached to me about addiction. See, he was incredibly rehab resistant and had always stated the failure rates of AA and most rehabs who ran on that model. Even though he wasn't a rehab rotator, he lived in that world of people who did. He saw people come out of them and almost immediately overdose-—one being his roommate and friend. He had a huge problem with the "I am powerless" part. We always thought that was just him, being in denial that he didn't have control over this monster, but as I read through the chapters one after another, I couldn't believe it. I found myself saying, "Dammit that kid was right!" Meaning MY kid, MY son. One of the most argued debates on addiction sites and posts consists of addiction being a disease or a choice. Of course, in all my searching and prying and prodding, I HAD to defend addiction as an insidious evil disease that takes over the brain rendering the user completely powerless. Coincidently that is step one of the twelve steps. But as I curiously read through chapter after chapter of common-sense descriptions of the "addicted brain," I was more than more convinced of the reality of this research. The main premise of the book is this: People choose everything they do based on the pursuit of happiness.

On Page 16 they state, "People exist in all sorts of voluntarily maintained engagements with which they are nonetheless dissatisfied-jobs, careers, relationships, living situations, and of course habits such as using alcohol and other drugs. But as dissatisfying and painful as these involvements can be, people do not move on from them until they believe they have a happier option available to them: a better job, a better career, a better relationship, or a better living situation. Until a credibly happier option is seen, they feel stuck. This applies to habits such as heavy substance use too."[63]

During my son's intervention: the interventionist told him, "Your freedom from the obsession to use drugs will be directly proportional to your willingness to surrender like ya know all those ideas the way you think your life is supposed to work out? If you can surrender that stuff and let go, then things can start getting better quickly. But if you fight, then the tougher it gets, right?"

"Right," my son agreed in the moment. But as I look back to his recorded voice in 2019, I see this.

"It's so unacceptable that people just want to feel good without there being a trauma behind it. There's not anything you can do to get an opiate high. There is NOTHING I CAN DO DIFFERENTLY IN MY LIFE THAT would give me that [high], and no one wants to admit that. That's why so many people don't succeed at recovery.... My addiction has not progressed at all. You're just like 90% of people who can't accept the truth that there are other things that affect people's lives badly."

He was stating the exact theory on happiness that this book explains. Bear with me here because this will blow your mind.

Each decade has its demons, and opiates are today's evil killers.... yet for thousands of years, they have served as miracle drugs to treat many ailments when medical technology hasn't yet delivered anything better. In the days when people

---

63

https://www.google.com/books/edition/The_Freedom_Model_for_Addictions/ru0_DwAAQBAJ?hl=enandgbpv=1anddq=the+freedom+model+Each+decade+has+its+demons,+and+opiates+are+today%27s+evil+killersandpg=PT304andprintsec=frontcover *literally died from coughing, the opiates offered cough suppression that enabled many to survive while their immune systems fought off deadly diseases....* [64]

This makes me think of my eating disorder patients. The reason that diets are a no-no for them is because we teach them not to demonize any food. Once we develop a war-like disdain for something, there's a strange obsession with it. Is that what D.A.R.E. does to these innocent kids? Makes them too curious? After all, if there's this much effort to NOT do something, it must be something spectacular, or something that might bring me some measure of joy.

This video explains the Positive Drive Principle, which is what the book is based on. It is what we ALL base almost every decision in our lives on: https://medium.com/@rschwantes/the-three-pillars-of-the-freedom-model-for-addictions-a-revolutionary-approach-to-addiction-ad68ed3d2722.

It basically centers on the three pillars of the Freedom Model, which is the opposite of everything treatment teaches.

Free Will - The ability to choose (it's not about LESS willpower)

Autonomy - You're your own person. (You are not "powerless") You have your own power. You get to choose your own life. No one controls you without your consent.

Positive Drive Principle: "What is my happiest option?"

It's easy to agree with this for a "normal" person, right? One who is unaffected by addiction. With all the chaos addiction causes, it's hard to swallow something as simple as free will, yet we are constantly told that they won't stop until they WANT TO STOP. So how can it be both ways? Either they are powerless or they have control. We want to believe it's a brain disorder because who in their right mind would CHOOSE to abandon their kids? Or ruin a million-dollar business, or a twelve-year

---

64

https://www.google.com/books/edition/The_Freedom_Model_for_Addictions/ru0_DwAAQBAJ?hl=enandgbpv=1anddq=the+freedom+model+Each+decade+has+its+demons,+and+opiates+are+today%27s+evil+killersandpg=PT304andprintsec=frontcover marriage where so much effort and time and children have been cultivated.

The problem with rehabs is the same as the D.A.R.E. tactic or the frying egg commercial. You could even say this is what we do to kids regarding sex. To instill fear of the consequences in them, which never works with sex, or overeating or even undereating. The freedom Model states it this way:

> *When you arrive for help in the addiction and recovery world you are hit immediately with a scary tactic. They say that you must never touch a single dose of alcohol or other drugs for the rest of your life, or else you will "lose control" ceaselessly consuming substances at disastrous levels. They try to make the issue a no-brainer by presenting you with a false alternative-either you abstain for the rest of your life, or get back on the fast track to an addicted-hell of jails, institutions, and an early death (as the popular phrase from 12-step programs puts it) ....*

Notice, YOUR pursuit of happiness isn't even mentioned. All decisions are based in fear and panic. They use the comparison of a mugger who points a gun at you and demands "your money or your life." If you hand over your wallet it's a coerced decision, one that you resent having to make. The ultimatum of "abstinence or your life" is similar. The decision is made out of negative emotions such as coercion. Yes, it may very well be "the best choice for your life" at the moment but who decided that? The mugger forced you to make a one-time decision, but the counselors in a rehab (and many family members) are trying to force you into an entire life decision. "It's no wonder this tactic fails so often. People end up miserable while abstaining, feeling deprived of joy, and eventually go back to the old pattern of heavy substance use." [65]

[65]

https://www.google.com/books/edition/The_Freedom_Model_for_Addictions/ru 0_DwAAQBAJ?hl=enandgbpv=1anddq=the+freedom+model+Each+decade+has +its+demons,+and+opiates+are+today%27s+evil+killersandpg=PT304andprintsec =frontcover

When Mason states that he doesn't want to be a "sheep" and falls for the rotating rehab lie this is what he means. He has seen too many friends come out of rehab and overdose or go straight back into use for him to believe in this model of treatment as having any type of success. Of course, everyone just puts the blame on the person, saying he didn't want it bad enough. So, which is it? A disease that you are powerless over or if you didn't try hard enough? Is it your choice of choosing happiness (aka feeling better in the moment) in every single person does with many different situations damaging behaviors but are not illegal of course. The same people who choose to employ tough love and to cut off the addict, with the theory they will *make them change;* still may say it's a disease and the person is powerless over it. The freedom model states that no one would scream at their child with cancer and that they can no longer support them if they "choose" to engage in the behaviors of their cancer.[66]

We can't have it both ways. I understand that anytime the disease versus choice argument comes up, people will say, "cancer doesn't have people stealing things and lying and abandoning their family." So, if that is a true statement then those people truly can't say that it's a disease and the person is powerless. And usually, they're not. They're the shamers and complainers who give the theory of choice in substance use a bad rap—in my opinion. It seems that society has decided we must be very divided black and white on issues and this is no exception. We have to believe in addiction being a full- on disease where brains are hijacked causing the person to sway far away from the true person they used to be or else we must go with the stigma that substance users are morally corrupt, and basically just assholes.

With the poisoned drug supply, and the rate of overdoses, it is easy to see why people get very passionate about abstinence and ultimatums. Fear is very powerful. Fear of dying, being fired, going to jail, family and friends shunning you. The Freedom Model book describes it this way, *"hardly a day goes by without the tragic stories in the news featuring pictures of beautiful young people who had so much promise but lost their lives to drugs. The*

---

[66] https://www.thefreedommodel.org/book/

cause of these deaths in these stories used to be kept secret. But now, the parents and other family members are warning others of the dangers and advocating for treatment. That's all they can do to try to help others through the loss of their loved ones. The hope is that the story of their children's deaths will serve to prevent further tragedies. It's a tough, courageous, and noble choice to be open about these deaths. *As if the tragedy of these overdoses isn't dark enough, there's an even darker side of the story that nobody sees. The news media, politicians, and activists are all using these stories to lobby for more addiction treatment. Yet what you'll often find is that the overdose victims had received every available addiction treatment, often multiple times. Their families had spent tens or even hundreds of thousands of dollars getting what they were told was the best available help, and yet their children still ended up dying. And the solution to this mess, according to the politicians, is more of the same treatment?* ***It just doesn't add up. Something is wrong here. Why should we be calling for more of exactly what does not work when the evidence that it doesn't work is right in front of our faces?'*** (Bold and italics are my doing.)

I can tell you what people will say. I've seen the discussions, "They didn't want it bad enough. They didn't have enough willpower. They were enabled by someone so they weren't desperate enough to recover." I mean all of these things are ludicrous in my (Samantha) opinion. I believe in the premise that an industry that has a ton to gain, is perpetuating all these nonsensical theories because it helps their cause. Follow the money. I don't want to get all conspiracy theory in this book, but rumor has it that the cure for cancer was found years ago, so it makes sense why an industry that makes billions would NOT want people to think they had a choice in the matter.

The Freedom Model states that the rehab industry often spouts these cliche statements in an effort to put the blame back on the patient when rehab doesn't work out. "You have to want it to work," they will say about someone who got kicked out of treatment. The Freedom model states that usually, if someone doesn't want to quit substance use when they go into treatment, they probably won't quit when they get out. So, when treatment centers say the choice is up to the addict- then they are saying it's voluntary! They are defeating their own disease model yet convincing many to go anyway. If you didn't have cancer, you surely wouldn't spend time getting Chemotherapy. It would be a waste of your time and very expensive. So, someone who disagrees with the disease model of addiction (like my son) yet is basically forced to enter into a commitment that they don't buy; and people wonder why they "relapse." (Page 31)

To help understand, we must go back to the happiness principle. The Freedom Model basically states that the treatment model works against this by insisting compliance not personal choice and happiness:

1. *Changing your wants and desires is autonomous. Each person must figure out this process.*

2. *To change your desire for substance use, you must weigh the benefits of heavy use against the benefits of moderate use of abstinence. Whichever option you come to see as most beneficial ... is the option you'll truly want, become invested in, and carry out.*

3. *Treatment providers don't usually address this autonomy. Instead, they circumvent it with fear by convincing you that you must become immediately abstinent and follow their program or die. Patients usually sober up for a short time out of these threats, but they're still left wanting heavy substance use. Eventually it all falls apart and they use again.*

Just to sum it up, the recovery industry guarantees repeat offenders by drilling in that patients are suffering from an incurable disease that requires treatment.

This disease requires constant effort which will result in periodic relapses that require more treatment.

They'll feel forever deprived and MUST avoid all triggers so as to not activate that deprivation.

Under this model, if you don't continually go to meetings and work on your "chronic disease" you will surely fail. Based on this doom and gloom prediction that is so well accepted, many people see that it's a losing battle and choose the option that is at least offering some measure of pleasure- to continue drinking or drugging. Especially if they "believe that they NEED substances to deal with anxiety and depression, then the stress, anxiety and depression most people feel when presented with this dire prediction is enough to make them turn back to substances."

They also state that the recovery ideology regularly compares addiction to "another" chronic disease—diabetes. So, in that sense, all diabetics should forever avoid all sugar, because their bodies can't handle it. But recovery in itself means to adjust "your life to accommodate your permanent handicap."

Insulin does that for diabetics. It's basically harm reduction. It's a reasonable alternative to abstinence, as most people can't avoid all sugar forever.

The argument of "why is Narcan free and my insulin isn't" is a completely separate argument about lifesaving Narcan. Narcan is like AED paddles, they bring someone back whatever their medical problem is, and no EMT, policeman or bystander should be playing God on who deserves to be saved.

Page 45 of The Freedom Model, explains further:

> It's not for anyone to decide whether another person's life has meaning and purpose. That is very personal to each individual and is not related to substance use at all. We concluded that we no longer needed to judgmentally prescribe goals, actions, and processes to our guests. It became clear that our goal needed to be to help people understand that they, and no one else, were the only cause of their use. We saw that people could find their own avenues to purpose and happiness in their lives (especially after they came to grips with the fact that they were choosing their use)." Once people understood their inherent power of free will and choice regarding substances, they naturally moved on with their lives; there was nothing they needed to artificially "replace" anymore. In the final analysis, all people have their own personal purpose in life, and no one else can make that purpose in life, and no one else can make that purpose.[67]

I believe the D.A.R.E. program and the egg frying commercial were too simplistic and threat-based. Turns out that fear mongering and

---

[67] https://www.thefreedommodel.org/freedommodelforaddictions/

ultimatums have little effect on someone already using or even beginning to use, because of the human denial of "it will never happen to me." I do wish the D.A.R.E. program would have stated the true facts such as why people want to use drugs.

The Anointed Appointed Ever Elusive Rehab— Finally

Have you ever seen sand magnified 300 times? It's a beautiful display of shimmering light and form in different sizes and shapes. It's dazzling to behold. Just like snowflakes and sand, people are like grains of sand. They take a long time to develop and sometimes under mysterious conditions. On the surface we see one thing, but only God can see the true beauty under the mess.

Then there's the opposite sand. My husband took me for a drive one day. I wanted to try to find oolitic sand that our rockhounding group had spoken of. It's only in a handful of places and one of them just happens to be in our backyard. Well not right in our backyard, but close.

I stood on the bank of the large lake just thirty-five minutes from my house, I gazed out at the pristine pink waters that spread from east to west. The barren brown mountain to the north was a stark contrast to the bluish Oquirrh mountains beyond the sparkling water. I walked toward the water, expecting to feel squishy sand on the beach. Instead, I felt the hardened salt crystals stand their ground under the weight of my sandals. The only sound to be heard was the crunching of the salty "ice" under our feet. The breeze was salty too, as if to not be left out. The crisp fall air that I had distinctly felt the last few days was noticeably gone- likely retreating back to its summer hibernation and graciously allowing the hot summer sun to have one more day of service. My husband and I were on the shores of the Great Salt Lake, the largest natural lake west of the Mississippi River and the largest saltwater lake in the western hemisphere. We were admiring the pink beaches that obtained their color from the 17 trillion brine shrimp that covered the area. The brine shrimp brought back a fond memory from my childhood. Remember the sea monkeys' ads? It was that day I realized that these brine shrimps were one and the same as my fond childhood memory! I was delighted! I remember the sheer curiosity and novelty of these mysterious little "people," not knowing that they were "made" right in my own state. I'm positive I tried ordering them more than once, patiently waiting four to six weeks for delivery. Our pink shrimp adventure was one of many weekend jaunts we took in the beautiful mountains and deserts surrounding our city and state. But this one was different. This time, I didn't have to force myself to not think of my son. I didn't have to wonder if he survived the night. I didn't have to wonder if he was in Vegas getting shot at. I didn't have to wonder if this mountain, or desert, or landmark would be the one where they call me to tell me my son passed away. Although time is not promised to any of us, this time, I knew my son was relatively safe. This time, after a series of miracles, my son was inside a rehab, (hopefully) starting his final journey of recovery. It had been almost two years since he entered his first and only rehab. He made it seventy-two days clean that time. The last two years have left me and those close to him swimming in darkness as we struggled to understand the terrifying grip this disease has on him. But just like the brine shrimp-their brine eggs remain viable in dry conditions for several years- because of desiccation tolerance; my son was being preserved in his "drought."

"Desiccation tolerance refers to the ability of an organism to withstand or endure extreme dryness, or drought-like conditions. This means that physiological or behavioral adaptations to withstand these periods are necessary to ensure survival." Oh, how my heart would weep at what conditions my son's life was in in the last two years. At his little kids not being able to know him, and in the real possibilities of harm or loss of his freedom through the correctional system. I would weep in joy at others' successes in the support groups, then turn to sorrow that my son and our family were still struggling. Little did I know that like the brine shrimp eggs in drought, or in their normal cold winter; those seeds of hope and love were being nourished in my son in the form of faith that he could pull through his "drought" period.

Just the day before, after not seeing my beautiful boy for 16 months- my husband and I embarked on yet another adventure- a midnight trek- driving 800 miles that ended in the sheer joy of watching my son walk willingly into a rehab and say, "Thank you." His (and mine) drought period had ended.

Many would say that this doesn't mean anything. Addicts go through rehabs like cars in McDonald's drive-through. But my son is very rehab-resistant (for many reasons) and his rock bottom is as deep as the sea that holds these microscopic shrimps. He acclimates to every new level of condition that this lifestyle has thrown at him. So, to see the willingness of him to go through the door of the rehab, made this mama's heart soar.

Oh, but I still had the oolitic sand to find. We drove a few miles down the road to the spot where the rockhounds mentioned that it could be collected. I took my container and ran to the mounds of sand. Stuck my hand in to get a big chunk of what I thought would be pink magnetic sand was completely black underneath. The smell was atrocious! I looked up at my husband with disappointment that my mission was a failure. It was only then that I Googled oolitic sand and found out that it starts out as brine shrimp poop! Sea monkey crapola! I could almost see the delight in the sea monkeys on those retro ads laughing at me. I am still unsure whether I just needed to scrape the sand off the top of the black but it didn't matter. My motivation and desire were gone. What a lesson in all that glitters isn't gold.

Frozen

Mason had called me the night before at 11:30 pm. His first day at rehab. When the phone rang my heart froze like the frozen ice "sand" on the beach. Had he left the rehab? It was all a scam to get out of jail! "Hello?" I cautiously answered. "Hi Mom." "What are you doing?" I asked, but feeling a sense of relief that it was him, from the rehab's number, which meant he was still there. But 11:30? What kind of place was this? He excitedly told me about his first day. How depressed he was at first (which I think meant 'scared') he had sat there for hours listening to what was expected of him and how many classes he would attend. But then he was able to go outside and lift weights and process everything. Now all the guys were doing the Friday night movie thing and they were able to stay up until midnight!" My boy. MY jail released, street running, rule resistant boy was excited about being able to stay up late. I was tired and told him I was so glad he was there and safe but I had to go to sleep. He apologized for the time not even realizing how late it was. The next day when he called, he told me how much food they had and that he went in and got his own cereal for breakfast. He was so grateful for the small things. My heart glowed in relief and gratitude. What are the chances that out of the 30 or forty rehabs I had researched the last two years, in anticipation of this day, that he would end up in one just up the street from me (I didn't know that campus existed when I first contacted this rehab last spring). It was a nondescript building across the street from one of the groceries stores I frequented. I had never given it a second glance before. Who knew this converted house with the white vinyl fence around it would be the "chosen one" of all my homework and insurance maneuvering.

Over the next few weeks, he would call me with his lists of needs and we would schedule a drop off time. I even rounded up an actual red weight bench with gold weights on Facebook marketplace and threw them over the fence after dark! One of my favorite photos of him and I was one month into rehab. He asked for a basketball he had seen in my garage. I bought a new one instead and went to drop it off. The staff

252

member in charge actually let him come out and see me, we were able to hug and take a picture. He looked amazing. So healthy and happy, I was in heaven. I gladly provided anything he needed because I didn't want him to have any possible reason to want to leave. I also had spent the last 16 months not knowing if I would see him again. I didn't know what the future held, so I wanted every interaction to be heart-centered, recovery minded, and validating where he's at emotionally.

I was thrilled that he was in an environment to learn how to take care of himself again. For years, yes years, he has been in pure survival mode. Trying to find a place to stay every night; trying to maneuver his substance use, trying to justify his substance use, trying to deny his substance use. Putting poison in his body TO SURVIVE, yes survive. Every day his body told him- SCREAMED at him in fact, "GET DOPE or DIE."

But now his focus is back on learning his body's other cues. Cues of revitalization. Healing. Repairing years of damage to cells. Brain and body. He has scars. He has a bullet hole. He has ingrained pathways in his brain that automatically go into the quickest way to feel better and the quickest way to obtain the resources in order to feel better. To slow the hell down, sit in class after class, face his demons, face the pain he has caused his family, and face losing his freedom, must be daunting. To refocus that energy on lifting weights, even with smoking; is a dream to me.

I gladly provide any of these items for the same reason as I picked out his baby food when he was little. As mothers, we are nurturers. It doesn't matter if they are grown, men. Everyone needs their "person." More and more studies are showing that even having one person believe in them makes recovery more sustainable. Plus, nothing is promised. No time, no future, no measure of success is promised, day to day, with anyone, but especially with substance use. If I can buy my grown son some protein bars, I will gladly do it. Anything to keep him focusing on recovery, contemplating new skills, and hoping for a better life.

He was both thrilled and cautious when after a few weeks, they made him a lead "steerer" who was in charge of the house schedules, others' chores, and attitudes. That was a game changer for his attitude because suddenly it wasn't about skirting around the rules– like the music iPod we had sort of snuck in for him in a carton of cigarettes. It had accidentally turned on so the carton of cigarettes was glowing as I handed it to the people in charge that day! He turned it in on the day he was made steerer and said, "I can't expect others to obey the rules if I'm not." He talked about going hiking to Donut Falls and how hard it was to keep 25 drug addicts in line. It was quite enlightening and refreshing to hear him bearing some responsibility for someone other than himself. I soaked it all in- knowing our time was short.

The day we picked him up from rehab was exciting. I had looked into some sober livings in the area, but he told me they had it all set up for him. He had told me a few weeks previous that a guy had hung himself in that very sober living recently, but I guess I ignored it and put it out of my mind, trying to let him lead his recovery. When we pulled up to the building, however, my heart sank to my knees. Not only was it in a bad area of town within blocks of the inner city, but the building was at least 100 years old with very poor upkeep. Even my son was shocked. He, Liam, and I stood there in disbelief as conflicting thoughts of: "are we being too picky? Shouldn't there be more funds somewhere for this? Don't judge a book by its cover." When my son went in to get his key, he found an empty mattress, with a curtain separating it from the kitchen. There were dirty dishes all over the sink and floor. The main floor toilet where they did their urine drug tests didn't work, so they had to urinate into the tub for their tests. I couldn't believe it. Yes, I emailed my contact with the rehab and said this was unacceptable. She completely disregarded all of my concerns saying that it's because he came from rehab where everything was nice and new. Okay. Whatever. She stated the female housing supervisor would meet him there at five and check on it. She actually never came. The male house manager was there and I found out nine months later that he actually sold meth out of the house. He had lived there for ten years, so no one obviously cared to stop him. There was a private sober living for $650/month that we had called and talked to that day, but we just couldn't swing it. Oh, how I wonder if that would have made a difference. I tried to back away and let him manage it. When I dropped him off at the door that first night after taking him grocery shopping, he had resigned himself to the fact that he had to stay there. He said, "Mom, it's okay, it's better than running and hiding like I have been." I made sure to validate that by sending him this text later.

I just want to tell you how amazing you are. For how resilient, yet kind, not hardened. None of this can be easy. Being tossed around and told what to do yet you are a warrior about it. I'm so grateful I get to be your mom and have a front seat in your journey to watch you grow through this.

To which he responded, "I forgot my bedding at rehab. We were supposed to bring it with us." I immediately turned around and went back to the store and delivered him clean, new bedding. The next few days I tried not to worry. Knowing the overdose and relapse rate of sober living was akin to giving birth the second time, now you are not clueless – you KNOW what you're in for and it's even more scary. When he didn't answer the next few days. I tried not to go there in the middle of the night in the darkened inner city, to see if he was there. I tried to not send Liam one day on his way to work when Mason didn't answer for 14 hours straight. (Both of which I failed.) I was so used to having access to him in sober living where I could actually call there anytime and talk to him. I had to learn to let him have his space and not be his parole officer and monitor his every move. I wanted to be a guidelight to his recovery, not another barrier that thwarts his autonomy and his personal search for the happier option.

For now, she need not think of anybody. She could be herself, by herself. And that was what now she often felt the need of - to think; well not even to think. To be silent; to be alone. All the being and the doing, expansive, glittering, vocal, evaporated; and one shrunk, with a sense of solemnity, to being oneself, a wedge-shaped core of darkness, something invisible to others ... and this self-having shed its attachments was free for the strangest adventures.
—Virginia Woolf, *To the Lighthouse*

The Red Bandana

Remind them who they are and sing them home.

A Beautiful African Accountability Practice

There's a story on social media called Ubunta, which depicts a group of African men encircling another man who has his hand over his heart. There's no proof it's genuine but it's a feel-good story, nonetheless.

In the Babemba tribe of South Africa, when a person acts irresponsibly or unjustly, he is placed in the centre of the village, alone and unfettered. All work ceases, and every man, woman, and child in the village gathers in a large circle around the accused individual.

Then each person in the tribe speaks to the accused, one at a time, each recalling the good things the person in the centre of the circle has done in his lifetime. Every incident, every experience that can be recalled with any detail and accuracy, is recounted. All his positive attributes, good deeds, strengths, and kindnesses are recited carefully and at length. This tribal ceremony often lasts for several days.

At the end, the tribal circle is broken, a joyous celebration takes place, and the person is symbolically and literally welcomed back into the tribe.[68]

Oh, how many times had I dreamed of this scenario. I wanted to repeat that hour of the intervention over and over again. I wanted to be like a football championship with never ending plays where we met together in a Ubunta-type circle on the sidelines, drawing plays on a white board and changing the course of action minute by minute until somehow, something WORKED!! And by working, I mean Mason is completely abstinent and healing. I knew that moment, that solution, was just around the corner and I wanted OUR TRIBE at the finish line cheering him on. I had begged and pleaded for others to feel the way I felt. I sent article after article on addiction to the family thread that was dwindling down by the minute. I sent articles for different treatments

---

[68] https://www.kindspring.org/story/view.php?sid=7535

and opinions on the cause and the cure of addiction. I sent pre-invites and on the spot zoom meetings for family recovery.

I mean, it seems silly now, but if I couldn't control the addiction in my son, what made me think I could control one, two or twenty more people? It's actually manipulation on my part.

One by one, they seemed to tire of my obsession. I was told that the addiction was ruining my life. I was told that every time I use "defensive language," or make arrangements for anything other than jail, I am enabling my son's behavior to continue. My husband was told that I just needed to "pick up the pieces and move on." Everyone had moved on with their lives and didn't seem to want to hear his name. This was made very clear in a dramatic way at a birthday party in the cold month of January. We had traveled our usual ninety minutes to Luke's house, which was the scene of the brothers' fight over a year ago. I made it through the party with the realization that this was our new life. New people, new houses, new traditions without any mention of the "other son." I smiled with tears welling up in my eyes and took pictures while I mentally processed the fracturing of our old life and how to welcome change gracefully. At the end of the party, I made the mistake of mentioning that Mason needed a truck. I thought that Luke might have an old work truck he wasn't using. I must have thought I could elicit some type of empathy–again. I never learn. After being told that no, they didn't want to talk about that and they didn't want any negativity around their new family, I completely went off the rails. This was not what I had anticipated. It had been 7 months since any mention of him and I mistakenly thought that was long enough. As we drove away with me in a complete meltdown, my husband had to pull over and calm me in the darkened winter night. I wanted to die right there and then. I couldn't believe how this horrible storm continued to hammer through the family with no end in sight.

Off the side of the road, in the deep snow, I tried desperately to grab Liam's gun. I wanted to run into the road. If I couldn't have my family, I was done with life. It seemed like hours of tears. Thankfully, my husband saved me from myself, but this episode took over a year of healing and minimal contact with Luke to even begin to repair.

Someone told me in a support meeting, "Can't you send your family the studies on science and kindness and connection being more effective than isolation?" I laughed. That exact scenario is what brought us here. I know some families can do it. They don't let the addiction take more victims. They are committed to figuring out solutions that show the struggling person they are loved and supported, just as if they had a fatal illness and their time was limited. They were like the friends of the paralyzed man in Mark 2 who had enough faith to convince Jesus to heal him; even after crossing many barriers to get there despite the man not believing in his own faith.

After these moments, just like a woman trying to get pregnant and all she sees are the pregnant women; I noticed all the people in the groups who had family support. One lady even said, "This requires all hands-on deck, your child will not survive if you don't have help to combat this evil." Great. They won't survive if you don't have family support. That's all I needed to hear. One lady in a group said this about her family's experience:

> *When we found out that my children were using drugs, just like anybody else, we fell to pieces. But one of the things that we did do as a family was to wear a bracelet. This bracelet was to remind us of our {addicted} child. Everybody in the family wore them. Aunts, uncles, nieces, nephews, grandparents ... Even some friends. One of my boys came to me not too long ago and said something about the bracelet. He said you know all these people in my family think about me and pray about me every time they look at their bracelet. It's really made a big difference. I know people are praying for me. We are and we did. He even wore a bracelet to remind him that we stood behind him. No matter where he was or the shape or condition, he was in he had that constant reminder. We didn't go out and buy these bracelets. We bought a red bandana and cut it into tiny strips. I have a picture of mine. It's not much but it means the world to us and our addicted children ... My boys are clean but I still wear my bracelet. It's one of my favorite pieces of jewelry.* —Used by permission

Oh, how I craved this. I wanted my red bandana. I wanted to drag my wooden pallet and put my "paralyzed son" upon it and beg God,

Jesus, or a higher power to heal him physically and then spiritually, if that's what he needed. How it tore at my heart to be called an enabler, or the reason for Mason's continued use. Or a codependent. Which felt ridiculous, unless maybe, my SUD person was a spouse and I had issues before the addiction. Then of course, personality problems will be made worse. Robert Weiss, the author of *Pro-dependence, Moving Beyond Codependency,* stated that codependency is sometimes confused with an actual diagnosis of *Dependent personality syndrome.* This is for people who are so "emotionally limited and impaired that they cling to other people for their emotional stability." I'm paraphrasing the following:

- *Codependency is not a diagnosis, but a pop culture label that was developed in the 80s and was carried over to describe people who love addicts.*
- *It states that if you have a deeply troubled person who struggles with substance use- then you are reliving your childhood trauma by trying to fix them.*
- *This creates more guilt because who wants to be told there is something wrong with caring and trying to get the loving caring person underneath the substance user back? There shouldn't be guilt or shame with trying to maneuver through the desperation and chaos that addiction causes to find peace again.*
- *We might be the only one who holds the vision of who that person is, who they were or who they could be.*
- *Most people who rescue others are heroes but yet those who love and want to save substance users are somehow flawed and a "part of the problem."*
- *When some of the things you try didn't work out so well, it's that's part of the insidious nature of the disease,* **not the cause of it**. *To try to help someone who's life is in danger is a noble effort. Even if they resist that effort.*
- *Codependency portrays the belief that if I can't make them better then maybe I'm the problem taking the blame off where it belongs- with the substance user.*

What Weiss proposes as a replacement to these words:

"*Enmeshed- viewed as an inadequate attempt at loving.*
Enabling- incredibly supportive
Lack boundaries- eager to help.

He offers the novel thought: *"When did love become a pathology? It's okay to love people who don't love you back….."*

> *"How can you love another human being too much? How can you love your grandma or your spouse too much? Why is there something wrong with me because I care for a person in crisis? Why am I being labeled an enabler -as part of the problem when in reality I have no control over another's actions. Sure, the way I act out my love might be reactive to the negative behavior's addiction causes. Yes, I'm obsessed with someone's life getting better. Yes, I will lay down my life for someone else to live theirs. To be willing to rescue and save another person is a strength not a weakness. If you run yourself ragged running your adult child to chemo treatments everyone would call you a hero, but if you run them to rehab and detox and court dates so they can get their life back on track, somehow there is something wrong with you.*[69]

I had to find a way to forge these Class 6 river rapids. I had to bridge this gap of torrential rains that wouldn't stop hailing on my family. I may not have a pallet from the town of Capernaum in Jesus's time, but I had a kayak. All my kids love to Kayak. We did it in Dr. Seuss Bay of La Jolla, in San Diego, California, and on our favorite lakes in our home state. Just like that time Luke and Callan and I kayaked to that little island in 2016 and marveled at the beauty of nature, the importance of family, the validity of stress relief. We could find our path back. One name I wanted for the title of this book was FIERCELY. I wanted it to represent how fiercely I fought this fight. I wanted to show how fiercely my son fought his battle.

I wanted to show a VICTORY. But now, as I near the end of telling my story. I want to show a battle of love. I want to show how fiercely humans CAN love. Not just my struggling son. Not just so he would recover. Not just so he can find his peace and his place and his own truth. But for all these other precious souls. The ones left behind. The precious kids. The "other brothers" of the Prodigal Son. The ones who didn't squander and sin, necessarily. Each one of my other kids and

---

[69] https://prodependence.com/

family members have their own battles. Their own pain. Their own longing for something. Their own beauty beyond the pain. I don't want them to suffer one more minute over this. I don't want them to miss out on a mom who has only been halfway there for these last few years. I don't want them to see how scared I am to forge relationships with the new family members. I want them to know that if it had been them, I would have fought the same fight. More than anything, I want ALL my kids to remember that beauty and strength inside them. The grit and humor and resourcefulness and vigor that they all possess inside them in different ways. I want all my grandkids to have a fighting chance. I want them to see how we worked so hard on this and how we approach other problems in life. I want them to know that every person is worth fighting for and every problem has a solution. There are always options that a skewed or depressed or anxious brain can't see. That's what families are for. Friends who care enough to drop someone through the roof to be given to Jesus. I want a huge red bandana that is big enough for all my family and their families after them, to tear into fierce loving pieces of hope that we can wrap all of us up in sweet joy, the sweet love and hope of family. That's all I hope for.

I wanted my patience and faith to eventually pay off for me. But if not, how grateful I am that I tried faithfully to keep an open loving heart for Luke and others through these challenging moments.

It's supposed to be hard. If it wasn't hard, everyone would do it. The hard ... is what makes it great. —Jimmy Dugan

I had this book almost finished when I read Gabor Mate's book Scattered. It was unbelievable how spot on his words were as they coincided with my experience raising my son. I know I'm not a doctor but I am a nurse, but in this case, I was just a mom. I was able to actually place a name with my summations of his thoughts and behaviors as a child struggling with ADD. My "ornery gaze" that I mentioned noticing on videos with my little son suddenly made sense when Gabor thought about the emotionally distracted mom. Then trying to follow my son's attempts through his growing up to seemingly change his "state" with humor, anger, work, then substances. Was it my fault? Should I have disciplined him more? Was it the curse of ADHD? Was it in our "genes"? My search took me into every crevice possible. From the deepest darkness to the brightest brightness. From quicksand to beautiful inland beach sand. Hopefully, this book will show my journey and help you with yours. Now, I wonder, what good does it do to find the cause? I had to believe that I didn't cause it and I couldn't cure it and I couldn't control it. The peace was slow to come. I continued my trudging through book after book, meeting after meeting, healer after healer; trying to find the magic cure, or the mysterious cause. I previously thought that I could only find peace if the outcome was in my favor. But I also knew that if I kept basing my entire life on him getting well, I would lose more than just him.

John Roseman from The Point of Grace Church posted this quote on Facebook: "Proper discipline does not guarantee proper behavior." Following the quote, he explained "The Jeremiah Principle" which is from this scripture:

They turned their backs to me and not their faces; though I taught them again and again, they would not listen or respond to discipline. —Jeremiah 32:33
(NIV)

"A principle that every parent needs to commit to memory: If a child does the wrong thing, and parents respond with a right and proper thing, the child may keep right on doing the wrong thing anyway. I call it the Jeremiah Principle because in the eponymous book of Scripture, the Lord of Israel laments that no matter what he does, His chosen people keep right on misbehaving. The story illustrates that proper consequences do not necessarily produce proper behavior.

When God created us, He gifted us with free will, the ability to make autonomous decisions. Interestingly enough, God has set things up such that He can control us but has chosen not to. Likewise, you can influence your children, but you cannot control them.

According to some psychology, bad parenting produces or leads to bad or dysfunctional adult behavior, and good parenting produces good or functional adult behavior. But common sense says that's just not so. Some kids raised in good families do really, really bad, or just downright stupid things (and don't seem to learn from their mistakes), and some kids raised in really bad families turn out well. Contrary to the psychological myth, parenting does not produce the child. Parenting is an influence, and your job is to maximize the positive aspects of your influence. But in the final analysis, your child takes your influence and he decides what he's going to do with it. It's all about free will, the ability to choose what the serpent tells us to do over what God tells us to do." [70]

Free will. I had completely forgotten about that in my attempts to control my son's behavior. I was taught in church that a battle was fought in heaven for the ability for us to come to earth to have free agency. On a particularly bad day, I was saddened and frustrated (again) that my son wouldn't take my advice and do the "obvious right thing." I had literally tried everything for three weeks to get him to handle things differently to save his freedom and many future headaches. I was, of course, starting down the rabbit hole thought process of *"why won't he listen? Why won't he do what I know he's been taught? I hate drugs, I hate my life, I hate the last three years."*

---

[70]

https://www.facebook.com/johnkrosemond/photos/a.435868033276/1015617520
5428277/?type=3

As I was going through a container in my storage to clear some things out, I came across some old papers from Haven's Wilderness adventure when she was fifteen. This is the program that the book *Beyond Addiction* is based on. There were two copies of "The Parent's Rabbit Stick Walk"—my husband's copy and mine. These were exercises on self-betrayal. Mine was full of notes of our then problem child teen daughter. I opened my then-husband's copy and saw his answer to the question, "What are situations in which you get offended easily?" He wrote, "When Mason won't do what I think he should. When Mason should know what I expect, because I've told him before. I want him to be a good worker and not half-finish things."

Keep in mind, we were there for our daughter. Mason would have been thirteen or fourteen and not particularly a "problem." Yet my then-husband's frustrations were EXACTLY the same as I was having twenty-five years later, after the severe drug experience. Things that I was blaming on his *hijacked brain*—a phrase which he despises and rejects. He was still essentially the same stubborn person as he always was! I'm not denying that drugs played a huge role in his problems, I mean it's ludicrous to think they didn't and I'm also not saying that my son was irresponsible and hopeless BEFORE drugs came into the picture. I'm saying that a lot of the things I'm spending so much energy on wanting to change, wouldn't work even if drugs were not ever involved. He was a boy and then a man who marched to his own beat. To always test the limits which later brought him trouble with compliance, but early on it helped a lot of people and blessed the lives of almost everyone he touched for many years.

In his book *Chasing False Highs and Running from Lows,* L. Michael Audley told a story about a Japanese airline pilot named captain Hokei Asoha, who landed his DC 200 yards short of the runway into San Francisco Bay with 180 passengers in broad daylight. Several days later the FAA was holding an investigation and had a news conference. The first question to the seasoned pilot was, "How could you land a plane 200 yards short of the runway into San Francisco Bay in broad daylight? We have examined the plane and there are no defects." Captain Asoh said, ***"Asoh F_____ UP!"***

That ended the investigation. He admitted defeat. A surrender in a way.

My son hadn't truly surrendered yet, but he has admitted how he messed up. How long should he pay?

Could I accept that my son's addiction was and is ugly, messy and mistakes were made in landing that portion of their journey? Could I just move forward without anger at WHY ME? WHY US? WHAT DID I DO WRONG? Could I resist making the struggling person feel like Shizz and continually rub in how much harm has been done? Could I, instead, hold space for him so wide that I'm standing in that gap? In that space–where on one side evil is slinging its fiery darts in the darkness hoping to hit dead center onto its vulnerable targets in order to continue their suffering in perpetual misery. On the other side is the pure love of God who sees my loved one as a struggling soul in which his love doesn't diminish in spite of their frailties and faults.

God is not ashamed of the lowliness of human beings. God marches right in. He chooses people as his instruments and performs his wonders where one would least expect them. God is near to lowliness; he loves the lost, the neglected, the unseemly, the excluded, the weak and broken. —Dietrich Bonhoeffer, God is in the Manger: Reflections on Advent and Christmas

Tough as Nails, Strong as Steel, Heart of Gold. Those are words I would use to describe my son. But what about us, those who are left behind, feeling weak, lost and in despair? Being told to get out of the way of God's work, stop helping, stop doing, stop trying so hard. To SOME that means to stop caring, stop responding. Let them sink further until surely, they come up begging and willing to do anything to fix it all.

Except most times they don't. I believe, to have the characteristics for addiction to develop; you have to have the strength of steel. I've always loved the analogy of comparing the heat used in tempering to strengthen the steel and the pain of trials to strengthen our souls. Tempering is where steel is reheated and rapidly cooled to make it stronger.

Good Lord we all must be the Empire State building at this point!

The person who gets entangled in addiction is not a weak person. I believe they have an iron grit so strong and beaming that it can't help being noticed by the enemy due to the ability to stand out. They have talents and an incredible mind. They have a certain desire and need to be different. They might be seen as rebels or even bullheaded, Or as my son says: "I'm either all or nothing. I have to be all in on a project". That's usually because they have passion. They have SOUL. They have depth. And sometimes those qualities leave them lost and unable to find their place. Sometimes this is because they are deeply sensitive people with an inability to place and process all their emotions adequately to society's standards. Or they might be unable to conform to certain relationship or political dynamics that are almost always committed to one party failing.

So, you see, society's idea that addiction is a moral failure or a sign of weakness couldn't be further from the truth. Sometimes there's the mental illness piece that might be at play too. Some had it before addiction and some developed it during and because of addiction. So now there's even more moving parts to address. To peel back the layers and heal slowly.

As I was writing this chapter, another tragedy occurred with a family of my kids' ages in our community. A 30-year-old man, after telling his wife he was going to get food, proceeded to go into his garage and shoot himself. This was very similar to the boy who hung himself a year and half ago who was very close to my sons. This time there wasn't any previous drug use involved. The man had a wife and two tiny kids. I had just been admiring their Facebook pages a few weeks earlier, because in our area, family pictures are huge. It's the thing for every season, usually fall and spring to have outdoor pictures done with all the extended family. This family, I had been classmates with, so I had known them my entire life, basically. I was doing the social media nightmare of self-torture by admiring their "perfect family' with their perfect pictures and all the fun family trips they went on. Trips that my family used to make an effort to do. Although there is always more to social media than portrayed, this death, like the previous one, seemed out of character and was a shock to everyone. As I read through all the sympathy comments to the family, I was overwhelmed with all the compliments and genuinely sad feelings. "He was such a great guy, the best husband, father, and son ever! A huge hole has been made on earth with his passing. He always had a smile on his face." This man seemingly had it all. He did the "family thing" that I so desperately wanted my son back doing.

Oh, how I ached and ached for my son to be with his kids.

My challenge, still, was to quiet these voices of despair and pain and see my son as a person worthy of love and of life and be given the opportunity and grace to be in their lives again. I also needed to honor HIS choices of being able to live in his own skin in the way only he can in order to survive. Maybe this guy who shot himself would be alive, if he had a secret drug habit that he could fall back on. My son told me after rehab, "focus on your other kids, something could happen to them too." Even while scraping the bottom of the proverbial barrel of life, he was trying to stick up for others in my life.

My challenge was to not so much have to stick up for him (which some might take as "justifying his use") but not be criticized for placing value on my unrecovered son's life. I needed to be proud of my courage to love him in spite of all the damage. I needed to be proud but not prideful for being committed to kindness. I needed to be able to advocate for him without sending the message that I approve of any of his actions. My son has the strongest heart I know. He is a fighter. He has survived situations that would blow people's minds. Yes, the substances helped him in a lot of ways. In fact, they probably saved his life. How many times, just like in my classmate's son above, have people snapped and caused a devastating tragedy either to themselves or others because they didn't have a desire or motivation to use substances-therefore there was zero outlet or "masking of the pain"? They just needed the pain to end. What sin is that? For a beautiful soul to want to feel better while being drawn into the mental illness tunnel of despair. It was their solution to a problem in the moment. How can we do anything but love for that effort? However, "wrong" and painful it turns out to be for those left behind.

I was beginning to truly see that the crutch of drug use to handle his stress probably averted many instances of tragedy. Even though, yes, the drugs themselves end up causing incredible hardship to everyone around him and himself; I have to give credit where credit is due. The spirit of survival.

So, the magic question: Would I be able to finally accept that my son may not "recover" in the way that I viewed recovery?

Could I use this as the opportunity to refine and define absolute unconditional love for others? Could I take the high road in becoming MY best self despite negative circumstances, like Matt Kahn suggests? Could I take Gabor's advice and say to my person, even if it's just me alone and not my family's recovery, "Thank you for being the sensitive one in the family, to manifest what's been hidden and misunderstood for generations; Thank you for giving us (me) the opportunity to deal with it and heal the entire family system essentially so that the buck stops here!" [71]

Could I soak in the gracious words of Reverend Dr Andrew Teal whom I heard on the radio one day?

"What if it wasn't about despising people who [use substances] and not about trying to be an example to them? What if it's about standing with them in grace? Grace abounds when we do the right thing. Not when we convince others to do the right. Nothing is going to happen on this day that is beyond the will of God. Nothing that is unredeemable. Can you stand with Radical Solidarity in honoring your loved one's journey with the dignity that a higher power would ask of you? What the enemy intends for evil, God desires to rescue and redeem. Will you let Him, dear one?"[72]
—Reverend Dr. Andrew Teal

Roman Dial was an adventurous dad who was used to navigating outdoor challenges, but not the two-year journey that would find him looking for his son in the Costa Rican Jungle. His twenty-seven-year-old son went to a remote Mayan archeological site in Central America called El Mirador. He had written to his dad and told him that he decided to change his plans and go into the jungle in another direction. The dad did not think he should go in that way so he started to send him an email, then another one trying to explain why he shouldn't go in that way but

---

[71] https://www.youtube.com/watch?v=VvQYwOlx0HY minute 29.47

[72] https://www.byuradio.org/defe938d-7df0-4f8a-89ab-c4264fffbb11 minute 18

he ended up deleting it and saying just be careful of the poisonous snakes etc. He did not hear back from him again. He spent two years looking for him and was featured in a National Geographical documentary highlighting his search. While embarking on this journey, just like me with my many rescue attempts, he imagined his child sitting in his tent waiting for his dad to come rescue him.

Out of all the dangers of the tropical rainforest, he found out that a tree had fallen on his son and killed him. Could he have saved him if only he had sent that email? Would his son have listened? These are questions that will never be answered for Roman. He has to learn to be at peace with his decisions, just as all parents must. Being okay with the risk they are taking by living the lifestyle they choose is hard for any parent. Whether it's adventure risk like Cody Dial or others, like Marc-Andre Leclerc of the documentary *The Alpinist*, it is THEIR risk even when it does affect us and our emotions. The similarities between what my son has said and what these adventurers say is uncanny. From memory, I share them below.

Alpinist – Marc: *People say [solo mountain climbing is] dangerous. I'm not deluding myself that it's not dangerous. But to me I probably just have a different view of everything. TO me it's not an unacceptable risk.*

Mason: *I am totally aware of the risk; I live it every day. But I just can't get down on my knees and beg for my freedom and for money for my kids, it's really easy to tell me what I should be doing cuz everyone thinks they know but it's not their life and they have no real idea what I am facing and there are only two ways to beat this………. When you constantly tell me to rethink my life, I'm not having fun or making irresponsible decisions. I'm literally fighting for my life and trying to get back what I lost.*

For those of us back home, wondering and waiting, it's excruciating. When we don't hear from them or even know where they are, we imagine the worst. My friend Joanne Richards, who is a family recovery coach and runs the Loving Your Child Facebook group, gave me so much comfort in those times:

Whenever I imagine my child hurt, beaten down, dead, or almost dead,
Whatever conditions on this earth that could possibly happen to your children,
Where's the safest place for them?
I have found the safest place for my child is in my heart, not in my imagination.
Questioning the very truth of my beliefs, coming to an understanding, where peace
comes in where peace enters in, how to envision my son in a different state,
in a different condition, send him love, a virtual hug
Just notice how much it hurts,
When they're alive for now, if they're alive for now, I have something I need to do.
When we imagine them dead, but they're not dead, and yet our spirit knows that, it is
our greatest pain to kill our children when they are not dead. When I don't remember
the beauty in him. When I'm in the future where he doesn't live and I don't live either
-that's going to cause a lot of pain. I'm gonna put my son right into my heart, where
he is safest. Fear cannot have us. Love always does. Love wins here!

—Joanne Richards

Could I do this? Again, and again? Would this deep, heartfelt, powerful advice serve me well in the next six months to who knows how long?

Can I let go just enough to allow God's rugged love for wayward souls [to carry] my son? In the chapter titled "Grace Wins," *Letting Go* authors Harvey and Gilbert write, "If you feel like you're dying each day, be encouraged. "Weeping may tarry for the night, but joy comes with the morning" (Psalm 30:5). In the fullness of time, dark nights end, cold winters subside, and hope heals. We live to laugh again because the One who showed us rugged love empowers us to exercise it. Even in the pain of letting go we remember the power that links the apostle John's story to our own: The God we rely upon who raises the dead.

What if you offered your loved one the grace and space to work it out while you offer zero judgment or scorn?

Can you look in your loved one's eyes and truly see them? Behind the web of destruction and chaos. Eyes that say, "Can you love me in spite of what I do? Can you? Even when I give you every reason to hate me? Can you show me love without that look of disappointment that flashes over your face? Can you offer a tinge of hope without your fleeting disdain for my life choices showing in your tone of voice?

So, yes, that space. That space I have been in for over four years now. Fighting not only the demons who now hold such power over my son; but fighting all of society that this effort is worth it. Trying to convey that it's worth more than the attention given to other projects, some that are far away and will hardly affect us. When we are in that gap of darkened light, we want to scream. We do sometimes. We just want to be heard, seen. We desperately want someone, everyone, to hold that space for us! For us. So, we can give up one of the fights that tear our soul. The fight to defend our position.

That same space that our addicted loved ones ask for. The space of non-judgment. The space of not arguing for their choices. The space of just being there. In all of the addiction's grimy mess. In its sadness. In its pain.

What would it take to get to that space?

Patience.

Grace.

Silent confirmation of their worth. Our worth.

Willingness to give up control.

Willingness to not be vested in the outcome.

Willingness to love.

EVEN IF things are not going our way.

EVEN IF they are acting suspiciously….

EVEN IF they haven't made contact….

I HAD to learn to do this. I HAD to be able to offer him enough grace to let this play out.

As Johann Hari states, "The opposite of addiction isn't sobriety. It's a connection. That's all I can offer. It's all that will help him in the end. If you are alone, you cannot escape addiction. If you are loved, you have a chance. For a hundred years we have been singing war songs about addicts. All along, we should have been singing love songs to them."

When we're in the story, when we're part of it, we can't know the outcome. It's only later that we think we can see what the story was. But do we ever really know? And does anybody else, perhaps, coming along a little later, does anybody else really care? ... History is written by the survivors, but what is that history? That's the point I was trying to make just now. We don't know what the story is when we're in it, and even after we tell it we're not sure. Because the story doesn't end.

— James Robertson, *And the Land Lay Still*

Chasing The Storm

My boy. It had been a flurry of movement after his sentencing. He was given 18 eighteen months' probation and thirty-days Outpatient therapy. He had been so excited. He actually went to his first ever job interview. The boy who had worked since he was 15 fifteen years old, for people who knew his talent and hard work ethic. He never needed an interview— a phone call and a shake of the hand would suffice for almost 14 fourteen years. The boy who always had a job before one ended, who never even had to have a resume. The boy who's loving big sister Haven, had helped him create one. She texted me one day: "How in the world do I create a resume for the hardest working guy in the world with no references or solid history/education? He could sell himself to anyone in person, but how do we create that opportunity onto a silly paper?"

He was looking forward to making up for lost time. He had them eating out of his hand in the interview. They couldn't believe their luck, but also couldn't offer what he needed. With his obligations, he needed at least $30/hour, or he wouldn't be able to get his own housing after ORS and IRS bills.

We had found an old truck on marketplace for him to go to the job interviews as we weren't able to drive him around. He was incredibly grateful and excited. He hadn't had a vehicle for 18 eighteen months, and the feeling of being back in control of his life and not at the mercy of the jail or the rehab was apparent on his face. He was going to pay us a little bit each check until it was paid for, which would have been just 4 four or five or 5 months. He was on his way. Until four days out of rehab on Thanksgiving.

It was an exciting day. He was to see family that he hadn't seen in over a year. It would be the first real Thanksgiving he had attended in over 3 years. He said he wasn't nervous but when he drove to my house from sober living, he kept asking what shirt he should wear and ended up changing into one of my husbands. The day went perfectly, albeit a bit awkwardly. His trepidation to jump right back in as the funny, loud guy was met with snippets of funny moments in jail that although were foreign to our normal family conversations, he made them entertaining. It was the life he had lived and known for years merging with our families' celebrations that went on as usual without him. Hugs were given, pictures were taken.

Momentum is a powerful thing. When it's interrupted there's a disconnect to the present and the future. Events will quickly spiral into a heap of unreached expectations.

The pink cloud of recovery fades quickly to a lightning storm of hail and brimstone about to reign down.

After a phone conversation regarding his kids, I felt the momentum change. It seemed the last few weeks of hope and promise suddenly seeped away. I think his mind was replaying his message of "I hate failure but mostly I hate failing people again and again. There's too much lost. Why even try anymore?" Bottom line is he needed money and he needed it fast. In his mind that was what would fix everything and he would be able to see his kids and get a good start with housing.

He called me on the road. He was in the middle of a long stretch of 400 miles between my city and his old one. It was a bad storm, worse than he had driven in and considering he hadn't really driven in over a year, it must have felt scary. He swore. He yelled into the phone in frustration, "This is awful. I can't see a thing! Visibility is about zero."

"Son, where are you going?" I asked, already knowing the answer.

"Mom, you don't understand, I can't even see the road! I got to go."

"Son... can you see the mile markers?" my voice faded as I knew he had thrown the phone on the seat. But he didn't push the end call button. I heard my son in one last attempt to cuss at the storm to stop ruining his plans. I heard him moan, "Oh God, good hell, come on!" Then the phone went dead.

After the storm's failed attempt at thwarting his plans, he went back to the same place he had been before his four-month jail/rehab sabbatical: our vacation town. Two days before Christmas 2021, I received a letter in the mail with a junk lawyer advertisement. "Charges have been filed against you for distribute/offer/arrange to distribute a controlled substance" This alleged time period was the previous year, before his last two jail visits and his 7-week rehab. These charges carried

274

one to fifteen years EACH (x 3) and a fine of up to $10,000. The possibility of forty-five years and a $30,000 fine was gut-wrenching.

We never received official court confirmation. Thank goodness for junk mail, however this completely devastated my son and me. He was crushed. He had just started to make a couple hundred a week for gas and food and was looking at housing. After breaking the news to him, I received this defeated message.

> *Mom, I'm done. They are taking their time-they have 3 years to indict so they will just keep throwing a couple out there just to ruin my life so that I can't start working or anything. It's just to try to keep me in the system. That's why this happened now, because they saw I went to rehab and they can't stand that. There are four cops who are determined to bring me down. They could have more things on me for how long I've been doing drugs. I am trying to figure out how to get enough money for a lawyer and for my kids and $500 for my license plus pay for outpatient and sober living -all with warrants hanging over my head so I can't drive or go anywhere or sign up for anything without getting arrested. It's impossible to fight them from the inside. I'm very pissed and ashamed of the decisions I've made the last few years that's got me where I'm at right now but I don't want you to consume your whole day worrying. Just try to have a Merry Christmas.*

He was gone again. Off to where he couldn't be hounded for things that he just wasn't capable of providing right now. My son is very resourceful at surviving on nothing. That's why tough love doesn't work with him. He tough loves himself enough by isolating and not taking care of himself, his life, and his obligations. One month turned into two then 6 months had passed. For the first time in years, he "went dark" off of social media, no phone, and no contact. I was beside myself with worry. Liam and I made several trips there tracking him down and connecting with local homeless advocates to help locate him. Private investigators wanted $150 per hour, and even if they did find him, what to do then? Despite a definitive plan, miracles happened in these attempts to ease my aching heart. I found an Arise interventionist who works with the family for this very reason: to help the person who wants to get better-not force them into an intervention where they feel obligated. This is done by teaching family members how to communicate and use their instincts and love in order to enable connection and hope to draw the person back into the fold. Oh, how I wanted that! But I needed family participation and I needed $6,000. I had neither.

I resumed my previous email and Instagram writing campaign basically begging everyone I could find for some help. People who had resources, where money was not an issue. Gary V, Russell Brand, Pew De Pie, John Assaraf from The Secret. Grant Cardone, business coach. Rich people donate to charities to help suffering people, not to families and kids suffering from a dad with the disease of addiction, but I still tried. I had no shame at this point. I knew my time frame was dwindling. I begged for just a few thousand, some for me to help him get out of there and some for his kids to relieve that struggle and tension. I know money doesn't solve all things and it can create a lot more problems, especially in families; but I just needed some relief from the debt. I needed him to be able to get back to his kids and the only way to do that was to get him legal and out of active addiction, out of jail and paying them. Every time he came up for air or out of jail or rehab, it was costing my husband and I about $5000 between, gas, flights, food, housing arrangements to get him stable etc. This is even buying all his clothes and bags and supplies at thrift stores every time.

But thank God for unseen miracles. Thank goodness for blank slates, and open minds and hearts. And thank goodness for his friends and acquaintances in Vegas who MADE him go get help that day-even when they weren't in a responsible mindset themselves. All those times I had prayed for wisdom and compassion from people he would meet and who he was around, would ultimately save my son's life.

On May 28, 2022, he finally walked into a clinic in Vegas unable to breathe. He had told me a few days before that he was getting an infection and needed antibiotics. He said he had felt sick for about a month. The clinic immediately called an ambulance and transported him to a local ER where he was admitted into the ICU unit for Acute diastolic heart failure, acute respiratory failure, Acute sepsis, Hypertensive emergency, hypoxia, Normocytic anemia, pneumonia, unspecified organism, and shortness of breath with parainfluenza virus type 4. The hospital stay was filled with layers of confusion and mixed information about his condition.

We were told that his heart was failing. Congestive Heart Failure. Originally it was only functioning at 10%, then they upped it to 25%. Nine days later they told us that his vessels were fine and he was being discharged. He was excited, thinking the previous diagnoses must have been wrong. If I had not demanded to talk to the resident on call, my son may have left thinking he could go to his previously scheduled "program" and he surely would have died.

She gave a grim picture of yes, his heart was functioning at 10%, but the vessels leading to the heart were fine. Oh but, by the way, he did need a portable pacemaker life vest in case his heart stopped. We were completely unhappy with mixed information. I had to specifically request to speak to a doctor almost every other day to talk about a plan. They acted like I was crazy each time for wanting to know what was evolving with his condition and plan for discharge. I couldn't seem to make them understand that he was homeless but actively using, so he couldn't just "go home with us" until he's somewhat recovered. He also couldn't go back on the streets with a heart condition requiring medication, testing, and access to treatment. He was also looking at prison time. They adamantly stated that he cannot go to jail anytime soon, if ever. One doctor stated that he would need a rehab that could take care of his heart too. Those don't exist in that state, so I looked into transferring him to the local renowned teaching university hospital in my state. They said they couldn't facilitate a lower level of care transfer, and with his state insurance, so he was better off just riding it out there. This was all before he had woken up, so I guess I sounded premature to them. Plus, I requested a letter to be written to explain to the court what they had told me—that he needed specialty care if he survived at all. The nurse straight out told me that the doctors don't have time to write letters like that. I then walked into the nurse manager office, very unhappily, and received a non-physician signed letter stating he was there, at least.

Those eight days were extremely stressful, expensive, and draining. There was the hassle of arranging for me to stay in Vegas, including switching hotels three times. Liam made the twelve-hour drive home and back to bring me clothes before he flew out to Texas to go back to work.

On the morning of discharge, the lady who was supposed to bring the life vest called to say he wasn't at the hospital. I flew into panic mode. I grabbed my things to check out of the hotel and set off looking for him, all while making calls to the hospital. The operator confirmed that his name was not pulling up. His nurse in the ICU was busy and couldn't talk. I desperately needed the time that he had left to see how far he could be from the hospital. I called Haven in a complete panic and drove recklessly to the east side of the freeway past the hospital, but north of the strip, which is the worst part of town. I knew it was the most likely way he would have walked to get back to where he thought his truck was. I could not imagine him being able to walk out of there without collapsing, no heart medication, nothing. I was beside myself, thinking I would surely now find my son collapsed on the hot Vegas streets.

After all this, he was going to die in Vegas anyway! Finally, the nurse called me back and stated that he was in the room and he was fine. I couldn't believe it!! I told her the operator did not have him listed and told that to three people! She didn't know what the problem was but didn't have time to listen to me. She said he is probably being discharged anyway, because there's nothing more they can do for him since he's too well to be in ICU. What a rollercoaster. I walked in his room and said, "You're in trouble!"

He smiled and asked, "What now?"

He laughed, we laughed, as I told the story of him 'leaving.' God help me.

This time, the goal was the same as previous attempts at recovery. To get him well, back to his kids, and legal again. There was no other way to accomplish all that–than to get him back working again. To do that we needed to spend the time and money to get his license back and get rid of warrants. Previous attempts had always resulted in impatience in achieving that. Money was always, always the issue. Every time, he had to figure out how to get money quickly. Each of these steps takes time, usually weeks, months. This time, however, was different. This time he had family support. The family rallied around him, all driving hours and hours to see him in the hospital. First, it was the fear that he would pass away, then it was relief that he was alive. Everyone covered him in love. He was blown away. He was able to see his daughter for the first time in years and he could hardly believe the grace and honor of that. He watched the video of that reunion over and over again for the entire six-hour trip home with a smile on his face. This time I received offers of help. Callen paid $700 to get his truck out of impound. Luke paid $600 to help me with expenses when all my credit cards wouldn't work while I was living out of motels. Haven was ready and willing to do anything she could to help. She made up non-sodium gift baskets for him and bought him brand new shoes from the internet, no dollar store shoes this time! The mother of his children seemed supportive, concerned, and caring.

I finally had my own Red Bandana.

Could this finally be *our* Ubunta?

However, this recovery was tricky. Due to his diagnosis of heart failure, he couldn't jump gung-ho back into working. Honestly, we didn't know how long he had to live. The goal was to get his heart to forty-five percent. The cardiologist made it clear that the heart can only heal once. That gave him a lot to think about. I stayed pretty much by his side every day for two more weeks. After six months of not seeing him; now with a possible death sentence; I was not going to let anything stop me from being a witness to this miracle. I wanted to help him find his light to be the man he was meant to be in the time he had left. Before this, I had to worry about him dying from his addiction. Now, added to that was the fear of his heart failing for an early death. I was not going to forget the last few weeks sitting by his bedside in the ICU where I prayed for his life to be spared. I was now going to celebrate his aliveness and not worry about the future. Of course, I wanted to help him find his groove, in spite of this new devastating news. I wanted him to find joy again, be with his kids, and be able to have plans for life, all with as little stress as possible on his heart. I had to let go of expectations for perfection in his path. This is where the family recovery part was crucial. I had to be ready for this. I had been to countless meetings (at least fifty), listened to over thirty live Zoom meetings of recovered SUD people, and read over forty books by this time.

I had to implement my skills of backing off, letting him lead his recovery, and his path. I had to give him the respect of his right to heal and take in this life-changing diagnosis. I had to not panic if he was sleeping a lot or if I saw a stick of gum wrapper in tin foil and not jump to conclusions and accusations.

The last six months of minimal contact was made clearer, when I saw how little he was on his phone. I saw how he hated texting. Especially with a cheap phone always with a broken screen that's hard to see and use. I saw how my constant demands for re-assurance must have been overwhelming due to all the moving parts of his life, and the need to overhaul every bit of it.

I now understood how much "easier" it would appear to be to go back to using and why so many do. To avoid responsibility? You could look at it in that negative aspect if you want to but comparatively, we all put off things in our life that seem overwhelming. Especially with the intense pressure that hits someone in recovery to fix everything.

Each day was one more day I had with him, one more day for his heart to heal a little, and one more day that I could help guide him toward better habits and a less stressful life so he could be there for his kids. We had our own Lazarus time. It was wonderful and everything I had imagined the last three years.

Mason's life was a 180-degree turn from what it had been. I was able to see his brain come alive and swirling with thoughts. I saw how he tried desperately to formulate a plan for his life for work again.

I now understood all those posts of moms who were impatient with their loved ones right out of recovery and that they seemed unmotivated or lazy.

Victor Hugo stated, "A man is not idle because he is absorbed in thought. There is visible and invisible labor. To contemplate is to toil. To think is to do."

Having a purpose and motivation to move toward something is huge for him, as for most people. His entrepreneurial mindset requires him to think big in order to "succeed."

In the 1964 book *The Transparent Self,* author Sidney M. Jourad states, "Frankl (1955) has argued that unless a man can see meaning and value in his continued existence, his morale will deteriorate, his immunity will decrease, and he will sicken more readily, or even commit suicide."[73]

This time, the allure of hustling and scavenging seemed like a death sentence and very well would have been. Instead, he slowly started to get his old mindset back—his entrepreneurial drive, his leadership skills, his lofty goals and dreams.

I witnessed his complete gratitude for his brother Luke who changed this entire course of this recovery for him. The Luke who told me this obsession was ruining my life. Luke who refused to hug me two years ago. He had told me when Mason was still unconscious, "tell him I'm coming to get him to pour cement." I thought that was noble of him, but I failed to have faith that he would offer him a few hours of work a week to get stronger and get back into the trade that they had started some 13 years earlier. This was a huge relief because what other company would let him work a few hours a day? Applying for disability or any services was out of the question with warrants and ORS back debt; not to mention the IRS massive debt.

He suffered during this time with painful teeth and jaw pain from the years of ignoring them. I tried to make him a dentist appointment knowing full well the connection to heart infections that teeth can quickly go to. He was overwhelmed and could only think of getting his warrants cleared. He was nervous about going anywhere, as he knew they were going to pull him into jail. Despite the devastating heart failure diagnosis, he was still facing three new felonies and a probation violation from his previous plea deal to two, third-degree felonies and one misdemeanor.

---

[73] https://www.amazon.com/Transparent-Self-Revised-Sidney-Jourard/dp/0442782713

We were unbelievably lucky to have found a wonderful lawyer for these new charges. He patiently waited this whole time but he now needed money in order to represent him.

Once again Luke came to the rescue for that. Mason started working a few hours every other day with nap breaks. As he increased his hours out in the hot summer sun, with frequent dizzy spells, it was clear that life was not going to give him a break despite his condition. He was dizzy often, and finally after a few weeks, when the pain was unbearable, he asked me to help him find a dentist. He had not been to a dentist in fourteen years but surprisingly there were only a few cavities, one root canal, three extractions, two of them wisdom teeth. He did a seven-day course of antibiotics first then had the extractions a few weeks later–on his own time.

In my poem to my son in the chapter ***Unfinished***, I write, "One day my son ... *will feel the warmth of **the sun on his tanned face.***

A few weeks into his post-ICU heart failure diagnoses and healthy sobriety, he sent me this text.

I really don't know if I agree with the serotonin level thing, because I've had no problem being happy doing nothing. Like sitting in a lawn chair, I'm perfectly balanced. Maybe almost dying, having my brain shift to basic survival for a few weeks, gave me a different scenario. I don't know. It might be different if I was in a different situation, like stuck in a hell hole still. If all your world has to offer is jail or being stuck with no clear option then it would be way different than your best option to feel better is obviously getting high. It all makes sense now.

*He finally had the **sun on his tanned face.***

My son was repeating the Freedom Model almost word for word. He was living it. He was proof that people have choice, and humans will almost always choose the happiest option. Who are we to judge that of another? Who are we to force someone into a treatment center that has methods of recovery that don't jive with them? Who are we to tell them "Haven't you had enough?" Haven't you learned your lesson?" And who are we to tell them what exactly is *best for them* and that complete abstinence is the only way they can earn our love back.

This will be my success story. I will think of my boy sitting on a lawn chair in the sun, having a moment of happiness. He will be reflecting on his journey and the future that only he can experience. Whatever the future holds, my wish for him is more moments of happiness than pain, more relief than strife, and more layers of love than hate. My job was never to change him or fix him. My job was only to love him. In that sense, like millions of other moms, I won.

You will teach them to fly,
but they will not fly your flight.
You will teach them to dream,
but they will not dream your dream.
You will teach them to live,
but they will not live your life.
Nevertheless, in every flight,
in every life, in every dream,
the print of the way you taught will always remain.
—Mother Teresa

Acknowledgements

Liam, thank you for doing things that you may not have believed in, but you believed in ME. From the tops of parking garages with binoculars and drones, to the middle of the night in the desert, you were my knight in the darkness hero and I will forever be grateful for the exact time you came into my life.

I know you showed up wanting to be the knight in shining armor that saves the day and rescues the maiden, but this isn't that kind of story.
I'm not saying you can't be heroic and amazing, but I don't need to be saved, completed or fixed.
I just need someone who'll stand beside me through the tough times when I'm fighting to make myself better and I'm doing my best to love myself.
Truth is, I would love someone to hold my hand and cheer me on when the going gets hard, because I'll need all the support I can get.
Maybe it's not the fairy tale ending you had planned, but it's real, it's genuine and it's the kind of love that lasts.
We don't live in a world of glass slippers and swashbuckling, and I don't want or need a hero.
I need someone to be real with me when the world gets hard.
I want someone who can love me when I'm not easy to love.
I need someone who will stand beside me, be strong and sometimes carry the load when it gets too heavy for me.
It doesn't mean that I'm weak or can't handle life. It's just that every so often, I get tired.
Not because I need more sleep, but because sometimes, I'm just weary.
So, if you really want to be a hero, those are the times you can step up, shoulder the load and let me rest for a moment.
Let me take a breath so I can come back stronger and better.
Because in the end, it'll be you and me versus the world.
It's not your job to do it all and there's going to be times when I need a hand.
Together, we can get through it all.

I know it's hard for you to stand aside and let me fight my battles, but I can overcome anything that comes at me.
Let me do what I have to do, struggle and rise again because you can't go there for me.
And I don't want you to.
Let me be the person I'm working hard to become and be my biggest cheerleader like I'll always be for you.
Because sometimes, at the end of a long hard day, it's just a great thing to just hear you say "way to go" with a long hug.
When it's all said and done, I don't need a hero or a knight in shining armor.
I just want you to be my safe place to lay my head ... where my heart will always be safe.
That's my best version of happily ever after.
—Ravenwolf, *Be a Voice, Not an Echo* (Used with permission.)

My firstborn, Haven: From identifying an earlobe on a blurry picture to driving 800 miles with me over and over, you never turned me down for help with your first best friend. Thank you for always bringing me back to reality. I will always be grateful for your ability to calm my frazzled mind and heart. Your love for your brother is palpable and I believe you suffered more than anyone knows with how to best help him.

Callan, I'm sorry for not seeing your silent pain for so long. The middle child who seems to get left behind, yet you never manifested victimhood. You agonized silently over how to help Mason and I see you and honor you.
You always have a special place in my heart for your sweet spirit and old soul whose love and concern spreads warmly through all who love you.

Luke, I can't even begin to tell you how you made me believe in heroes. I never would have anticipated your strength, honor, and level of maturity you fostered after Mason's diagnosis. You have my undying gratefulness for stepping up to the gate and showing up in love. I begged many famous and rich people to take Mason under his wing and bring him back to the fold, not knowing that it would be you who would be the one. My faith was weak in times of strife. Thank you for renewing that faith and hope and allowing Mason to reunite with all his nieces and nephews and make memories for a summer that won't be forgotten.

Rylee, in the midst of some of the hardest struggles you've faced, you still showed up many times for Mason and for me. Your silent love and admiration and concern for your brother was evident many times to me as you struggled with what to say or do. I will always be grateful for our adventures and for the unspoken acceptance of each of us. You are a beautiful soul.

To my grandkids' mother, thank you for taking care of the babies. I will forever be grateful that you had family around and the stability to give them safety and lots of love. I am always sad that I couldn't be more helpful and supportive in your journey. I hope you will someday forgive me. I cherish our many years of sweet memories and fun adventures.

To *The* Kevin Gates fan, thank you for allowing the time and space for my intense fear and emotional outbreaks. You patiently watched and listened to my verbal montage of anger, mixed with hope of some new idea or plan. You brought me back to center with reality without ever dishonoring Mason. Your emotional strength and fortitude grounded me and kept me from sinking further. You are a true friend to him who understands loyalty and unconditional love with boundaries.

To Mason, what can I say? This book is a testament to your strength, persistence, and true grit that you needed to survive through many dark moments. Your deepest thoughts and struggles may never be written on a page but just know that many times I saw your pain. I saw the tears you wiped away. I saw the lump in your throat. I saw the far away lost look in your eyes when you were hurt by words and actions that cut deeply. You still amaze me with your courage through all of this. You are some sort of enigma who never gives up. When I told you that once you said, "Is that a person who has seizures?" No, that's a different E word. I always say I don't know where you came from and I am not sure where you are going, but I know wherever it is, my bond and love with you and for you will never end.

To my editor for your unyielding patience, I would have quit many times over if not for you. Your charity, clarity and encouragement of my skills were a game-changer. Your ability to pull me back to earth and appreciate my own story and the need to share it was paramount.

To my early readers and supporters who always asked about my state of mind and how Mason was doing, and to all the people who kept supporting me through all my questioning and confusion: thank you.

Maureen, Denise, Mickie, Carrie, Rebecca, Justin and Christopher: thank you.

To the people who didn't support me, I understand. Addiction is a crapshoot, but also a unique opportunity to discover new ideas and communication skills that transfer into other areas of life. Even if addiction doesn't affect you, the face of adversity and darkness will hit everyone at some point in time. Luckily, we all get to choose how we respond with what skills we have learned.

Tidbits of Wisdom

If you are an unwelcome new participant in this journey of navigating through addiction, here are some things I've learned that might help you, depending on your situation. But first, what WASN'T helpful to me when I was looking for answers was the one size fits all answers such as:

He/she will never change. Hogwash. People change all the time.

Thirty days of rehab is not enough. Sometimes, one day/minute/hour is enough to change a mind/heart. Let them lead their recovery and be there to celebrate every step forward with them.

Marijuana slash alcohol slash Xanax slash any mood-altering substance isn't as bad as XYZ. ANY. THING. That takes you away from being your best self is just as bad. Don't compare experiences or pain. Pain is pain.

"They made their own bed; they can sleep in it", as my dad used to say. We have no way of being in someone's mind to see what choices they "perceived" to be the "only" choices. Their behaviors make sense to them
Mental illness and drugs skew thinking into narrow tunnels that they perceive as their only option.

Addiction is a choice. I used to lie out on my roof on the old silver tanning blankets, WITH ONLY CRISCO ON MY FACE. I never once thought this might lead me to die of melanoma. This is how I think of the consequences of a person in chaotic drug use. We all have heard of the consequences, but we never ever think they will happen to us. I do believe we all choose the happiest option at the time regardless of whether the brain is functioning fully or not.

Don't believe anything the person with a substance use disorder says. If you understand the compulsion and obsession that they must have in order to continue to use, then it becomes clearer why everything they say and do goes toward their main agenda. That agenda is **to get more drugs to reach their dopamine levels and not be sick or achieve some sort of balance emotionally**. The problem is that in severe chaotic use, the brain doesn't have the reasoning or executive functioning to weigh risks versus benefits. The dopamine levels that most drugs reach are unattainable with normal everyday pleasures until almost a year without use. I believe this is one reason they relapse. The hard part is not accusing the person with a substance use disorder of lying every single time, because they will defend themselves fervently. We have this mistaken belief that if we can just PROVE what they are saying is untrue, they will suddenly give up their whole game, like a cop trying to elicit a confession. Addiction isn't like that. By using the substance again and again, it creates the neural pathways that are REQUIRED for the drug *and the lifestyle or support the drug use*, thereby causing the person to fall into these habits of deceit and dishonor over and over again. They *must* believe that they are telling the truth for it to keep working. Its survival. Just like an old dirt road during a storm, its thirsty dust welcomes the fresh water to come along for the ride, forcing it into the two sections that the car needs to put its tires into. This occurs over and over, forcing the grooves deeper and deeper down the mountain. The grooves are filled with untruths and poor choices. To clear out those grooves requires complete repaving and grading of that road. Continuing to insist to them that the sky is blue only pushes relationships apart and pushes them deeper into their defensiveness.

We do the same thing with our conditioning. When someone hits our triggers, we start getting defensive, if we haven't worked through them. We see a name on our phone text and our feathers start rising to be ruffled. It's 11 o'clock-time, time to be offended or stressed or worried. It takes a lot of inner work to create blank slates of love, intention and giving someone a whole lot of grace.

Ok. Now, the helpful tips.
Please seek out professional advice regarding taxes, insurance, and custody issues. I am only sharing what I have learned.

Be non-reactive but concerned. Acknowledge every move forward without adding loads of suggestions and expectations. Don't act like they are going to relapse any second. They need hope and the benefit of the doubt but not to where it will set YOU back financially or emotionally because you are again basing your emotions and finances on their entire recovery. **Consult a physician about antidepressants or a non-addictive mood stabilizer.**

Don't confuse boundaries with cruelty. It's always about the delivery. What we enforce can be a bridge to a more loving connection or can nullify hope. Shutting someone down may feel freeing in the moment but it has an underlying tone of moral superiority. Reducing this "heart of war" can drastically improve relationships and therefore outcomes. If nothing else it offers dignity to our person that they are worthy of figuring out a better way–if only just for today. There is zero evidence that being mean and nasty and treating someone in a dehumanizing manner leads to lasting change. In fact it does more harm as it pushes them deeper in shame, regret and isolation. Boundaries can be shown in a healthy, dignified manner which offers hope and compassion. I love Nicole Labor's YouTube talk: The Neurobiology of Addiction Addiction 101 in Olson because she talks about the brain changes which drive their personality and behaviors.

If your addicted child is a minor, you have more options, even if it seems like you have no control. Let them know actions have consequences by taking away privileges with kindness, not anger and disdain. If you start feeling resentment and vindictiveness, counseling for you is a must to help turn your "heart of war" into something more helpful. Enlist counselors to help recommend programs that are a fit for your child.

Make sure they are properly evaluated for underlying conditions which almost always contributes to continued desire to use. I am convinced part of my son's addiction started with an Adderall prescription. I truly believe that the drugs actually helped him "feel" normal for a minute. Or did "taking a pill" make it worse? Maybe had he kept taking it as directed, he would have felt better. I wish I could have known about evaluation with a mental health professional using the health relief model or theory of planned behavior.

It might have warned us of his higher risk, but then again, it might not have. At the least, have them evaluated by a neutral, competent psychologist who is an expert in personality disorder and can test for depression and anxiety disorders such as conduct disorder. At the same time, be cautious about throwing a fix-it-all drug on them too. The strategic marketing of a fix-it-all product, pill, vacation, car, or house to solve all our problems is one of the things we need to have constant conversations about when they are small and impressionable. Use experiences and achievements to work through how they feel. These accomplishments are great for self-esteem but does it make them dependent on outside sources for their happiness? Teach them about healthy sources for dopamine. I think this is HUGE! Especially with more and more electronic stimulation to take up the time of kids and teens. Teach them to trust their own bodies and minds as to when they need self-care and self-regulation. Not what a commercial or TikTok video says they need.

Don't buy them anything expensive. When my son was in rehab out of state, I sent him an electric razor that I found out later he tweaked (sorry) it into a tattoo gun and sold it. Use thrift stores for clothes and necessities.

Don't downplay a "lesser" addiction. Every kid HAS TO try alcohol, right? Or pot, or smoking. No, actually they don't, but if they are one of the many teens who do try it, AND they have the propensity for addiction (yes there may be an actual gene[74]), they are at an increased risk to move onto other drugs at worst, and at least they are more likely

---

[74] https://www.sciencedirect.com/science/article/abs/pii/S000689931200813X

to have a dozen other problems that underage drinking causes. Keep having the conversation over and over, not just once.[75] Don't buy into the idea that every kid has to try it. They don't. And the effects on the prefrontal cortex of alcohol before it's fully developed at twenty-two or twenty-six, is becoming more known. I wish I had paid more attention to this.

What recovery looks like to you may not be what it looks like to them. Most of us who have been through the wringer have been told what offers the most success. Voluntary detox. Voluntary rehab, thirty to ninety days. Sober living six months to a year. MAT,[76] buprenorphine, methadone, naltrexone (opioids), acamprosate, disulfiram (alcohol), Vivitrol (opioids and alcohol), Sublocade, Campral (for alcohol), and/or a plan to increase the dopamine levels naturally without relapse. But remember our method for recovery and theirs are completely different. Even though we probably do know best in this case (ha ha), it's not going to work long-term if they don't have a say in it. Actual true *lasting* recovery involves the addict's autonomy and full participation in what **HE PERCEIVES AS THE BETTER OPTION**. Rehab isn't for everyone, my son especially. ANY FORWARD MOTION is (or should be) considered recovery.

Don't go buy a pink elephant and put it on the front lawn. So many times, I read a new article, or watched a video, or saw a motivational quote and sent it to my son excitedly, "Look what I found!" Hijacked brain or not, no one wants to be told what to do, what to read, and where to go and how to get there. So, even if you saw a giant pink elephant in a vacant yard, and you got permission to buy it, and you hired a crane company to come and lift it out and put it on a big truck that you also hired, and then you had the big truck haul it to your house, and you sprayed it off with the hose then called your loved one and said, "LOOK! LOOK at what I got you! It's perfect, it will change your life!"

---

[75] https://learn.genetics.utah.edu/content/addiction/genes/
[76] https://www.samhsa.gov/medication-assisted-treatment

and he or she says, "What am I gonna do with that?" To us, we take great pleasure in getting things done, cleaning, finding the perfect candle smell, getting our car registered, going to the dentist (well, maybe not that), and taking out the trash. These things are normal, boring things we take for granted, but not every brain derives any kind of purpose for doing those things. When the brain is hyper focused on what it sees as the most important for survival; other things that give pleasure and a sense of accomplishment are meaningless. This fact causes so much strife in families because we just can't see why they don't care. Not to say that we can't plant a seed, but if you can **"meet them where they are,"** with compassion and hope, then maybe you can draw them into wanting those things again. Right now, to just be there when they do talk, so that they'll talk more, is progress. (Look up motivational interviewing).

Understand the job of attorneys and court officials. Stick to facts. Your child broke the law. As unfair as the laws may be. The lawyer isn't there to plead how unfair a law is and to change it. They are not your counselors. They are not your child's counselors.

Hire a lawyer or use a public defender? This is different for everyone. There are times that a public defender will do just fine but remember they are paid by the state like the prosecutors and *may* have their own agendas and quotas to meet. My daughter said they do all eat lunch together. We couldn't afford the 2 attorneys we hired but we chose to do it anyway due to certain situations such as having warrants and needing them to pull them and schedule a hearing. Public defenders are available once you are arrested and sometimes you can't wait for that. There are lawyers that are invaluable and worth every credit card statement and there are other ones who are against their own clients from the start.

The legal system is expensive, so don't get mad when they won't do the leg work. YOU DO all you can to get info. They usually don't know anything about rehabs, insurance, withdrawals, suicide or overdose rates, co-pays, relapse rates etc. They are in the courtroom all day and usually only see that perspective. That's what they get paid to do.

Get Power of Attorney as soon as possible. It is paramount in talking to rehabs/banks/bill collectors/insurance/pharmacies if they are in jail or the hospital or in active chaotic use with no phone etc. This lets you advocate for them. Don't be afraid to use it proactively especially when you feel embarrassed that your person won't take care of things. Say, "My child has severe substance use disorder and is unhoused. I am trying to help them get stable with basic necessities so they can move forward. Can we work out the details beforehand to help facilitate this?"

Get your child on state health insurance asap or keep them on your policy as long as possible. Documented substance use is protected under the Americans with Disabilities Act so they can be on your insurance policy AFTER age 26. You just have to actively ask for the right paperwork to fill out prior to their 26th birthday and get them to a clinic or detox at least once before then. Some states may vary.

Get a life insurance policy or at least burial costs for your child as early as possible. Do this BEFORE treatment shows that your child has a SUD. Otherwise, he or she may have to be clean for five years for some companies.

Car insurance is a case-by-case basis and is a lot riskier. I would always make sure to have liability– preferably **in your child's name,** even if you have to pay it.

Save any money possible for rehab expenses (copays and needed items), sober living expenses, and early recovery. This is needed because until your child can get on his or her feet while still going to inpatient, outpatient, and court; they don't have the time or means to earn money in the short term. Give gifts of bus passes, laundromat usage, regular food delivery or anything to keep some measure of dignity and health.

Don't be public enemy number one. The best advice I received, from all my reaching out for help, was from a man in long term recovery. "Listen, your son is NOT going to listen to you. He HAS TO FIGURE IT OUT ON his own. He KNOWS he's an addict. He KNOWS he's in debt. He knows he has failed. He knows he has hurt people. But he sees YOU as the gatekeeper to all that because YOU ARE ALWAYS ON HIS CASE. YOU are the face of the enemy in his eyes. Yes, everyone else has given up on him, but YOU, throwing it in his face every day (disguised as a solution because yes, we think we have all the solutions for them) just makes him withdraw." Craft methods and Beyond addiction workbooks help facilitate these conversations.

Be kind. The more of my own recovery that I accessed and the more I conserved my energy away from negative support sites and doomsday thinking–the more empathy I had and less anger. The unnecessary cruelness and constant lecturing just pushed him further away. Beyond Addiction, Craft methods, and Anatomy of Peace help humanize addiction and soften hearts in order to be more effective. The success rates of these methods are measurable and documented. The goal is to strengthen bonds, not weaken them. The addiction does enough of that, it doesn't need our help.

Self-Compassion

When I was going through my dark times, the few people who I confided in all said the same thing. "You have to take care of yourself, girl! Self-Care, Self-Care". I hated that word! I didn't want it to be about me. I wanted my son better. I told them "don't worry about me. All I do is self-care. I go home from work to my comfortable house on my comfy couch, watch TV, read, cry, cry, and cry. All I do is CARE about MYSELF. Because that's all I CAN do."

I learned that I had to use this time to focus on something FOR ME, not just sulking in misery. No one in my circle was asking me how I was doing with all this, but I wasn't asking them how they were doing either. We were all in our own silent pain, secretly wondering why the other didn't feel the way we did. Slowly, as I learned more and more about addiction and the devastating effects it has on the family, I realized how important boundaries are. Boundaries that I regularly blurred. I was constantly trying to stick up for my son by begging people to have compassion for him. Each of those relationships imploded. I thought they didn't care what his problem was, or why, or where. That was a double stab into my already bleeding heart. I wonder now why did I insist everyone have my same experience?

Everyone views the world and particular situations through their own lens. Some through a wounded lens that everyone is going to hurt them eventually. Some through a childlike lens (like my sweet mama) without any real data or information. It's like the dog with the cone around its neck. Until those areas are healed, they will only see what they want to see. This applies to people who are addicted and every other personality who isn't.

To a hammer, everything looks like a nail.

When I finally dropped the martyr syndrome that I was my son's save-all, I was able to let others feel as they may. I learned that my relationship with each of those people DID NOT HAVE TO BE BASED ON WHETHER THEY UNDERSTOOD AND FELT THE SAME AS ME, and it certainly did not hinge on whether he was recovering or still out there using. I had to force myself to re-get-to-know my other family members without the topic being the prodigal son.

Emotional Energy

People who haven't lived in daily grief or trauma can't fully understand the concept of harnessing emotional energy. Emotional energy is everything. It's fueled by dopamine, which drives motivation, direction, priorities, and purpose. Nutrition and exercise help immensely. When we are not taking care of ourselves AND are hyper focused on one particular problem we become very imbalanced in our lives. I can't stress enough to find a system of habits to restore serotonin and other neurotransmitters that are needed in this rollercoaster ride. It took me quite a while to convey to my husband that my lack of effort or neglect of his feelings and needs wasn't due to being cruel or lazy. At one point in working out the kinks to our new marriage and discovering each other's triggers, I found myself in my bedroom with a mouthful of bullets that I had put there myself in an attempt to self-regulate how I was feeling. Even though our fight that day had nothing to do with my addicted son, my conflict resolution skills were zero. My emotional stores were empty. I had nothing left to give. Any new or perceived problem or situation requiring my attention seemed too daunting to even address, let alone solve.

Some people call it buckets. Fill up your own bucket so you have something to take out. I see it as a reservoir. Reservoirs are meant to store water for future needs. They are usually built or formed for a good purpose. The reservoir of our human body and mind is amazing. I work with eating disorder patients whose bodies handle months and years of abuse through binging and purging and restricting food. It's not until they see blood in their vomit or until a parent notices their behaviors or sees their self-harm marks and/or doctor insists they get help that they come to us for help. They think their bodies will adjust to their self-abuse. After seeking help, just like with addiction, trying to unravel the thought patterns that kept them ill and in their behaviors requires time and various methods of treatment. They may become hyper focused on their secret, and nothing may seem to matter. As loved ones, we get hyper focused on saving them and meanwhile lose ourselves little by little along the way.

It wasn't just my husband who got what was left of me. It was my other kids, my grandkids, and my job. I literally had to count my walking steps into work just to force myself to get through the doors. I once told my boss to please tell my coworkers not to talk so loud and not to talk in a sing-song voice and please don't do this or that. I mean, who did I think I was?

My co-workers at that job only knew me as this strained, nerve wracked, saddened, pathetic person. This person who completely hid her personal life from them. I avoided any small talk, family talk or joking around. This was not who I had been in years past. I used to be a fun person. A driven person. I always had a second job or a project I was working on. But the past 4 years, I had nothing to give. The emotional energy it takes to grieve daily and wait for the other shoe to drop is exhausting.

I remember sitting at my grandson's baseball game with my daughter when her friend came up and started talking about her problems with housing. As I listened to her frustrating story of having to move so her husband, a highway patrolman, would be in the boundaries of his work (within fifteen miles, and they were seventeen miles or something ridiculous like that); I actually felt another person's problems for a minute! I had been so immersed in my tragedy the last eighteen months, without any patience or regard for others' (seemingly minor) problems, that I had lost my empathy for others. It was a wake-up call to forge new and better relationships and listen, for heck's sake!

I had to find a way to get emotionally healthy. Besides the therapy and zoom meetings, I started with painting rocks. I bought a bag of river rocks and all the fancy paints. Soon, I found that I sucked at it. Plus, the activity kept me home with my miserable thoughts, so I became interested in rockhounding. I already loved hiking in the mountains on the weekends, and this was a great addition to that. Rockhounding brings out the treasure hunter in all of us. It's basically being an amateur geologist by searching for and studying of rocks, gems, minerals.

My dad was a huge rockhounder and I remember roaming the hills with him as a child.

It didn't take me long to be completely immersed in it. I can truly say that it saved me from my own self destruction. Hey, some people cover their feelings with substances; I collect rocks. I don't just mean pick up a rock or two here and there. I mean buying the pickaxes, the chisels, the rock hammers, guidebooks and joining a rockhounding club. Liam and I went to Wyoming to dig for blue, sixty-million-year-old, petrified wood, to Texas for three-foot walls of oyster fossils, and to

Yellowstone in Montana. When Liam was out of town, I took my youngest daughter or my grandsons with me to the desert and walked around in the hot sun with buckets and a shovel. Liam and I paid $100 and took the grandsons to go chip off colorful bubble opal in the middle of Utah's desert. I would climb mountains and slide all the way down because my fifty-three-year-old legs couldn't maneuver the descent while Liam climbed to the top to get my treasure. I made friends with geologists and had them on speed dial to ask what a particular gem was. I would go visit mine tailings with the risk of old explosives buried there, and Liam would bring his pickaxe and patiently chip vesuvianite off the hard granite wall of rock. Interestingly, vesuvianite has healing properties tied to the heart chakra. It releases pent-up anger in a gentle way that helps an individual find emotional balance.[77] *I needed emotional balance.*

Sometimes, out in the mountains, I would be overcome with sadness because I knew how much my son loved the outdoors. My heart would ache knowing he wasn't doing anything remotely like that. He had called me on the 4th of July one year, normally one of our favorite holidays. My family members were all still sort of fighting, so Liam and I went camping in Idaho that weekend with friends. My son rarely asked me for anything except once in a while a hamburger when he was out on the streets for a long time. This time he said he wanted to do something for the holiday. I think he was asking for money, but I was not sure. I asked what he wanted to do. He said to go swimming or something fun. A glimpse of my old, adventurous boy. I think he was desperately missing his kids but couldn't do anything about it except bury the pain. I hung up the phone and just cried. I wanted us to all go camping again. His favorite person and hero had just died, his grandpa, and I know he was still deeply hurting from that. He wasn't able to go to the services because of his addiction circumstances. I would have gladly given him a shuttle ride the three hours to the service, but he never asked. Because of Covid that year, his court cases were delayed, which took the pressure

---

[77] https://www.firemountaingems.com/resources/encyclobeadia/gem-notes/ha5x

off him having to comply with anything. That left me with several months of so-called "freedom".

The rocks gave me an obsession to fill that time, besides my son. I still had my days. Wondering where he was, what he was doing, if he was eating. But that Messenger obsession of not seeing him online and panicking lessened. I could actually go a week or two without too much panic.

In the early morning hours, I would sometimes wake up in a panic, wondering if he was shot or overdosed somewhere. I would do one look at my phone to make sure there wasn't a missed call or message, then have to get up and go wrap myself in my weighted blanket and lay on the couch. There in the dark, I would stare at my porcelain, lit wax melter as it cast its shadows on the wall. While I cried in a fit of sadness, I soon noticed that it made a huge glowing heart on the wall. That glowing heart gave me (and still does) such warmth and hope that everything would be okay as I drifted back to sleep.

One night as I was lying in the dark, I looked toward the distressed end table where another candle warmer sat among the many frames holding childhood pictures of my kids. I saw with surprise as another spotlight pointed at one of my favorite pictures of my kids taken many years ago in our backyard with the beautiful Utah mountains rising behind them. My five innocent children, who were soon to be shown the realities of the world stood smiling in the summer son next to my sweet dad, may he rest in peace. I noticed the glow of the tiny light shown exactly onto my eldest son's tall teenage face. Out of six people in that picture, why him? Because he was the struggling one. He was the prodigal right now. I wept in tears at this sign of hope. A heart of light projected onto the wall and now a glow spread onto my son's young face full of such hope and laughter.

Soothe Yourself in Love

The story *The Velveteen Rabbit* was written in 1922 by Margery Williams. It shares the process of getting a real Heart by being loved by its owner. By becoming strong and worn out, willing to be burned to save its owner's life it transcends into a real heart, knowing true love.

> *"Real isn't how you are made," said the Skin Horse. "It's a thing that happens to you. That's why it doesn't happen often to people who break easily or have sharp edges, or who have to be carefully kept."*
> *"Does it hurt?' asked the Rabbit.*
> *"Sometimes," said the Skin Horse, for He was always truthful.*
> *—Velveteen Rabbit*
> *"When you are real you don't mind being hurt." – Velveteen Rabbit. `*
> *"Does it happen all at once, like being wound up,' He asked, "or bit by bit?"[78]*

I think we can all agree that being hurt and can be very depressing too. Scrolling through the posts is like a twilight zone of drama, chaos, fear and even death. Every few days someone would post that they got THE CALL. I knew it was time to close up Facebook for the day then. Some groups are also very toxic as unhealed people who are full of fears, say very horrible things about their struggling loved ones. This creates a depressing environment where it's hard to find hope and figure out how to be effective in helping the situation. Your nervous system can't relax if you are in the fire wondering where the exits are. Turn it off. Distance yourself from toxic people and places. Triggers that bring out your worst fears or insecurities. Take a bath. Breathe through your belly. Do box breathing.. (think Pacman). Get a massage. Yin Yoga, Medication, mindfulness, music that relaxes you. When you find yourself getting worn down and depressed, then it's time to upload your nervous system to move forward. Dancing is one of my all-time favorite activities. It

---

[78] https://everydaypower.com/velveteen-rabbit-quotes/

used to be going out to singles groups and country music dances, but now it's at home in my living room. Going for a nature walk, hike or bike. Vinyasa style yoga. I have a native American dance I do in the mornings called Dallas Arcand Pow Wow dance aerobics. I even bought a hula hoop with lights in it to use with his hoop dance. Painting is a great stress reliever. Go get some cheap canvases at Walmart, some cheap brushes, and a pack of the little jars of paint and just paint anything. You can start with a rainbow. Paint over it if you hate it. Or throw on some 80's music or some Don Coen music and paint a wall. Seriously, so relaxing. One of my favorite YouTube videos to watch is Traveling Robert. Especially the Original *Traveling to the West Episode* in 2018 I believe. I promise you will forget your problems for 2 hours. Another video that will keep you relaxed and peaceful is: *2 years alone, Building log cabins like our forefathers.* He is a 21-year-old from Sweden with no building experience. Even if you don't like cabins or dogs, you will find yourself enthralled at what he is doing and building next. Creativity is a great stress reliever, even if it's watching someone else create something wonderful. If you need some background music videos and are not scripture savvy like me, a YouTube video I love is INRI motivation. It is a spiritual vibe but so soothing to listen to and watch. It is geared toward anxiety, depression and worry by using short scripture stories to show strength and faith. It uses parables that a motivational speaker might use to help with struggles. It's very soothing, even if you need to replace the word God for your own beliefs. Maybe the word Truth, Or My Higher Self. My husband and I giggle a little at the apparently easiest videographer job on the planet. They get to just point and shoot at every single person's side profile in front of a blurred-out background while rotating a little to the front. If you just want peace, watch "Music That Is NO Longer on the Radio" on YouTube.

I started a website Samantha-waters.com where I could post all my articles on addiction even if no one was reading. Trying to find the balance of "saving him" and "saving me" was the goal. One post I wrote was called white on rice. It's about spilled rice and how each grain represents one problem in life. When there is a pile of problems they become so overwhelming, it's paralyzing. It takes excruciating patience to focus on picking up one piece at a time. I wrote it in relation to my son, but it also applies to everything else we, ourselves are unable to pay attention to because we are so hyper focused on this "problem.

By far, my best therapy for help in my constant obsession with my son's addiction was writing this book. It saved my sanity when I felt lost and alone with no one to talk to.

A thought would come to me while driving or at work, and I couldn't wait to get home to write it down. I spent hours listening to audiobooks on addiction and mental health.

I found myself aching to use all that I was experiencing for good— to help others feel hope, to teach that it's okay to feel all these tormenting emotions. You CAN be in this space of chaos, not knowing how the story will end but living out *your* story of finding beauty and peace while helping your loved one and others have a morsel of hope. Or at least make someone's journey less painful.

When you become comfortable with uncertainty, infinite possibilities open up in your life. — Eckhart Tolle

A Final Note of Encouragement and Hope

In summary, this journey is exhausting. I get it. In all the madness and despair, please don't forget where your power lies. *Your power lies in you.* Your power lies in your ability to turn pain into love. Not by changing others, but by changing yourself. You can't feel hopeful when you are always in fear and moping in sorrow and agony. Movement is SO important to feel relief, hope, faith. Make your body move. It frees your mind and clears your head. Let the tears fall to clear out all the feelings of despair. Imagine them washing your fears away. Just like the smell of the air after a rainstorm, its freshness holds the promise of a new breeze of hope, of the faith of sunlight in the morning. Use your tears to empower yourself. *Breathe life into your loved ones.* Pray, send good vibes *constantly.* Not by begging, which only brings back your powerlessness and lack of control. *DECLARE* health and healing. Say: "*I can't wait to see you (shine, feel proud, feel loved and content, smile, feel free, feel respected, again)*". Manifest life and love to everyone in your family, free of expectations and judgements. You will never have to fear the last goodbye because your loved ones will always be safe and loved in your own heart.

You may not know the **HOW**,
But you always know the **WHY.**
Because of Love.
That's why.

Hope is like the sun. If you only believe it when you see it, you'll never make it through the night.
—Leia Organa *Star Wars, The Last Jedi*

About the Author

Samantha Waters is a wife, nurse, mother of five, and grandmother of thirteen. She describes herself as a "selective empath and book hoarder." A lifelong private journalist, Waters is a lover of photos and keeper of memories. Waters lives with her husband in between the steep Wasatch Mountain Range and the Great Basin Desert. She strives to help parents of loved ones advocate for addiction and recovery reform and to remove stigma and judgment from those struggling.

Helpful Books on Addiction:

This is just a quick summary of books that I read in my two-year deep dive into this treatable condition. These might be helpful depending on where you're at in your journey. Obviously, the books about ADHD, entrepreneurs, and prison caught my attention more. Different authors and different formats will appeal to everyone individually. I know it gets expensive, so I hope this helps others decide what would be beneficial to their situation. I feel a little like Gabor Maté with his addiction to classical music. I had to really control myself when it came to buying addiction books. This doesn't include the dozens of books I shipped to my son while he was incarcerated. They had to be all from Amazon, brand new, and paperback).

- *In the Realm of Hungry Ghosts* – Gabor Maté, MD
  It's so descriptive of my son's ADD personality. The author offers great insight into childhood trauma and personalities that may precipitate addiction.
- *The Freedom Model for Addictions: Escape the Treatment and Recovery Trap* – Steven Slate and Mark Scheeren with Michelle Dunbar

This book contains a refreshing alternative that resonated so well with me because it used exact words my son has said regarding twelve-step recovery models. My son and I talked about this book many times during this journey. There's also a freedom model for families.

- *Chasing The Scream: The First and Last Days of the War on Drugs* – Johann Hari
  This takes you through the criminalization of drugs and the damage it causes. Made into a movie called The United States Vs Billie Holiday. Johann coined the phrase: *Addiction is the opposite of connection*, a new model for compassion for substance users instead of stigma and shame.

- *Pro Dependence: Moving Beyond Codependency* – Robert Weiss
  This book debunks the overuse of the word and diagnosis "codependent" and changes it to a way of acting with interdependence with your addicted loved one.

- *Loving Lions: A Guide for Families Struggling with Addiction* – Michael J. Wilson Jr.
  Wilson, Jr. shares a helpful explanation of how the person with substance use disorder is chained and drawn to drugs in a "love affair" and how families need to realize they are NOT dealing with a house cat but a full-blown LION.

- *The Taste of Cigarettes: A Memoir of a Heroin Addict* – Jon Vreeland
  Vreeland writes very graphic descriptions of a heroin addict's daily life on the streets. The text can be triggering, even for this mom who has never used drugs. Sadly, Jon passed in 2020.

- *It's Monday only in your mind. You are not your thoughts* - Michael Cupo This book delves into what most rehabs don't. The WHYs. Why the addictive behavior? Very introspective and self-reflective of the author's patterns.

- *Cover My Dreams in Ink* – Jessie Dunleavy
  A true testament of a mother's devotion and willingness to seek out help for her son in a parenting world without roadmaps. She described her son in such a loving way that I

found myself rooting for him in every new endeavor he took on.

- *Son Down, Son Up: How One Mother Battled Her Son's Addiction, Found Hope, and Survived* – Brenda Seals
Seals inspires readers with her message of hope for recovery. She is the mom of a recovered son whose addiction started early in life.
- *Unhooked: A Mother's Story of Unhitching from the Roller Coaster of Her Son's Addiction* – Annie Highwater
This story of hope comes from a single mom with twelve "rounds" of boxing acronyms symbolizing her child's recovery journey.
- *Sincerely, Addison's Sister* – Jessica Akhrass
Jessica is a champion. Read her in-depth look at Tennessee's prescription laws and how she battled the opioid epidemic which caused her brother's death.
- *The Addictoholic Deconstructed* – Dr. Nicole T Labor, Kevin Kolankowski, et al.
Great explanation of the reptile brain and what drives substance use, especially dopamine. She is the one who taught me to say "other people in pain aren't the enemy" in response to people who compare chronic pain sufferers or diabetics getting insulin for free.
- *Chasing the High* – Michael G. Dash
This is great insight into high achievers and the love for money and all things addictive. This fits my son to a "t".
- *Scattered Pink: A Diary Of A Woman In Recovery*–Honesty Liller
A breath of fresh air in recovery! If you need a feel good, hopeful, happy, resilient, story of redemption and forgiveness, this is IT!
- *Shape of a Woman* – Jen Elizabeth
The author shares a touching memoir of her life. "Here's the funny thing about emotions ... no matter how awful and treacherous the road is to walk through them ... they will never kill you the way avoiding them will." Her Instagram is fantastic.

With great quotes on the worth of someone using drugs. She has been so helpful to me on my journey of offering respect to those whom society shuns.

- *Have I Had Enough?* – Ryan David Hiatt
This is the first book I read on addiction after learning my son had a "problem with pills." It's a valid, real, addiction story from the eyes of the one using. He started writing it while in jail on a four-year sentence, I believe. I was given this book and told that my son will have to lose everything before he realizes it's a problem. I adamantly rejected that idea at the time, because I couldn't fathom it happening or it being "the only solution."

- *You Are Not Alone: Hope for Hurting Parents of Troubled Kids* – Dena Yohe
This book is from the mom of the girl who the non-profit and movie *To Write Love on Her Arms* was started for her daughter. A great book about self-harm, cutting, and addiction, the book gives so much HOPE. You will need your highlighter. Dena is the kindest, most gracious soul I have had the privilege of meeting.

- *Stay Close* – Libby Cataldi
A mom with a son as stubborn as mine, the author thoroughly describes her heartbreak and indecisiveness as to the right thing to do to help with every sinking hole her son got into. I related to this woman's tormented heart so much, sans having the resources that she did.

- *When I lay my Isaac Down* – Carol Kent
The book details the journey of a mom whose son was charged with murder. Inspiring. Just when you think she had it all, you realize how easily this could happen to anyone. Great reminder of what the value of a life is and how to find peace in God's word. I found myself strangely jealous of the support she had even though the severity of the situation was awful and of course I would not want to be in her shoes. Carol is a class act.

- *Unhooked*– Jason Coombs

A stark and helpful look into the mindset of those struggling. It details "The Stages of Change" which helped me understand that their current behaviors may not reflect their true desire to change. They just haven't worked it all out yet. Jason is brutally honest about his journey through addiction and how he is able to help others.

- *Dreamland*– Sam Quinones
  A stark look at the drug cartel and distribution in America. Great read along with Chasing the Scream, and watching The Business of Drugs and Crack on Netflix

- *Broken Gifts* – Tyler Auck
  A raw introspective beautiful journey of turning extreme pain and child abuse into purpose and joy. Hard subject matter but proof that the human spirit longs for life no matter what circumstances it is subjected to. It gave me such hope that people are never too far gone.

- *American Prison: A Reporter's Undercover Journey into the Business of Punishment* – Shane Bauer
  Strikingly raw look at how inmates have been treated over the years in America. This reporter was told in training to never eat the food that's served to inmates. My son had told me previously that the food packages in jail say: Not for human consumption.

- *Understanding Addiction, Know Science, No Stigma* – Drs. Chuck Smith and Jason Hunt
  Both were Physicians who were addicted and both crossed the line many times and came back strong. The reader's digest condensed version of addiction. If you buy any book for family members who may not have the emotional connection and just want straight facts (like maybe a man), this is your book.

- *Overcoming Opioid Addiction* – Adam Bisaga, MD
  Very strong support for all paths of recovery and the false statistics of abstinence-based programs' success- mostly the anonymous ones. Very thorough look at Medication assisted treatment and how drugs work in the body.

- *I am Not Sick; I Don't Need Help* – Xavier Amador
  This is geared toward how to get someone with mental illness help, but as I listened to the examples, it was pretty close to substance use disorder.
- *Praying our Loved Ones Home* – Pam Jones Lanhart.
  Invaluable offering of peace and comfort through daily prayers in written form. This gave me so much relief and peace when I could hardly function.
- *Strung Out: One Last Hit and Other Lies That Nearly Killed Me* – Erin Khar
  A raw and authentic look from the eyes of addiction and the cycle of pain and loneliness that it brings. Erin weaves a heartfelt and authentic memoir of her life and career in and around Hollywood that will have you longing to help this troubled soul burst out of her pain and chaos to a life of joy. No worries though, Erin is a true survivor as she looks hard at her patterns of addiction. I loved her from the first few pages and even more so after.
- *Why Don't They Just Quit?* – Liam Herzanek
  The author was addicted then became a therapist. He then had a son who became addicted and also recovered. I listened to this on CD in my car over and over again. A bit of slanted opinion and possibly outdated info on legalization of drugs, mostly marijuana, the efficacy of AA, and the correctional system and addiction. But I used his words on my son while in jail: Make it known to "them," that you are NOT a criminal with a drug problem, but an addict with a criminal problem.
- *I Love You - But Not Your Addiction: Stuff You Need to Know for Family and Friends* – Nan Reynolds
  Twenty-one chapters are jam-packed full of resources and ideas for every situation, including quizzes and info for Al-Anon. I couldn't even get through all of them.
- *Crawling to God (...and my toxic relationship with myself!)* – Steven F. Gray II

Gray shares over twenty very detailed chapters of his traumatic childhood and battle with addiction. It took him ten years to write it. Excruciating journey. Raw vulnerability at its darkest hour; there is NO sugar-coating the man's torturous life of abuse and trauma. Even with all his pain and rejection, turning to drugs and all that goes along with that, even when trying to do the right things: turning to God, trying to keep employment, continually trying to have a relationship with his children, he was shot down over and over again. What a testament of strength, courage, and perseverance. It lays truth to the fact that drugs are not the only evils in the world, but they will always be blamed as the fall guy.

- *How to Grow an Addict* – J. A. Wright
  The refreshing and almost delightful-considering the subject-but raw viewpoint of a child raised in a dysfunctional world, which shows how she survived and recovered with apparently only a thirty-day stay in a recovery center.

- *Never Enough: The Neuroscience and Experience of Addiction* – Judith Grisel
  Judith writes a scientific account of her addiction from getting drunk at age thirteen to her research as a scientist for twenty years. The book is poignant and offers easily understood descriptions of every drug and their effect.

- *How to Murder Your Life* – Cat Marnell
  This is the very first addiction book I read long before it hit my life. Cat is a talented, quippy adorable writer but I would hesitate to recommend this book to anyone under the age of 35 because of the glamorization of her addiction. But then again anyone over 35 will not know who she's talking about when name-dropping and gushing about all the glamor mags and sites. She lucked out big time with having a grandma who was able to afford her and dare I say it– Enable her? But she probably saved her life in the process.

- *If Only Your Heart Would Listen* – Elise Schiller

Beautiful memoir written in true honor of her daughter's struggle. Very tender and detailed tribute of a journey that is often so painful. I loved this book.

- *Keven's Choice: A Mother's Journey Through Her Son's Mental Illness, Addiction and Suicide* – Barbara Legere
  Between the darkness of addiction and the hidden halls of mental illness, there's a mom like Barbara, who will do anything to save their child. What a raw, emotional look at the struggles of one boy turned man who tried and tried to maneuver his jumbled thoughts into some sort of peace. Barbara is a great example of having no regrets on a journey that has no real answers.

- *Welcome to the Tribe, Sorry You're with Us: Surviving the Traumatic Loss of a Child* and *Still Welcome, Still Sorry: The Second Year of Traumatic Child Loss* – Both by Susan Sek
  Invaluable to those who have lost a child to overdose or poisoning. Susan walks readers through her grief by honoring and acknowledging her son's decisions and struggles.

- *Courage to Change* – Al-anon family groups.
  A daily reader/meditation to navigate through the maze of addiction.

- *The Cross and the Switchblade* – David Wilkerson
  A book written in 1963 that highlights New York's gang life and one ministry's attempts to bring gang members to God. There was also a movie made in 1969. Written by the founder of *Teen Challenge* and with his brother who founded *World Challenge*, along with the co-authors who wrote *The Hiding Place*, it has sold over 15 million copies.

- *Anatomy of Peace* – Arbinger Institute
  The family of this book's author took my daughter under their wing twenty years ago and helped her come out of her rebellion stage. It's a must read to change how we view others. Do we see people as objects, as a means to something, or as humans?

- *Chasing False Highs and Running from Lows* – L. Michael Audley

A bit of a quirky book that will trigger your ADD and OCD
tendencies, but if you skip to chapter 3 it will save your brain.
If you can ignore the editing (or non-editing),
you can enjoy the author's attempt at explaining how it's okay
to stay in the middle. There are a few interesting anecdotes that
I've included in the book.

- *Joey's Song* – Sandra Swenson.
  A raw memoir of a mom of a very defiant young adult son who
  struggled with SUD. She learned how to use her version of
  tough love strategies to find her peace. I'm not going to lie, this
  book made me feel sad and depressed for both of them,
  mother and son, but I admire her eloquent writing and I aspire
  to be so talented.
- *My Journey with Nathan: A Mother's Story of Her Son's Life and
  Struggles with Drug Addiction* – Dottie Wise
  This is a short but sweet memoir of a mom whose son
  struggled (from age thirteen to twenty-two) with addiction and
  epilepsy, which ultimately claimed his life.
- *Life of Kayos: My Opioid Journey through Hell, Hope and Healing* –
  Chekesha Kay Ellis
  Short but to the point memoir of the author's nine-year
  addiction that started when she was twenty-seven.
- *The Weight of Air* – David Poses
  His journey with addiction. A lot of dialogue throughout the
  first half. My ADD brain struggled with it. But the last chapters
  on harm reduction are GOLD. David is HUGE on treating the
  cause of addiction and NOT putting suffering people in jail.
  Unfortunately, David passed away in 2022 less than a year after
  his book came out.
- *Chasing A Flawed Sun* – Daniel McGhee
- *From The Bottom Up* – Samuel Hunt
  Hunt teaches mostly about the journey of his career while
  addicted.
- *Don't Let Your Kids Kill You: A Guide for Parents of Drug and
  Alcohol Addicted Children* – Charles Rubin

Very stoic and harsh, written by a man with two sons who battled SUD.

Non-addiction Books That I have Loved

- *The Untethered Soul: The Journey Beyond Yourself and The Surrender Experiment* – Michael Singer
- *The Power of Now* and *A New Earth* – Eckhart Tolle
- *Loving What Is: Four Questions That Could Change Your Life* – Byron Katie
- *Life's Healing Choices* - John Baker
  The book describes eight choices that promote true happiness and life transformation.
- *Who's in Your Room: The Secret to Creating Your Best Life* – Ivan Misner, Stewart Emery, Rick Shapiro
  This entire book is about emotional energy, which is PARAMOUNT in addiction support.
- *Healing the Shame That Binds You* – John Bradshaw
- *How to Stop Worrying and Start Living* – Dale Carnegie
- *Psycho-Cybernetics* – Maxwell Maltz

Books I Sent to My Son in Jail

- *Leadership and Self Deception* – The Arbinger Institute
  These are the same authors of Anatomy of Peace. My son told me almost a year later that *I* needed to read it in the context of our (*my*) attitude toward certain particular people and how it sways our view of them and how we treat them. What a crazy twist—him giving me resources and advice.

315

- *For Whom the Bell Tolls* – Ernest Hemingway
  Apparently, my son was lifting weights to the song by the same title (Metallica), when they came and handed him this book that he didn't know I sent. He's always so nonchalant when he tells me these divine *coincidences.*
- *The Peaceful Warrior and The Life You Were Born to Live* – Dan Millman Excellent Read! He's a fellow quote collector. Check out his YouTube videos and tell me how old you think he is.
- *The Greatest Salesman in the World* – Og Mandino

Recommended Resources:

https://samantha-waters.com/about/

https://cmcffc.org/

https://helpingfamilieshelp.com/

https://www.smartrecovery.org/

https://addictionthenextstep.com/resources/

https://www.nmmitc.com/events/robert-j-meyers-phd-presents-craft

https://www.thefreedommodel.org/the-addiction-solution-podcast/

https://thrivefamilyrecoveryresources.org/

https://drugfree.org/article/craft-approach-encouraging-healthy-constructive-positive-changes-family/

https://www.youtube.com/watch?v=WT8ywN2o44U

https://www.samhsa.gov/find-help/national-helpline

https://www.ncbi.nlm.nih.gov/pmc/articles/PMC3181920/?fbclid=IwAR12QD2LBlm8-mHBhZEnqW9liISJAJSvh0vGsl236tALnK1EG9yBpaOUmc8&fs=e&s=cl

https://nida.nih.gov/nidamed-medical-health-professionals/screening-tools-resources/chart-screening-tools

www.ingramcontent.com/pod-product-compliance
Lightning Source LLC
Chambersburg PA
CBHW061558120626
46550CB00004B/1532

* 9 7 8 1 9 5 8 5 3 3 2 8 4 *